בס״ד

A project of

TorahLive

www.torahlive.com

"Commentaries note that the reason the blessing for Torah study is 'Blessed is G-d Who *gives* the Torah' rather than 'Who *gave* the Torah' is because the Torah is eternally present. In *Relevance*, Dan Roth shows us how *Pirkei Avos* can serve as a behavioral guide in the 21st century. *Relevance* is a beacon of light in the haze of current moral and ethical confusion."

Rabbi Dr. Abraham Twerski

Relevance

Relevance

*Pirkei Avos for the
Twenty-First Century*

Rabbi Dan Roth

ISBN 978-1-58330-935-3

FIRST EDITION
First impression 2007
Second impression 2009

SECOND EDITION
First impression 2015

For questions regarding this book or any other parts of Pirkei Avos, please contact:

D. Roth
20 Sheshet Hayamim
Jerusalem 97804
d.roth@torahlive.com

Distributed by:
FELDHEIM PUBLISHERS
POB 43163 / Jerusalem, Israel
208 Airport Executive Park,
Nanuet, NY 10954

Printed in Israel

Book design by:
Ben Gasner Studio

Cover design by:
Yael Knochen

To my wife

שֶׁלִּי וְשֶׁלָּכֶם שֶׁלָּה הוּא
כתובות סג.

*"What is mine
and what is yours
is really hers."*
Kesubos 63a

בס"ד

י' אלול תשס"ו

"כאשר תקום מן הספר תחפש באשר למדת אם יש בו דבר אשר תוכל לקימו...."

"When you rise from studying a *sefer*, ponder carefully what you have learned in order to see what there is in it that can be put into practice...."

The above words, written by the Ramban in a famous letter to his son, instruct us to search for the practical application of everything we learn in Torah. As lofty and essential as this goal is, however, it is one that often eludes us.

We tend to perceive our Torah study as an intellectual pursuit, divorced from the reality of our lives. Even when we do try to relate what we study to everyday living, it is not always easy to do so. The concepts discussed do not seem to pertain to the modern world or be applicable to our daily lives.

In this excellent book, you overcome both these hurdles.

First, you approach each Mishnah with the attitude of "I have to get something out of this." Instead of letting the Mishnah's message remain a theoretical ideal, you show how it relates to the practical world.

Secondly, by analyzing the Mishnah in depth, you prove how every word of Torah is eternal. Taken superficially, the words of the Mishnah may at first not appear applicable, but when one looks beneath the surface and understands the true wisdom of its teachings, one realizes that the lessons are as relevant and pertinent as if they were given to us today.

This work has a tremendous amount of wisdom to offer both the novice and the advanced student, each of whom will enjoy and benefit from the wide array of sources employed.

Hachosem lichvod haTorah,

Rabbi Zvi Kushelevsky

92 Katzenelbogen St. P.O.B 43106 Jerusalem 91430, Israel   91430 רחוב קצנלבוגן 92, ת.ד. 43106, ירושלים

Tel: 6519402 Fax: 6524402   טלפון: 6519402 פקס: 6524402

Rabbi Zev Leff   הרב זאב לף

Rabbi of Moshav Matityahu   מרא דאתרא מושב מתתיהו

Rosh HaYeshiva—Yeshiva Gedola Matityahu   ראש הישיבה—ישיבה גזולה מתתיהו

D.N. Modiin 71917   טל' Tel: 08–976–1138   פקס' Fax: 08–976–5326   ד.נ. מודיין 71917

כ"ח חשון תשס"ז

Dear Friends,

    I have read many portions of the manuscript of *Relevance – Pirkei Avos for the Twenty-First Century* by my friend and colleague Rabbi Dan Roth. Rabbi Roth has also discussed with me many of the subjects contained in the book.

    Rabbi Roth himself is an accomplished *ben Torah* and *talmid chacham*. He has taken various subjects dealt with in *Pirkei Avos* and presented a broad view of the various commentaries as well as a deep but practical explanation of the issues themselves.

    I find this book informative and illuminating. It contains a wellspring of Torah knowledge that can be applied to many very relevant current issues and provide true Torah guidance.

    I highly recommend *Relevance* to all who seek wisdom and understanding and direction in developing a true Torah outlook and way of life.

    May Hashem grant the author and his family long life and health, and may he continue to benefit *Klal Yisrael* with further Torah works.

Sincerely,
With Torah blessings,

Rabbi Zev Leff

My dear friend הרב דן רוט שליט"א,

As I read your commentary on *Pirkei Avos*, I increasingly saw the uniqueness of your approach to the important life-issues dealt with in the Mishnayos. In trying to analyze what makes your work so original, I realized that you do not preach the truth out of a cold, academic knowledge, but rather you explore the issues based on your search for truth in your own life. Through the many sources you quote, and the inspiring stories you tell, you show the practical application of each Mishnah.

This approach to studying the Mishnayos is contagious; it stirs the reader to search within himself, to examine his own deeds, and to hopefully integrate the message of *Pirkei Avos* into his own life. There is no better expression for this than the title you chose for your *sefer: Relevance.*

It is my hope that many people will see how these "old" words of wisdom are really fresh and relevant to us in our time, and I am sure that your great *sefer* is a substantial contribution toward this goal.

B'chavod rav,

Reuven Leuchter

Rabbi Reuven Leuchter

Contents

Preface

When I began writing this book several years ago, I visited the Jewish National Library in Jerusalem, which contains the largest collection of Jewish books in the world, in order to find out which other *sefarim* had been written on *Pirkei Avos*. The librarian explained that I could only access a particular *sefer* by first finding its call number in the computer database. She typed in "Pirkei Avos" to bring up a list of all available books on the topic. The result? 1,128. The look of disbelief on her face was unmistakable. Restrained by etiquette, she could not express her unspoken question, which was "And you want to write *another* one?!"

And my unspoken response was "Why, yes, I do."

Each generation has its own challenges and its own unique set of circumstances, and as such needs its own commentary. The *nisyonos* of the Jews in France in the eleventh century were not the same as the *nisyonos* of the Jews in Poland in the eighteenth century, and neither are the same as the *nisyonos* we face today: Internet, drugs, assimilation, consumerism, the loosening of moral constraints.... The *yetzer hara* has many faces and appears in many forms, unhindered by the passage of time.

Thankfully, we have the lessons of our Sages to guide us. The teachings of *Pirkei Avos* are timeless; they contain answers to the moral challenges of every generation. The manner in which those messages are best expressed, however, and the particular application of those messages to the needs of each generation, changes according to the times. As such, every generation needs to delve anew into the words of Chazal to discover how to apply the eternal truths of the Torah to the challenges of the day. Our bookstores are filled with "how-to" books, but *Pirkei Avos* is the classic "how-to" book: how to live; how to grow old; how to be satisfied; how to treat other people; how to love and be beloved; how to live a life of contentment, peace, and fulfillment.

My goal in this work is to show how each Mishnah is as applicable today as it was throughout the millennia and that, far from being an outdated 2,000-year-old document, its teachings are vibrant and relevant today, containing lessons and ethics that far surpass the wisdom of modern thinkers.

In undertaking this task, I have been inspired by the words of the great Rabbi Shimshon Raphael Hirsch:

> *I intended to show that this full and authentic Judaism —* תורת ה' תמימה *— does not belong to an antiquated past but to the living, pulsating present; nay, that the whole future, with all its intellectual and social problems whose solution mankind expects of it, belongs to Judaism, the full and unabridged Judaism.*[1]

A work such as mine, which sets out to focus on all 128 Mishnayos of *Pirkei Avos*, would fill many volumes.[2] Rather than undertake such a Herculean task, I thought it wiser to begin this project with a more humble offering. The result is what you hold in front of you: a collection of essays on selected Mishnayos from *Pirkei Avos*.

The reader will soon notice that many of the essays do not deal with an entire Mishnah, but rather discuss only a specific line or phrase. Highlighting only one part of a Mishnah permits the reader to see for himself the profundity and wisdom that can be discovered even in a few choice Mishnaic words.

If there is one lesson I have learned over the course of writing this book, it is this: despite the many *sefarim* that exist on *Pirkei Avos*, the most powerful impression does not come from that which one reads in books, but from that which one thinks about on his own.[3] The commentators are there to guide and lead us around the pitfalls of misreadings and uninformed interpretation, but the teachings of the Mishnah become our personal possession only after we ponder, struggle, and grapple with the text by ourselves. The insights that emanate from within — unlike those that come from outside — penetrate deep into our being and remain with us forever, forging a lasting impression on our soul.

Among the vast corpus of Mishnah and Gemara, the Mishnayos of *Pirkei Avos* are the most widely known and beloved. In shuls around the world, they are studied and discussed for several months every summer after the Shabbos afternoon davening. As such, they are often familiar to us before we even open the text. By delving into every Mishnah with fresh eyes, treating it as if it were the first time it's being read and scrutinizing every word relentlessly, we will uncover hidden treasures and reveal Chazal's instructions for living.

It is my fervent prayer and hope that this modest work will enable the eternal words of *Pirkei Avos* to become an integral part of our consciousness — so that ultimately each one of us, through the way we live our lives and relate to our Creator and our heritage, will not only understand the text and its commentaries, but will ultimately himself become a living and enduring commentary.

---

[1] *Jeschurun* [1861], quoted by Dayan I. Grunfeld in the introduction to his translation of *Horeb*, lxxxv.

[2] The Mishnayos are divided differently in various printings of *Pirkei Avos*. Throughout this book, I have followed the system of division used in the widely acknowledged ArtScroll siddur.

[3] See *Sha'arei Teshuva* 2:§26.

A NOTE ON THE NOTES

Unless otherwise stated, citations of commentators refer to their comments on the Mishnah under discussion.

The symbol § refers to a section of a work and could refer to *ois, sicha, perek, siman,* or paragraph, depending on the system of division in that particular *sefer*.

Thank You

To R' Dovid Orlofsky for encouraging me to devote the bulk of my time to this project and for suggesting the book and essay titles.

To R' Reuven Leuchter for pushing me to think about the Mishnayos in an original way and showing me that there is always more depth to uncover in Torah.

To R' Zev Leff, R' Chaim Yitzchak Kaplan, R' Hillel Copperman, R' Immanuel Bernstein, and R' Shaul Goldman for sharing their vast knowledge of Torah with me and pointing out sources I would not otherwise have come across.

To my brother-in-law, R' Reuven Poupko, for being the first sounding board for the essays, and providing insightful comments and corrections that helped me clarify my thoughts.

To R' Emanuel Feldman and Mrs. Malka Winner for editing the manuscript with such talent and precision.

To Ben Gasner for his gifted artistry.

To R' Hanoch Teller for his insights into the publishing world, gleaned from his many years of experience.

To R' Chaim Neumann for meticulously verifying the accuracy of each endnote, and to R' Dovid Solomon for advising and helping me regarding the many technical aspects of producing this book.

To Adam Sheps, Arye Schreiber, Avraham Solomon, Ayala and

Jonny Finn, R' Boruch Peritzman, Ben Rosenfelder, Benji Schreiber, R' Dovid Tugendhaft, R' Hadar Margolin, R' Jonathan Taub, Meir Rabinowitz, R' Nesanel Kelaty, R' Shimon and Rachel Verbov, and others for offering feedback on various parts of the manuscript.

To my parents and parents-in-law for their love and support.

To my wife, Becky, for allowing me to be married to *Pirkei Avos*, and to think and talk of little else. Your devotion and self-sacrifice are second to none, and you are the strength behind everything I do.

Finally, and most importantly, to the Father of all *avos* for orchestrating the many people who helped in this work, and for letting me taste the sweetness of His Torah. May this work bring all His children one step closer to Him.

Understanding
Current
Events

פֶּרֶק א' מִשְׁנָה ב': שִׁמְעוֹן הַצַּדִּיק הָיָה מִשְׁיָרֵי כְּנֶסֶת
הַגְּדוֹלָה. הוּא הָיָה אוֹמֵר, עַל שְׁלֹשָׁה דְבָרִים הָעוֹלָם
עוֹמֵד, עַל הַתּוֹרָה וְעַל הָעֲבוֹדָה וְעַל גְּמִילוּת חֲסָדִים:

Chapter 1, Mishnah 2: *Shimon Hatzaddik was
one of the last survivors of the Great Assembly. He
used to say: The world stands on three things — on
Torah, on tefilla, and on kind deeds.*

I magine archeologists finding the following fragment of an
ancient newspaper:[1]

*Sodom — Shortly after sunrise yesterday, four cities in the
eastern basin of the Mediterranean were destroyed by fire. The
cities, known as the most fertile and productive in the Jordan
Valley, now lie blackened in cinders and ash.*

*Emergency forces arrived on the scene immediately but have
not yet found any survivors.*

*Government officials have declared a state of emergency
and have issued a statement announcing the formation of a
special committee to investigate the cause of the tragedy. The
committee intends to report its findings within seven days. It
also hopes to include plans to ensure that such a disaster will
not be repeated.*

*Speaking on condition of anonymity, several investigators say
that three possible causes of the disaster are being considered:
a volcanic eruption from one of the many mountains in the
area; an explosion caused by the buildup of hot air; or an act of
terrorism.*

*This last theory is thought to be the most likely, given eyewitness
reports that claim a man and three women fled the area just
minutes before the explosion. The four escapees are thought
to have some connection to the terrorists and were apparently
warned to leave in time.*

*Army personnel and volunteers are searching for the fugitives,
who may be able to provide the police with significant leads.*

Anyone reading this article would be exasperated by the investigators' audacity in suggesting that the calamity came about through natural causes, when the Torah clearly tells us that Sodom was destroyed because of its sins.

But the reality is that had Sodom been destroyed today, the experts and investigators would propose the same types of explanations. Newspapers would sensationalize the gruesome details of the disaster, and government officials would look into methods of ensuring that it not reoccur.

Why is it, then, that we laugh at the article and marvel at the foolishness of the investigators when we read similar reports all the time and take them seriously? It is because the real reason for Sodom's destruction — the intense cruelty of its inhabitants — has been drilled into us from our earliest years and has become so deeply ingrained in our psyches that any purely physical description of the event leaves us incredulous. We know beyond any doubt that it was Sodom's spiritual failings that caused its downfall, and the physical particulars that led up to the event — the rain, the fire, the exact time of the calamity — are just the methods that G-d used to mete out Sodom's punishment.

This strong, practically innate feeling we have about the reason for Sodom's destruction can be used to teach us the proper perspective on world events today. We live in a physical world, in which one can find physical explanations for nearly everything that happens. The more our knowledge of the world increases, the greater our ability to explain in scientific terms why things happen, and why certain actions cause certain reactions. Our understanding of cause and effect has become so sophisticated that many people erroneously believe the world is governed by physical factors alone.

Rising Above the Physical

In our Mishnah, Shimon Hatzaddik tells us that the health of the world and its continued existence rests on these three pillars

— Torah, *tefilla*, and *gemilus chasadim*.[2] The breakdown of any pillar, such as happened in Sodom, results in destruction. Just as a building that has faulty foundations cannot stand, so, too, a physical world devoid of its spiritual base cannot exist.

This concept is illuminated by our Sages. Chazal comment that when Nevuchadnetzar destroyed the *Beis Hamikdash* he was merely "grinding already-ground flour."[3] In other words, he only had the power to destroy the *Beis Hamikdash* physically because its spiritual counterpart had already been destroyed in Heaven by our sins.[4]

Mordechai and Esther grasped this idea on a fundamental level. When they went about fighting the decree to annihilate the Jews, the first thing Mordechai and Esther did was assemble the entire nation for a day of fasting and prayer, actions that transcend the physical. They understood that until the decree had been eradicated at its root, which was in the spiritual realm, any effort to go to Achashveirosh and beg for mercy in the physical world would be in vain.

These sources demonstrate that the physical world is only a reflection of the spiritual world, and what unfolds down here on earth is just an enactment, a playing out, of what has already been decreed in Heaven.

With this as a cardinal principle of their lives, the *Tanna'im* lived with a deep feeling that the factors that really affected and controlled their lives were not physical ones, but rather their spiritual counterparts.

For example, when the *Tanna'im* were asked how they lived such long lives, they didn't respond with a list of natural explanations — a good diet, country air, and the like — but instead suggested praiseworthy behaviors, *middos*, that they had maintained throughout their lives.[5]

When Rav Huna's stock of wine went sour, his friends told him to take a spiritual accounting of his deeds to determine what had brought on the loss.[6] They didn't try to find a physical cause for the loss, such as the room temperature or the presence of bacteria, but went directly to the spiritual source of the problem.[7]

To be sure, physical explanations must be dealt with. One must not ignore the natural world and neglect one's body or business ventures, saying that everything is *min haShamayim*. To do so would be both foolish and sinful. But it is important to understand that one of the tenets of this Mishnah is that the root cause of everything that happens to us is determined by the strength of the three pillars — our Torah study, *tefillos*, and *gemilus chasadim*.

Looking back at our news fragment from Sodom, we see that the government's report on explanations for Sodom's destruction and possible preventative measures for the future would not have had any lasting effects unless it had investigated the problem at its roots and addressed the spiritual reasons for the tragedy. Similarly, it would be foolish for us to try to resolve the difficulties in our lives by dealing only with the visible causes while ignoring the underlying reasons.

Without prophets, it is impossible for us to know with certainty which spiritual faults are causing which particular troubles. Anyone who points to specific tragedies, claiming that he or she knows the reason G-d does what He does, is sadly misguided.

Nevertheless, by strengthening our Torah study, *tefillos*, and *gemilus chasadim* in general, we will alleviate much of the suffering in our lives. As the Mishnah teaches us, these are the three basic areas of life upon which everything stands.

Let us focus on the pillar of *chesed*, the pillar that crumbled in Sodom.

Understanding *Chesed*

A wealthy businessman, who was noted for his extraordinary generosity, once became completely overwhelmed by the countless requests for *tzedaka* he was receiving. He went to consult the Chofetz Chaim on the matter. As he entered the room, the Chofetz Chaim happened to be expounding the verse "*Ach tov vachesed yirdefuni kol yemei chayai* — May only good and kindness pursue me all the days of my life."[8] The Chofetz Chaim explained that no man can live out his life in total tranquility, without any headaches or worries. Everyone is chased by some bother, be it repaying creditors, raising children, or battling sickness. Fortunate is the man who discharges his "obligation" by being pursued by charitable causes, such as institutions that harass him for support. This is what the verse means when it says, "May only good and kindness pursue me all the days of my life."

The businessman understood the message. He returned home reassured and doubled his charitable efforts.[9]

A person often thinks that he will lose out by helping others, that it will drain even more of his already low energy. But the above story demonstrates that a person does not lose by helping others — he only gains by removing some of his own headaches. The hassles and the errands will always be there, but by making the hassles *chesed*-related, one relieves himself of additional personal problems.[10]

One woman spent several hours a week shuttling her young daughter from one appointment to another, taking her from speech therapy one day to occupational and play therapy the next. The stress began taking its toll, leaving the mother nervous and fatigued. Inspired by this lesson from the Chofetz Chaim, she decided to increase her involvement with *chesed* and volunteered to drive people to and from hospitals as part of a *chesed* organization. Her chauffeuring headaches gradually dissipated as she became more involved with *chesed*, and her daughter's appointments became unnecessary. Although she had virtually no free time on her hands to do more *chesed*, she realized that it was precisely then that she stood to gain the most.

We see that for every extra ounce of effort we invest in helping others, we are actually helping ourselves. On the surface, this may seem illogical. After all, if I am already overburdened with my own chores that need to be taken care of, taking time to help others will just consume more of my time and energy. But upon reflection, one realizes that this *is* logical. We are all G-d's children and, as any parent will tell you, when one child looks after his sibling or a friend, the parent is filled with greater compassion for the child who extended himself. Thus, by looking after other children of G-d, He in turn looks after us. The *midda kenegged midda* is obvious: when we do *chesed* with others, G-d does *chesed* with us.

Putting *Chesed* Into Action

Chesed need not necessarily be done outside of the home. Sometimes we overlook those closest to us who may need our help the most — our own brother or sister, son or daughter, husband or wife. Before seeking to help people far away, we should look within our own families.

Furthermore, the *chesed* need not be enormous. Sometimes the large-scale *chesed* projects that we plan do not get off the ground, and as a result we miss the smaller, more manageable opportunities that are right under our noses, like smiling at people or giving them a word of encouragement. In a way, these small *chasadim* are really the most significant. When a person does public acts of *chesed* and he knows he will receive great honor, his motivation may not be so pure. Because small acts of kindness will not be known to anyone, they are often the truest tests of a person's character.

One of the greatest forms of *chesed* is *hachnasas orchim*.[11] Chazal say that performing *hachnasas orchim* is even greater than receiving the Shechina,[12] and we are told that whoever fulfills this mitzvah carefully will be blessed with children.[13] Indeed, when someone once asked the Chofetz Chaim for a *bracha* to have children, the Chofetz Chaim advised him to bring more guests into his home.[14]

When Chazal spoke of *hachnasas orchim*, they were referring to inviting people from out of town who had nowhere else to eat or stay.[15] Most of our guests today, however, are people who have their own homes, and our inviting them is more of a social affair. While this is certainly a *chesed*, it would be an even greater *chesed* to invite people who really need the company, like widows, orphans, those new to Judaism, or students who are far away from home.

What about the Sodom investigation committee? Undoubtedly, it would propose investing great sums of money in developing an early warning system which would prevent another tragedy. But according to what we have learned from our Mishnah, such a proposal would miss the main point. The real cause of the destruction was not a dormant volcano come alive, hot air buildup, or terrorist activity. A lack of *chesed* destroyed Sodom.

Imagine, however, that one of the members of the committee would have recommended inviting downtrodden individuals for meals in order to ward off disaster. He would have been laughed out of the room! The other members would cry out, "What on earth will hospitality do? We are talking about implementing the best, most sophisticated, multimillion-dollar surveillance equipment, and you're sitting here talking about having company?!"

But we know the truth. Had they been hospitable, their city would never have been destroyed. Similarly, by strengthening the *chesed* we do with one another in our lives, we reinforce one of the pillars of our existence, thereby meriting a greater level of *chesed* from G-d.

---

[1] The idea for this newspaper article and much of its content comes from *Yalkut Lekach Tov, Chaim Shel Torah* 1:31–34.

[2] Throughout this piece, I follow Rambam, *Peirushei Rabbeinu Yitzchak ben Harav Shlomo MiToledo*, and Rabbeinu Yisrael (quoted in *Peirushei Rabbeinu Yitzchak ben Harav Shlomo MiToledo*), who explain the phrase "*ha'olam omed*" as "the world continues to exist." This is unlike Rabbeinu Yona and *Bartenura*, who explain it as "the world was created for." See *Tosefos Yom Tov* ד"ה ועל העבודה and *Tosafos Chadashim*.

[3] *Sanhedrin* 96b; *Eicha Rabba* 1:41.

[4] *Nefesh Hachaim* 1:§4.

[5] *Megilla* 27b–28a. See *Tnuas Hamussar* 2:113.

[6] *Berachos* 5b.

[7] See *Tnuas Hamussar* 2:113. The reason his wine went sour was because he had not given vine branches to his sharecropper. As soon as he paid his worker, the wine returned to its former state.

[8] *Tehillim* 23:6.

[9] R' Avrohom Chaim Feuer, commentary to *Tehillim* (*ArtScroll Tanach Series*), 293.

[10] This principle is also stated by the Chazon Ish, *Pe'er Hador* 2:168, and R' Elchanan Wasserman, *Kovetz Ma'amarim V'igros* 1:62.

[11] Meiri to *Shabbos* 127a says there is no greater mitzvah.

[12] *Shabbos* 127a.

[13] *Kad Hakemach*, s.v. אורחים. This is learned from Avraham Avinu and from the Shunamite woman, both of whom were originally childless but merited offspring as reward for their *hachnasas orchim*.

[14] R' Moshe Aharon Stern, quoting his grandfather R' Yaakov Yosef Herman, *Bayis U'menucha*, 226.

[15] *Beis Yosef*, *Orach Chaim* 333; *Rema*, ibid. 333:1; *Shulchan Aruch Harav*, ibid. 333:6 and 510:20. R' Yosef Yitzchak Lerner, *Sefer Habayis* 435–436, says that while this is the view of the majority of *Acharonim*, there is a lone opinion of the *Sefer Hachaim* that disputes it. See also *Beis Yechezkel*, 346.

Friends
for Life

פרק א' משנה ו': יְהוֹשֻׁעַ בֶּן פְּרַחְיָה וְנִתַּאי הָאַרְבֵּלִי
קִבְּלוּ מֵהֶם. יְהוֹשֻׁעַ בֶּן פְּרַחְיָה אוֹמֵר, עֲשֵׂה לְךָ רַב, וּקְנֵה
לְךָ חָבֵר, וֶהֱוֵי דָן אֶת כָּל הָאָדָם לְכַף זְכוּת.

Chapter 1, Mishnah 6: *Yehoshua ben Perachia and
Nittai of Arbel received [the tradition] from them.
Yehoshua ben Perachia says: Make for yourself a
Rav, acquire for yourself a friend, and judge each
person favorably.*

Recent advances in communication have made it easier than ever to keep in contact with friends. Cell phones, e-mails, and text messages mean that friends are never further away than the touch of a button. At the same time, advances in transportation have led to greater distances between friends, with more people relocating than ever before. In the last five years of the twentieth century, close to half the American population — some 120 million people — packed up and moved to different homes.[1]

This ease of mobility affects everyone's friendships in one way or another. Those who move find themselves having to gain a new circle of friends, while those who are left behind lose some of their oldest and closest companions. The number of adults enjoying the luxury of living nearby their childhood friends is far less than in the past, and people must establish new friendships increasingly often.

Technology has thus made it both easier and harder to maintain friendships, presenting our generation with a unique challenge. Let us look at what Chazal had to teach us about making friends, applying their lessons to our day and age.

The True Purpose of Friendship

The Mishnah tells us to acquire for ourselves a friend (*keneh lecha chaver*). Being that the need for friendship is a basic human need, existing in people of all races since time immemorial, Chazal do not seem to be revealing any new ideas or instructing us to do something we wouldn't have done anyway. But upon examining their words more carefully, we see that their every word is imbued with wisdom and, like all their insights, everything they say reveals a depth of understanding we might not have perceived on our own and from which we have much to learn.

The first novel idea about friendship that we learn from the Mishnah is what the purpose of a friend is. As the commentators explain, the purpose of making a friend is to have someone to learn from and grow from spiritually, someone who will encourage you to keep the mitzvos properly and point out areas that need improvement should you fail.[2]

This way of looking at friendship is not the way friendship is usually perceived. Most people look to their friends to strengthen already existing parts of their personality. The areas about which the two of them agree are what bonds them and forms the basis of their friendship, whereas the areas about which they disagree are politely avoided.

Chazal, however, teach us that the purpose of a friend is to expand our personalities and broaden our way of thinking. It is precisely the areas in which we don't think the same or see eye to eye that offer us room to grow and provide us with the opportunity to develop areas of our personality that are as of yet undeveloped. It is our dissimilarities that generate growth.[3]

The Torah alludes to this idea in its account of Adam and Chava — the first "friendship" that ever existed between people.

G-d looked at Adam and said, "*Lo tov heyos ha'adam levado* — It is not good that man be alone."[4] G-d ended man's loneliness by creating woman, a being with a vastly different temperament than man. We see that true companionship doesn't come from being with someone who is identical to you, but from being with someone who is different from you. By virtue of the different ways our friends view the world, they can open our eyes to new understandings.

Of course, the point is not to look for friends who are totally unlike ourselves and with whom we share nothing in common.[5] It is just important to understand that instead of feeling uncomfortable when differences arise, we should appreciate that the prime purpose of a friend is our personal growth and that it is the differences that make this possible.

Making Friends Chazal-Style

Having looked at what Chazal saw as the correct motivation for having a friend, let us look more closely at the way they phrased their instruction: *"keneh lecha chaver."*

The word *keneh* literally means "buy." Chazal's choice of words is interesting since one usually speaks of buying an object, not a friend.[6] In using the verb *buy*, Chazal teach us several things.

First, they teach us that one should look into whom he chooses to be his friend. Just as you would research an item before you buy it to make sure it is not poor quality, so, too, when picking a friend you should consider the type of person he is, ensuring that your friendship will be mutually beneficial.[7]

Chazal even offer specific advice for picking a friend, telling us to look for someone who is a level above ourselves.[8] Bearing in mind that the purpose of a friend is personal growth, it is logical that we should choose someone who we feel will inspire us to grow and who has traits we would like to emulate.[9]

Having chosen a person who we feel is suitable, we need to make him interested in becoming friends with us. After all, just because we want to become friends with him doesn't mean he feels the same way about us. We need to create in him the desire to pursue a relationship with us the same way we want to pursue one with him.

This is the second lesson Chazal teach us by using the word *buy*. Buying always entails sacrificing one commodity in order to gain another. When buying a product, for example, one sacrifices time, effort, and money in order to gain ownership of the item. Similarly, in order to acquire a friend, one must make sacrifices on behalf of the friendship. This includes giving up time for him, making the effort to speak kindly to him, and spending money on gifts for him. All these things will have the effect of drawing our chosen friend close to us and making him want to become our friend.[10]

One also needs to show that he cares for the person and is aware of his needs. It is essential that each friend be considerate of the other and put the other one's wishes before his own. Instead of thinking about what I want — be it where I want to go or what I want to talk about — think of what he wants. As the *ba'alei mussar* put it, "When you love someone, don't love him according to your preferences and desires but according to *his* preferences and desires."[11]

Choosing Your Friends

Chazal's approach to making friends, as outlined above, is particularly fascinating in how it differs from the customary approach to making friends. Most of our friendships occur by themselves, without our actively pursuing them or paying too much attention to whom we are befriending. We happen to be taking the same class with someone or happen to be living close to him, and before we know it, we're friends. Chazal are teaching us, however, that friends need to be consciously chosen — both in regard to the type of person we choose as well as in regard to the whole process of becoming friends.

The difference between how we tend to go about making friends (the haphazard approach) and how Chazal teach us to make friends (the conscious and active approach) leads to a major difference in the commitment the friends will have to one another.

To be sure, all friends give something to one another. If they didn't, they wouldn't remain friends for very long. But there is a vast difference between the level of self-sacrifice that exists between people who "happened" to become friends and the level of self-sacrifice that exists between people who consciously chose to become friends.

This is because the latter group recognizes their friends as essential to their self-perfection. Their chosen friend isn't someone who simply came into their lives, but someone whom they deliberately decided to become close to, someone who possesses character traits they look up to, someone in whom they have invested money and emotional energy in befriending. They will therefore extend themselves for their chosen friend beyond the level of ordinary friends, exerting themselves to the utmost to fulfill his wishes and see to it that the friendship endures.

The Gemara says that when Iyov's friends heard of the tragedies that befell him, they traveled 300 *parsas* to comfort him[12] — a distance of approximately 700 miles (1,200 kilometers). In those days, a trip of that length probably took about two weeks each way. That means his friends took off over a month of their time to console him.

It is hard for us to fathom taking off such a huge block of our time to support a friend in his time of need. Sure, we would make a phone call or even pay him a visit, but who ever heard of taking off a month to comfort a friend? Once you appreciate the importance of a particular friend, however, and how crucial he is to your self-growth and perfection, you will be willing to bend over backward and do almost anything to build and maintain the friendship.

One's Enough

This leads us to the last word in the phrase "Buy yourself a friend." The use of the singular word *friend*, as opposed to the plural form, *friends*, seems strange. After all, most people have more than one friend and, if asked, would probably say they have "lots of friends." Why, then, do Chazal limit us by telling us to make one friend?

The answer is that Chazal are speaking about a close and intimate friendship, a friend with whom one shares his innermost secrets[13] and for whom one would travel across the world. It is hard to have more than one such friend.[14] When people say they have many friends, what they actually mean is that they have many acquaintances, people they share a casual relationship with, but not the "soul mate" Chazal had in mind.

This distinction between friends and acquaintances is especially relevant to our generation. On the one hand, people today cross paths with more people than ever before because of the changes in transportation and technology that we discussed earlier. At the same time, loneliness is more prevalent today than in previous generations, with the *New York Times* calling it a "national epidemic."[15] The reason for this conundrum is that instead of building a solid friendship with any one person, people's relationships with one another are becoming superficial.[16]

Thus, a person can be in the haunting position of having "lots of friends" without really having even one! He can be in a room full of people, surrounded by those who are ostensibly his friends, and still be very lonely. Perhaps he should take Chazal's advice and search for a friend who is able to help him grow, whom he then commits to befriending by investing time and money in order to build a sturdy relationship.[17]

Chazal teach us that the more spiritual a friendship is, the longer it will last.[18] When friends are bound only by circumstances, then when the circumstances change — they stop attending the same course or move away — the friendship is lost. However, when friends are joined by the desire to grow together, their souls are bound with one another and the friendship will last throughout their lives. This is possibly the most pleasurable and rewarding aspect of what Chazal are teaching us about "buying" a friend — namely, keeping a friend for life.

---

[1] U.S. Bureau of the Census, *Census*, 2000. Jane E. Brody, "Personal Health," *New York Times*, April 6, 1983, reports that the average American moves fourteen times during his lifetime.

[2] See Rambam, Rabbeinu Yona (on this Mishnah and in *Iggeres Hateshuva* §22), *Peirushei Rabbeinu Yitzchak ben Harav Shlomo MiToledo, Ruach Chaim.* Rambam (commentary on *Demai* 2:3) notes that *talmidei chachamim* are referred to as *chaverim* (friends) because their friendship is for Heaven's sake and hence a true friendship. Rambam's words "for Heaven's sake" imply a shared striving for spiritual growth.

Ta'anis 23a deduces from the story of Choni Hame'agel the somewhat startling conclusion that "death is preferable to life without companionship." R' Eliyahu E. Dessler explains that to righteous people, spiritual development is the essence of all life, and since they cannot grow without friends, they prefer death over life without friends (*Michtav Me'Eliyahu* 4:209). This underscores the great spiritual benefit Chazal saw in having friends.

[3] See Meiri (*Mishlei* 27:17) and *Mirkeves Hamishneh* (on this Mishnah), which also bases itself on the verse in *Mishlei* 27:17.

[4] *Bereishis* 2:18.

[5] Looking again at the example of Adam and Chava, Chava may have differed in many ways from Adam, but at the same time she was formed from his rib (as opposed to the other female creatures, which were created from the ground) so that she would have as much as possible in common with him (*Akeidas Yitzchak, Bereishis, Sha'ar* 8, *Perek Hachibbur*; Malbim, *Bereishis* 2:18).

[6] This is very likely what prompted Rashi (in his first explanation) to define the "friend" in the Mishnah as meaning books (see *Magen Avos*).

[7] Based on *Binyan Yehoshua* to *Avos D'Rebbi Nasan* 8:3.

[8] *Yevamos* 63a.

[9] See Rashi, *Yevamos* 63a ד"ה שושבינא.

[10] That the word "buy" refers to spending money to gain a friend is stated by Rambam (with the Bach's amendment), Rabbeinu Bachya, Rabbeinu Yona, and Bartenura. (*Peirushei Rabbeinu Yedaya Hapenini* mentions spending large sums of money.) That the phrase also includes kind words is mentioned by Rabbeinu Yona and *Mirkeves Hamishneh.*

[11] Rambam. See also *Sha'arei Teshuva* 1:§31.

[12] *Bava Basra* 16b. In taking this measurement literally, I have followed the interpretation of the Maharsha. Cf. *Chiddushei Ge'onim* on *Ein Yaakov.*

[13] *Avos D'Rebbi Nasan* 8:3. Meiri describes the friend mentioned in the Mishnah as one who is as close to you as yourself.

[14] *Lechem Shamayim.* See also Meiri. *Lechem Shamayim* goes on to say that even though one should not feel even a thousand friends to be too many, that is in regard to being friendly with people and giving them a pleasant smile. However, in regard to having a close relationship with people, one friend is adequate. This point is made in *Sanhedrin* 100b. (The idea that the Mishnah refers to specifically one friend fits in with the first phrase of the Mishnah, that of making oneself a Rav, which many of the commentators explain to refer specifically to one Rav. See *Nachalas Avos, Mirkeves Hamishneh, Midrash Dovid,* Meiri, *Bartenura,* and *Midrash Shmuel.*)

[15] *New York Times,* loc. cit. See there for contributing causes.

[16] "Too Busy for Real Friendships?" *Mail on Sunday* (London), December 19, 2004.

[17] See *Sifri* to *Devarim* (*parashas Nitzavim, piska* 2) that a (true) friend can be obtained only with great difficulty. Meiri makes a similar point, saying that a friendship of the type referred to in the Mishnah — where the friend is as close to you as yourself — requires a great deal of effort. That is why, he says, the Mishnah uses the word "*keneh.*"

[18] *Avos* 5:19 with Rambam, Rabbeinu Yona (MS ed.), and *Rav Yosef ben Nachmias.*

Beyond "Is the Chicken Kosher?"

פרק א׳ משנה ט״ז: רַבָּן גַּמְלִיאֵל הָיָה אוֹמֵר, עֲשֵׂה לְךָ רַב, וְהִסְתַּלֵּק מִן הַסָּפֵק, וְאַל תַּרְבֶּה לְעַשֵּׂר אֲמָדוֹת.

Chapter 1, Mishnah 16: *Rabbi Gamliel says: Make for yourself a Rav, remove yourself from doubt, and do not give excess tithes by estimating.*

T he Mishnah tells us to make for ourselves a Rav in order to remove uncertainty from our lives.[1] There are several reasons a person needs a Rav: to teach him Torah, to answer halachic queries, and to act as a guide and mentor in life.[2] In the following piece, we will look at the benefits of having a personal connection with a Rav who can advise a person on fundamental questions of how to conduct one's life. Sadly, this aspect of having a Rav is often missing in today's world, sometimes with unfortunate consequences.

The advantage of having a personal connection with a Rav was brought home to me recently when my family and I were thinking of joining a new community. It was to be a small group, with no more than seventy families. Obviously, it was a difficult decision to make, as it would have meant moving from a large, well-established setting — with over 2,000 families, as well as many shuls, schools, and yeshivos — to a small start-up community.

I discussed the matter with my Rav. As he listened to my concerns, he reassured me that many of them were nothing to be afraid of. On the contrary, he felt the move might be a very positive one for me. What struck me about our conversation, however, was how he addressed my needs as an individual and thought about how the move would affect me personally. I realized that someone else who discussed the very same question with him would probably receive a completely different response. An absolutely right decision for one person could very well be an utterly wrong one for someone else. Without having a Rav who knew me personally, I would never have been able to make such a major decision with such clarity.

In my case, the decision involved where to live, but the same is true of any life decision, be it finding the right marriage partner, how to educate one's children, or deciding what to do in life. It is much easier to discuss these issues and reach the right conclusion when you have a Rav who knows you well and understands your background as well as your strengths and weaknesses.

Perhaps the Mishnah wants to stress this aspect of having a Rav in saying, "Make for *yourself* a Rav." It doesn't say that your shul or community should have a Rav, but that you personally should have one.[3]

Acquiring a Rav

The practice of making a Rav for oneself is not so common today. As Torah becomes more easily accessible, people relate to it in a more and more depersonalized manner. *Shiurim* can be downloaded and listened to electronically, questions can be e-mailed to "Ask the Rabbi" forums, and books can be read on virtually any topic in *Yiddishkeit*. Rarely does a person have to meet a rabbi face-to-face, much less build up a real and meaningful relationship with him. While there certainly are positive aspects to this new accessibility of Torah (especially for people in out-of-the-way places who don't have direct physical access to Rabbanim), the loss of personal contact that comes with it has become an unfortunate casualty.

Many people wish they had a personal connection with a Rav but don't know how to go about making one. The *talmidei chachamim* they would like to be close to — those who have deep insight into human nature and whose opinions they value and want to hear — have busy schedules and are not easily accessible.

It is perhaps with this in mind that the Mishnah tells us to *make* a Rav for ourselves. The word *aseh* — make — suggests that we have to extend ourselves to create a situation that did not exist before. In this context, says the Meiri, if we don't find a Rav ready to teach us Torah, we have to work to acquire one.[4] Similarly, in order to obtain a personal relationship with a Rav, one has to be prepared to make some effort. One cannot expect great Rabbanim to have time to pursue a relationship with all their *talmidim*. It is up to the *talmid* to seek the Rav.

In this regard, one must use his own initiative. One of my friends has developed a close connection with his Rav by offering to drive him to his various engagements. That way, he spends time talking to his Rav in an informal setting without interfering with the Rav's packed schedule. But one doesn't have to have a car to develop a relationship with a Rav. Someone else I know of turned up on his Rav-to-be's doorstep every *erev Shabbos* with a bunch of flowers. After several weeks of this, the Rav announced, "Congratulations! You've just got yourself a new Rav!"

At first this may sound like bribery, but when one considers that a Rav of a large community has numerous *mispallelim*, many of whom are not interested in a personal relationship with him, one realizes that giving flowers or benefiting the Rav in some other way has nothing to do with bribery. It is just a way of letting the Rav know that unlike the other members of the shul, you are interested in more than a casual acquaintance with him.

Rabbi Dovid Morgenstern, one of Rabbi Yosef Shalom Elyashiv's closest *talmidim*, began building his connection with the Rav twenty-two years ago by walking him to shul every morning.[5] Rav Elyashiv didn't approach Rav Morgenstern asking him to escort him to shul! Rav Morgenstern thought of the idea on his own, arising every day before dawn just to be able to spend a few minutes speaking with Rav Elyashiv.

These people used initiative to build a personal connection with their Rabbanim. They probably felt a little uncomfortable at first, but in time their uneasiness subsided and they were able to build a relationship with the leading Rabbanim of our generation.

For those who don't feel comfortable coming up with innovative ways of spending informal time with Rabbanim, the Torah provides an opening in the requirement to visit one's Rav on *chol hamo'ed*.[6]

This gives everyone the opportunity to spend time with his Rav without feeling awkward.

By Association...

People who have a close relationship with a Rav generally achieve more in their lives than those who do not. With a Rav to guide them, they often surpass even people who are more educated and talented than they are.

This point can be observed from Yehoshua bin Nun. In his earlier years, Yehoshua's heart was not "open to wisdom," to the extent that people ridiculed him for his lack of comprehension.[7] Yet it was Yehoshua who was chosen to lead the Jewish people after Moshe Rabbeinu passed away, and, as Chazal make clear, it was his devotion to Moshe that led to his inheriting this position.[8]

There are several reasons why a close connection with a Rav and mentor is a sure predictor of success.

Firstly, closeness with a Rav helps a person utilize his talents and energies more effectively. When problems arise, he has someone with wisdom and experience to turn to for counsel and direction. Rather than being consumed by doubts, which sap his energy, he can face life's challenges with calm reassurance. Instead of having to reinvent the wheel, he can benefit from the experience of someone who has dealt with similar issues and who has guided many others through similar situations over the years.

Secondly, having regular contact with a great individual inspires a person to become great himself. Instead of measuring himself against his friends, whose accomplishments are more or less on the same level as his own, he can look up to someone who is above himself. This pushes him to strive ever higher, safeguarding him from complacency. Continual exposure to someone who thinks with more depth than he does also helps him expand his way of thinking, leading him to attain a level of greatness he couldn't have reached on his own.

Apart from these practical reasons, there are also spiritual reasons why someone who is close to a Rav will most likely surpass his friends. For one thing, the Rav will pray for him, just as Moshe prayed for Yehoshua.[9] Also, by being close to a *talmid chacham* he will merit more wisdom. This is because wisdom comes down to the world through the wise people of each generation, who act as conduits for it. Although these wise people bring down wisdom to the whole world, those who are close to them are able to absorb a greater portion of wisdom than everyone else. Thus, one who is close to a Rav is able to attain higher levels of wisdom than he would be able to attain on his own. The closer he draws to the Rav, the more wisdom he will be able to absorb.[10]

Food, Shelter, Clothing, and...a Rav

Having a connection to a Rav has always been an integral part of a Jew's life, to the extent that if a *talmid* had to be exiled to a city of refuge, his Rav was required to go into exile with him. Chazal derived this law from the Torah's description of the city of refuge as a place where people need to be able to live,[11] from which they learned that people in exile must be provided with whatever they need to live.[12] Since having a Rav is an essential part of life, this included providing him with his Rav.[13]

A *talmid* in exile would have been deprived of many conveniences. Without his friends and away from home, he would have lacked many comforts. Yet Chazal didn't require that any of these things be provided for him. The reason is that the Torah only obligated us to provide him with what he needed to live, in other words, items that were crucial to his existence, not ones that would merely make his life easier and more comfortable, but without which he could still survive. If Chazal insisted that his Rav go into exile with him, it can only be because having a Rav was vital to his existence, a necessity of life without which he could not survive.

This halacha is particularly interesting in that the city of refuge was a place filled with *talmidei chachamim*. The *Levi'im*, who devoted their lives to learning and teaching Torah, lived in these cities, so the *talmid* could easily have found another Rav. The reason his personal Rav had to come along with him was that he would feel more comfortable learning from someone he already knew and with whom he had a connection.[14] Once again we see the vital importance of the close rapport that exists between student and teacher.

For many decades Rabbi Yehoshua Neuwirth, author of *Shemiras Shabbos Kehilchasa*, was a close *talmid* of Rabbi Shlomo Zalman Auerbach. When Reb Shlomo Zalman passed away, Rabbi Neuwirth asked Rabbi Yosef Shalom Elyashiv to become his new Rav. Rabbi Neuwirth was almost seventy at the time and an eminent sage in his own right, but nevertheless even he felt a pressing need to make a Rav for himself.

Thus it is that no matter how old or wise a person is, he is never beyond the stage of making a Rav for himself. In fact, the wiser a person is, the more he seeks the perspective of an expert and devoted outsider who gives guidance, inspiration, and objective evaluations. This is a gift that is far too valuable to pass up.

---

[1] Rashi, Rabbeinu Yona, Rabbeinu Bachya, *Bartenura*, *Tiferes Yisrael*. Cf. *Magen Avos*.

[2] The phrase *aseh lecha Rav* appears twice in the first chapter, here and in Mishnah 6. Rambam explains that Mishnah 6 refers to a Rav who teaches Torah, while the Mishnah here refers to a Rav who rules in halachic matters (see *Magen Avos*, which elaborates on this distinction; see also Rabbeinu Bachya, who makes the same distinction, as well as Rabbeinu Yona and *Bartenura*). *Baruch She'amar* on Mishnah 6 adds that the Rav serves not just as a teacher of Torah but also as a mentor in life. In a similar vein, *Mirkeves Hamishneh* says that the Rav is responsible for protecting a person from incorrect beliefs and teaching him how to think properly. In the following discussion, we will focus on the idea of *aseh lecha Rav* in general, without reference to how our Mishnah relates to the earlier one.

[3] See *Tiferes Yisrael* (Mishnah 6), which derives a different point from this wording.

[4] Meiri to *Avos* 1:6.

[5] Heard from R' Dovid Morgenstern.

[6] *Sukka* 27b. Some authorities say this requirement is no longer in force, but all agree that it is a commendable practice. *Noda BiYehuda* (*Mahadura Tinyana, Orach Chaim* §94) writes that the obligation to visit one's Rav during the festival does not apply when there is no *Beis Hamikdash*, but he concludes that it is still commendable even now. *Aruch Laner* (*Sukka* 27b) maintains that the requirement applies now as it did in former times, while *Ya'aros Devash*, §12, asserts that the requirement is in force only when the *Beis Hamikdash* is *not* standing. Cf. *Orchos Rabbeinu* 2:112; *Ateres Paz* 3:§15.

[7] *Yalkut Me'am Lo'ez, Devarim* 34:9, quoting *Shusa Dinuka*. *Yalkut Shimoni* (*Mishlei, remez* 959) relates that they called him a "fool."

[8] *Bamidbar Rabba* 21:14; *Midrash Tanchuma, parashas Pinchas* 11.

[9] Rashi, *Bamidbar* 13:16. In a letter to a *talmid*, R' Shimshon Dovid Pincus mentioned how he prayed for him almost every day (*Nefesh Shimshon, Igros U'ma'amarim*, 38).

[10] *Drashos HaRan*, §8, as elaborated on in *Divrei Chanina*, 23 and 69.

[11] *Devarim* 4:42.

[12] *Makkos* 10a.

[13] *Matnas Chaim, Kinyanim* 1:23.

[14] Ibid. based on *Nimukei Yosef* to *Makkos* 10a.

Very *Early Childhood Education*

פרק ב׳ משנה י״א: הוּא הָיָה מוֹנֶה שְׁבָחָן. רַבִּי אֱלִיעֶזֶר
בֶּן הָרְקְנוֹס בּוֹר סוּד שֶׁאֵינוֹ מְאַבֵּד טִפָּה. רַבִּי יְהוֹשֻׁעַ
בֶּן חֲנַנְיָה אַשְׁרֵי יוֹלַדְתּוֹ. רַבִּי יוֹסֵי הַכֹּהֵן חָסִיד. רַבִּי
שִׁמְעוֹן בֶּן נְתַנְאֵל יְרֵא חֵטְא. וְרַבִּי אֶלְעָזָר בֶּן עֲרָךְ מַעְיָן
הַמִּתְגַּבֵּר.

Chapter 2, Mishnah 11: *He [Rabbi Yochanan ben Zakkai] used to enumerate their praises: Rabbi Eliezer ben Horkanos is a cemented cistern that does not lose a drop; Rabbi Yehoshua ben Chananya — happy is she who bore him; Rabbi Yose HaKohen is pious; Rabbi Shimon ben Nesanel fears sin; and Rabbi Elazar ben Arach is a spring that flows increasingly stronger.*

I n our Mishnah, Rabbi Yochanan ben Zakkai recounts the praises of five of his students. All of the praises except one point to an outstanding quality in the man he describes. But the description of Rabbi Yehoshua is different — it praises his mother.

Rabbi Yochanan commends Rabbi Yehoshua's mother, attributing his spiritual greatness to her. Why does he do this? Upon becoming aware that she was carrying a child, Rabbi Yehoshua's mother immediately went to the *battei midrash* in order to expose him to the sounds of Torah.[1] During each day of her pregnancy, she would ask the *talmidei chachamim* learning there to pray that her son grow up to be a tzaddik and a *talmid chacham*.[2] And after he was born, she brought his carriage into the *beis midrash* so that his ears would become saturated with words of Torah.[3] In fact, according to some commentators, she never took his carriage out of the *beis midrash*, so that he would only hear words of Torah.[4]

Rabbi Yochanan ben Zakkai recognized that it was this special upbringing, suffused entirely with holiness and purity, which caused Rabbi Yehoshua to surpass his colleagues and become the leading sage of his generation. Thus Rabbi Yochanan praised Rabbi Yehoshua's mother, crediting her with her son's major achievements.[5]

The Greatness of Rabbi Yehoshua

In order to fully appreciate the significance of Rabbi Yochanan's praise, we must first understand the greatness of Rabbi Yehoshua.

Rabbi Yehoshua possessed all the admirable character traits a person can possibly have,[6] and was renowned for his pleasant manner.[7] He was also extremely learned, earning himself the much sought-after position of *av beis din*.[8] He had great insight, often proposing ingenious solutions to problems that no one else was able to solve.[9] News of his wisdom spread so far that the Roman emperor Hadrian frequently summoned Rabbi Yehoshua to his palace to answer a variety of questions,[10] ranging from the absurd ("What will I dream about tonight?")[11] to the philosophical ("How did G-d create the world?").[12] In addition to going to Rome, Rabbi Yehoshua also traveled to Athens and Alexandria, spreading Torah and defending Judaism against Greek attack.[13] In fact, when he passed away, his friends exclaimed, "What will become of us [now] at the hands of the non-believers?"[14]

Rabbi Yehoshua was also a master of Kabbala. He once used his knowledge of the supernatural to lift himself up in the air.[15] Another time, while walking with a friend, he began expounding the *ma'aseh merkava*, the most secret and profound section of Jewish mysticism. The intense *kedusha* emanating from his words caused the sky to cloud over, which was most unusual for that time of year, and scores of angels gathered around him to listen to his every word.[16]

Bearing Rabbi Yehoshua's greatness in mind, Rabbi Yochanan's statement takes on extra meaning.

The Power of Influence

When an ordinary person looks at a great sage, he cannot surmise what experience led to his greatness. Yet Rabbi Yochanan did exactly that, attributing the greatness of Rabbi Yehoshua to the efforts his mother made to raise him in an atmosphere of *kedusha*.[17]

The idea that a child benefits from hearing Torah even before he is old enough to understand the words is clear from the mitzvah of *hakhel*. The Jewish people were commanded to gather in Jerusalem every seven years to hear the king read from the Torah. Although too young to comprehend, babies were also brought, in order to instill *yiras Shamayim* in them.[18]

Everything a person is exposed to as a young child has the potential to influence him positively or negatively. This is indicated in the Torah, which informs us that Esav's wives worshiped idols and that this was a great source of anguish for both Yitzchak and Rivka.[19] The verse mentions Yitzchak before Rivka, and Chazal explain that this is because Yitzchak was more troubled by their idolatrous ways than Rivka was. Never having been exposed to idolatry, Yitzchak was more sensitive than Rivka, who had grown up in a house of idol worship.[20]

Rivka had left her father's house when she was only three years old,[21] and the incident with Esav's wives did not take place until she was sixty-three — sixty years later.[22] Thus we see that exposing a child to negative influences leaves a permanent mark on his soul;[23] even as an old man, he will never have the same sensitivities again.

The soul is very fragile. It is affected by subtle, intangible influences. The sound of Torah that Rabbi Yehoshua heard as a baby was not something that could be felt, yet it had the power to mold his future and lay the pathway for his greatness. Similarly, the idol worship in Rivka's house was not something in which she actively participated. She never worshiped idols; she just watched others worship them. Nevertheless, the mere sight of it desensitized her revulsion for this sin, leaving a permanent scar on her soul.

Looking at an infant in a carriage, it is hard to believe that he could grow spiritually by hearing words of holiness or be scarred spiritually from hearing words of impurity. After all, he is only an infant, who cannot speak or understand anything being said. Even once he's a toddler and walking around, it is still difficult to imagine that he could be affected by exposure to sights and sounds that are beyond his understanding.

The story of Rabbi Yehoshua hearing Torah as a baby, the mitzvah of *hakhel*, and Rivka seeing idol worship as a three-year-old demonstrate that a child's *neshama* is affected by what it experiences well before the baby is old enough to understand the experiences. His childish behavior and immaturity stem from physical limitations. He may be unable to talk, walk, or behave appropriately, but these are all aspects of his physical immaturity. His soul, however, is not limited by these physical constraints and discerns every bit of *kedusha*, benefiting from even the smallest pinpoint. Similarly, it discerns every bit of impurity, and is impoverished accordingly.

Controlling Input

Although rare, there are people today who make heroic efforts to enact this principle positively in their daily lives. One family in Jerusalem hosts a weekly *shiur* in their home specifically for the benefit it brings to their children. Despite the fact that their oldest child is only in second grade and is far too young to understand the contents of the *shiur*, they feel that the sounds of Torah permeating their home will make a lasting impression on all their children and instill in them a deep love for Torah.

Families such as this are few and far between. Sadly, many parents leave their young ones with babysitters and housekeepers who dress immodestly and listen to coarse, inappropriate music.

The parents would never willingly expose older children to such influences, but while the children are still young the parents feel that no harm is done. Similarly, some mothers take their little boys with them to a women's swimming pool or beach, rationalizing that they are too young to be affected by what they see.

For this reason, many contemporary halachic authorities rule that it is improper for a mother to take her young son swimming in a ladies' pool.[24] Other Torah authorities stress the harm in letting young children hear songs with immodest lyrics, saying that it creates a spiritual coarseness within them,[25] even though the child is too young to grasp the meaning of the words.

Researchers are just beginning to discover what our Sages have known all along, that fetuses are affected by outside influences on them.

Anthony Casper, a psychologist at the University of North Carolina, had expectant mothers read aloud Dr. Seuss' book *The Cat in the Hat* twice a day to their unborn children. A few days after birth the newborns were given the opportunity to hear another Dr. Seuss story. The infants were outfitted with a special feeding contraption that let them change the story read by altering the speed of their sucking.

As demonstrated by their sucking speed, the newborns remembered *The Cat in the Hat*, liked it better than the new story, and adjusted their sucking speed to hear the familiar one. They preferred the story read by their mother over another female reader, and they preferred it read forward instead of backward.[26]

Scientific research is able to prove that a fetus is affected by what it hears, which is impressive. But these discoveries still leave many questions unanswered. For example, what about the effect of inadvertent sights and sounds on an infant — things that are not done deliberately and are thus not measurable scientifically? And what about their effects on a person later in life? For example, how will they affect his refinement of character or his understanding of Torah as an adult?

These are areas that scientists cannot address, and that only our Sages, with their great wisdom and depth of vision, could perceive. They teach us that the sights to which we expose our children and the experiences in which we involve them play a major role in molding their characters and determining what kind of adults they will become.

Rabbi Yehoshua's Mother: A Second Look

In all this, we must not overlook the crucial role of Rabbi Yehoshua's mother. Beyond what Rabbi Yehoshua heard and saw as a child was the unalterable fact that he was blessed with a mother who was perceptive enough to expose him to Torah as a baby. Such a mother, with a passionate love for and belief in Torah, molded Rabbi Yehoshua as much as the sights and sounds to which she exposed him. Consider: here was a woman who was so certain about the impact of Torah on her baby that she put aside her own needs and sat with him for endless hours in the *beis midrash* — oblivious to any other consideration. Her yearning for her son to become a Torah giant was so profound that it overrode all else — even to the point of asking others every day for nine months to pray for his spiritual growth. To be raised by this kind of mother was almost a guarantee that the child would become a spiritual and intellectual leader of Jewry.

Thus we see that more than what parents say or do with their children, it is the parents themselves, and who they truly are, that has the greatest impact.

Rabbi Yehoshua's *neshama* heard Torah; what he saw with his own eyes was a mother who reinforced it.

The most powerful teaching that a parent can provide children is a living example. As an infant, Rabbi Yehoshua was exposed to the sounds and sights of Torah. But as he was growing up, he saw with his own eyes and sensed with his own heart that his mother not only preached about the power of Torah, but fully lived it.

Therefore, Rabbi Yochanan ben Zakkai, instead of praising him, praises his mother: "Happy is she who bore him." She persevered in the face of many difficulties; she possessed deep insight and profound faith; but primarily it was her personal example that transformed that infant into the light of all Israel. Truly happy is she who bore him and was responsible for his greatness — and truly deserving of fulsome praise.

---

[1] Vilna Gaon (commentary to *Shir Hashirim* 1:8). See also *Pele Yo'etz*, s.v. תורה. The precedent for exposing a fetus to Torah is Rivka, who, Chazal say, stood outside the *battei kenesses* and *battei midrash* while pregnant with Yaakov and Esav (*Bereishis Rabba* 63:6; see *Oznayim LaTorah*, *Bereishis* 25:22). Indeed, *Shevet Mussar* (chap. 24) advises a pregnant woman to sit in holy places, look at holy people, and listen to holy things.

[2] Rashi and *Tiferes Yisrael*.

[3] *Tiferes Yisrael*. Although according to most of the above-mentioned commentators it is possible that R' Yehoshua's mother did only some but not all of these actions (see also note 5 to Rashi, Mossad Harav Kook edition, regarding variations in *Yerushalmi*, *Yevamos* 1:6), *Pele Yo'etz* (s.v. תורה) credits her with having done all of them.

[4] *Magen Avos*, Bartenura.

[5] See Rashi and *Magen Avos*.

[6] Rabbeinu Yona.

[7] *Midrash Shmuel*.

[8] *Bava Kama* 74b.

[9] See *Nidda* 61a; *Bechoros* 8b.

[10] See *Chullin* 59b–60a; *Bechoros* 8b; *Bereishis Rabba* 28:3.

[11] *Berachos* 56a.

[12] *Bereishis Rabba* 10:3.

[13] His discussion with the Jewish community in Alexandria is recorded in *Nidda* 69b–70a. His debate with the elders of Athens is found in *Bechoros* 8b.

[14] *Chagiga* 5b.

[15] *Bechoros* 8b.

[16] *Chagiga* 14b.

[17] Based on Rashi, who writes, "She [his mother] *caused him* to become a *talmid chacham*." *Magen Avos* uses a similar expression.

[18] *Devarim* 31:12–13. That the Torah is referring to babies, as opposed to children who are old enough to understand, is clear from *Haksav V'hakabbala* and *Oznayim LaTorah*. Cf. Ramban and *Ohr Hachaim*. *Chagiga* 3a says that the young children were to be brought in order to provide *their parents* with reward. This implies that the benefit was for the parents, not for the children. The explanation offered above follows the interpretation of the Chasam Sofer (*Drashos Chasam Sofer* 1:26a), *Oznayim LaTorah*, and *Nachalas Yaakov* (on *Maseches Soferim* 18:6).

[19] *Bereishis* 26:35 with Rashi.

[20] *Bereishis Rabba* 65:4.

[21] Rashi on *Bereishis* 25:20.

[22] We know it was sixty years later because Esav was forty at the time (*Bereishis* 26:34) and was born twenty years after Rivka was married (from *Bereishis* 25:20 and 26).

[23] *Chinuch Habanim L'mitzvos V'dinei Katan*, 39.

[24] See *Halichos Bas Yisrael*, 101, and *Children in Halachah*, 32.

[25] Chofetz Chaim, *Sha'ar Hatziyun* 560:25, in the name of the Shelah.

[26] Dr. Frederick Wirth, *Prenatal Parenting* (New York: Regan Books, 2001), 36–37.

The Lost Art
of Thinking

פרק ג' משנה ה': רַבִּי חֲנִינָא בֶּן חֲכִינַאי אוֹמֵר, הַנֵּעוֹר
בַּלַּיְלָה וְהַמְהַלֵּךְ בַּדֶּרֶךְ יְחִידִי וּמְפַנֶּה לִבּוֹ לְבַטָּלָה, הֲרֵי
זֶה מִתְחַיֵּב בְּנַפְשׁוֹ.

Chapter 3, Mishnah 5: *Rabbi Chanina ben Chachinai says: One who is awake at night or who travels alone on the road, but turns his heart to idleness, bears guilt for his soul.*

*A*pollo 9 astronaut Rusty Schweickart reminisced about a special moment in his life that occurred as he was floating outside the spacecraft, testing equipment. His fellow astronaut, Dave Scott, had been photographing him when suddenly the camera jammed. Scott had to return to the capsule to repair the camera, leaving Schweickart dangling alone for a few introspective moments. What does he recall thinking about while traveling at 17,000 mph in absolute silence, looking down on the beautiful, blue Earth? "Questions," he replied. "What does this mean? How did I get here? Who am I?"[1]

Floating alone in space is certainly an ideal time to contemplate the meaning of life, but, as the Mishnah teaches us, we don't need to wait for such rare occasions to engage in introspection: we can enjoy the same pleasure each night in the comfort of our own beds.

Night: A Time for Thinking

Dovid Hamelech instructs us to "think in our hearts while lying in bed" (*Imru vilvavchem al mishkavchem*).[2] The reason he singles out time in bed as an opportune time for thought is that, away from the daily grind, one's mind is free to reflect on the important things in life without disturbances.[3] It is for this reason that our Mishnah criticizes someone who wastes his wakeful moments in bed contemplating irrelevant matters: he fritters away time that is best suited for serious reflection.[4]

Although the words "*Imru vilvavchem*" refer to thinking,[5] their literal translation is "speak in your heart." The reason Dovid Hamelech uses the seemingly indirect expression "speak in your heart," instead of a direct word for thought like *machshava*, may be to convey the following idea: We each have an inner voice that lies at the depth of our consciousness. During the day, amongst the hustle and bustle of the physical world, that voice is muffled and cannot easily be heard. But in the darkness and stillness of night, free from all distractions, that voice becomes audible, filling our minds with all kinds of thoughts. Alone with nothing but our own consciousness, the "speech of our hearts" becomes clearly discernible, occupying the entirety of our minds.

Thinking on the Road

The Mishnah mentions a second stretch of time that is conducive to uninterrupted thought: traveling alone. This does not refer to today's "traveling alone," which means going by ourselves on a plane, bus, or boat amongst throngs of people and a stream of distractions. In earlier times, "traveling alone" meant going by foot or donkey along secluded country roads.[6] Away from civilization and without anyone to interrupt his concentration, one could reflect with unmatched peace of mind. Nowadays, however, modern transportation has stripped us of this serenity and we need to seek alternative opportunities to be alone with our thoughts. The contemporary version of *mehalech baderech yechidi* could be driving alone in a car, or walking to and from one's various destinations, both of which can be used for quiet reflection.

The Mishnah does not demand that we learn from a *sefer* at these times.[7] Lying in bed in a dark room and traveling along a road are hardly suitable occasions for studying a book. The Mishnah only admonishes us not to *turn our hearts to idleness*. It expects us to use these times to think Torah-related thoughts, be they *divrei Torah*, how to refine our character, or how to bring joy to others.[8]

Mind Control

We often wish we had the ability to think about important matters in an abstract way — indeed, we may even manage to begin doing so successfully — but inevitably our minds drift to unrelated topics, and before we know it, we are thinking mundane thoughts, lost in them entirely or, at best, wondering how exactly we ended up on the subject we did. Instead of controlling our thoughts, we find our thoughts controlling us.

In this regard, the Mishnah's phraseology of "turning his heart" is very revealing.[9] It teaches us that the ability to control our hearts, which in this context refers to our thoughts, lies within our grasp, and that we can "turn" our thoughts from one topic to another. In the same way that the person in the Mishnah "turns" his thoughts to idleness, so is he also capable of "turning" them to meaningful matters.

One man who worked on developing his ability to direct his thoughts found that as time passed he became better at it. He described the immense satisfaction and enjoyment he derived from being able to steer his thoughts as he wished.[10]

Besides the inherent fulfillment a person feels at being able to control his thoughts, there are also other pleasures that come from directing one's mind inward.

When you use your ability for creative thought, life is never boring. You could be waiting at a red traffic light or sitting in a waiting room — it makes no difference: You always have something to turn around in your mind, reaching new insights and understanding things that never occurred to you before. Instead of seeking constant stimulation, you are content just to be with your own thoughts and to spend time with yourself.

Little wonder that people in earlier generations looked forward to those parts of their day when they could spend time alone, contemplating important matters and connecting with their Creator without interruption.[11]

Today, this ideal has been almost entirely forgotten and whenever we find ourselves alone, we make frantic efforts to escape. When walking alone in the street after having been in a place where our cell phone had to be turned off, the first thing we do is switch it on. Upon entering our cars, we immediately feel the need to turn on the radio, play a tape, or phone a friend. It rarely enters our minds to use these times for uninterrupted thought and self-reflection.

Society impels us to act this way, teaching us to fill any quiet moments with noise and disruption so that we are never alone with ourselves. Many things society calls relaxing — novels, cinema, television, sports, and card games — are, in truth, nothing more than diversions. Being busy, rushing from meeting to meeting, stuffing our ears with headphones, and scurrying to check e-mail from handheld devices are often just ways of avoiding oneself.

Sometimes we find ourselves alone quite unexpectedly; at other times it is anticipated. How we use such moments reveals a great deal about ourselves. It is a barometer of our spirituality, and the degree to which we are in touch with who we truly are. To some, the thought of being alone with nothing to do is frightening. Having nothing to do, watch, read, listen to, or play with is a nightmare. They become very uncomfortable, for being alone with themselves means coming face-to-face with their own reality. Their lives are filled with so many distractions that the most important person in their lives — themselves — remains a stranger, and they feel uneasy in their own presence.[12]

In light of this ethos, our Mishnah is particularly refreshing. It restores a rare and almost forgotten ability — to use one's time alone for serious reflection. You are up at night anyway. Do not squander the precious moments. Use them to get in touch with yourself. You are walking along the road. Do not kill the time. Use it wisely to give voice to your innermost thoughts. We should scout out such opportunities, and certainly, when they arise we should utilize them — for these opportunities have the potential of becoming the most worthwhile moments of our lives.

[1] Louis Pollack, *Fingerprints on the Universe* (New York: Shaar Press, 1994), vii–viii.

[2] *Tehillim* 4:5.

[3] Radak and Meiri to *Tehillim* 4:5.

[4] *Milei D'Avos, Nachalas Avos*. Like many commentators, they learn that נעור בלילה is talking specifically about time awake at night in bed. Rabbeinu Yona, however, writes that the uniqueness of the night is that then a person is free from work and is not disturbed by noise, which could include any part of the night.

[5] Radak, *Tehillim* 4:5.

[6] This is clear from *Milei D'Avos*, which mentions being away from civilization, and also from *Nachalas Avos, Roshei Avos*, and *Peirushei Rabbeinu Yosef ben Shoshan*, which say that this refers to where nobody else is present.

[7] See Rabbeinu Yona and *Tiferes Yisrael*, who say that he should utilize his time to *think* Torah thoughts.

[8] Many commentators discuss thinking *divrei Torah* (Rabbeinu Yona, *Bartenura, Mirkeves Hamishneh*, and others). Others mention thinking about mitzvos (*Milei D'Avos*), contemplating G-d's wonders (*Pirkei Moshe*), and thinking about *avodas Hashem* (*Tiferes Yisrael*).

[9] See *Milei D'Avos*, which translates *u'mefaneh* as turning, as opposed to vacating.

[10] It is not within the scope of this work to explain how to direct one's thoughts.

[11] See *Peirushei Rabbeinu Yitzchak ben Harav Shlomo MiToledo*; *Kad Hakemach*, s.v. (א) תורה; Shelah, *Maseches Yoma, Hilchos Teshuva* §50; *Kuzari*, beg. §3.

[12] *Alei Shur* 1:178 and 2:415.

Before You React, Consider This...

פרק ג' משנה ט"ו: רַבִּי אֶלְעָזָר הַמּוֹדָעִי אוֹמֵר, הַמְחַלֵּל
אֶת הַקֳדָשִׁים, וְהַמְבַזֶּה אֶת הַמּוֹעֲדוֹת, וְהַמַּלְבִּין פְּנֵי
חֲבֵרוֹ בָרַבִּים, וְהַמֵּפֵר בְּרִיתוֹ שֶׁל אַבְרָהָם אָבִינוּ, וְהַמְגַלֶּה
פָנִים בַּתּוֹרָה שֶׁלֹּא כַהֲלָכָה, אַף עַל פִּי שֶׁיֵּשׁ בְּיָדוֹ תּוֹרָה
וּמַעֲשִׂים טוֹבִים, אֵין לוֹ חֵלֶק לָעוֹלָם הַבָּא.

Chapter 3, Mishnah 15: *Rabbi Elazar HaModai
says: He who desecrates holy things, who degrades
the festivals, who humiliates his fellow in public,
who renounces the Covenant of Avraham our
forefather, or who distorts the Torah contrary to
halacha — even though he may possess Torah
and good deeds, he has no portion in the World
to Come.*

R abbi Meir Chodosh was once in the hospital for surgery
when a doctor came in to perform some blood tests. Reb
Meir asked his visitors to step outside while the blood
was drawn. When they returned, his visitors asked him why he
had wanted to be alone, but Reb Meir did not want to discuss the
matter and changed the subject.

Some time later, a student was alone with him and pressed
him to reveal what he was hiding about the incident. "The doctor
is a good doctor," Reb Meir explained reluctantly, "but he is not
proficient at locating veins. He has to poke several times before
succeeding. I realized that he may be self-conscious about this in
front of others, and I wanted to save him from being embarrassed
in public."[1]

Let us further examine the idea of not embarrassing others in
public.

The Severity of Shame

It is forbidden to shame a person any time, even in private.[2] The
reason our Mishnah specifies shaming *in public* is because the severe

punishment of losing one's share in the World to Come applies only when one shames someone in front of others.[3] "Public," in this regard, is not necessarily a hall filled with people: even three people suffice.[4] Since the instigator also counts as one of the three,[5] shaming a person in front of two other people is already sufficient to forfeit one's portion in the World to Come.[6]

The idea of not shaming another is derived from the story of Tamar and Yehuda. When it was learned that Tamar was expecting a child, Yehuda sentenced her to death for committing harlotry.[7] Yehuda didn't know it at the time, but he was actually the one responsible for the pregnancy. Tamar had in her possession Yehuda's ring and staff, which he had left with her as a pledge. Using these items, she could have proved that the child's father was Yehuda, thus saving herself from death. But she did not.

Instead, she sent a vague and ambiguous message: "By the man to whom these belong did I become pregnant."[8] She preferred to let herself be thrown into the fiery furnace rather than embarrass Yehuda publicly by naming him as the one responsible. From her behavior, Chazal learn that it is better to die than to publicly embarrass another person.[9]

Considering that the punishment for publicly embarrassing another person has eternal consequences, it makes sense why one should rather die than do so. Better to die a physical death and spiritually survive forever than to die a spiritual death and continue an empty physical existence for a number of years.[10]

We also learn this concept from Yosef. Before Yosef revealed himself to his brothers, he asked all the Egyptian guards to leave the room.[11] By being left alone with his brothers, Yosef was putting his life in danger. The brothers had the power to kill Yosef; they were in fact so powerful that they were capable of destroying all of Egypt.[12] This, coupled with the fact that they were angry with him for antagonizing them and threatening to keep Binyamin as a slave, created a situation rife with danger for Yosef. When they saw that they were alone with him they could easily have killed him, putting an end to all the pain and hardship Yosef was causing them. Before he even had a chance to reveal himself, he would be dead.

Yosef was fully aware of the danger. Although he realized he might be killed, he asked the Egyptians to leave so that his brothers would not be embarrassed when he revealed his identity to them. He said to himself, "I would rather die than embarrass my brothers in front of the Egyptians."[13]

Applying the Lesson to Everyday Interactions

Chazal instruct us to aspire to reach the levels of our ancestors and to ask ourselves, "When will my actions reach the actions of my forefathers?"[14] That means that we, too, should say, "I would rather die than publicly embarrass another person."

Applying this to our daily lives would mean that if someone upsets us we should prefer to die than embarrass him. It is hard to control ourselves, however, when we feel the other person is to blame. When another's negligence causes us harm, we feel that any embarrassment he suffers is his own fault and is totally justified. We rationalize that he deserves what he gets. For example, people expect a certain level of service in a restaurant or on an airplane. When that level is not forthcoming, it is tempting to speak sharply. One feels justified berating the employee even in front of others, as he is at fault. His lack of efficiency caused harm.

Again, let us look at Yosef. His brothers were in the wrong. Their mistake caused Yosef great suffering — 22 years of separation from his father, 12 of which were spent in prison. Yosef had every right to be angry with them, to deliberately shame them for all the pain they had caused him. He could easily have justified any embarrassment that he caused them. Yet he said, "I would rather die than let my brothers be shamed."

It is clear, therefore, that even if the other person is at fault, there is no justification for shaming him.[15] So, if a guest breaks an expensive ornament in your home, or accidentally wipes out all the photos from your digital camera, before you groan out loud — which would embarrass him in front of those present — take a deep breath and remind yourself, "I should rather give up my whole life, never seeing my family again and destroying all my dreams, than embarrass him publicly."

Haste and impatience also make it hard to refrain from embarrassing another person. When in a hurry, it is difficult to weigh every word and make sure that no one will take offense.

Picture the following: You are late for an important business meeting. Hundreds of thousands of dollars are at stake. Your presence is essential. You climb into a cab with two of your partners, give the driver the address, and begin discussing the details of the meeting. Half an hour later the cab is still driving around. The driver is lost. What should have been a ten-minute trip has turned into a fiasco. Under such pressure, it is hard to stay calm. It is much easier to lash out with a fierce remark and to scold the driver for his incompetence than to think, "I would rather die than shame him in public."[16]

Consider Tamar and the pressure she felt as she stood by the fire.[17] She knew that in a few minutes she would die. She felt the intense heat and watched the soaring flames. And yet she managed to keep her presence of mind to such an extent that she could carefully word her message to Yehuda. Instead of saying, "You are the father of my unborn child, and here are your belongings to prove it!" she said, "I am pregnant by the man to whom these belong."[18] To weigh each word under such stress demanded heroic strength of character. When we reflect on her behavior, we are inspired to reach ever higher levels — even in everyday situations.

Rabbi Yehoshua Leib Diskin used to deliver a weekly *shiur* in his home, and before each *shiur*, his attendant would prepare tea for him. Once, the attendant mistook the salt container for the sugar bowl and put salt into Reb Yehoshua Leib's cup. Since Reb Yehoshua Leib's doctor had prescribed that he use a lot of sugar in order to increase his energy, the attendant stirred several heaping spoonfuls of salt into the glass.

Upon discovering the error, Reb Yehoshua Leib's wife quickly tried to warn him. But Reb Yehoshua Leib had already drunk the tea, making sure to hide any signs of distaste. After the students left, his wife asked him how he had managed to show such self-restraint.

"What?" he wondered. "And shame a Jew in public?"[19]

---

[1] *Hamashgiach Reb Meir*, 395–396.

[2] Rambam, *Hilchos De'os* 6:8; *Chofetz Chaim, Hilchos Lashon Hara, Pesicha, Lavin* §14. *Arachin* 16b implies that the prohibition of shaming someone is only transgressed if he is shamed to the point that his face changes color. From Rambam (loc. cit.), however, it seems that any embarrassment falls within the transgression's purview.

[3] Rambam, *Hilchos De'os* 6:8, with *Pri Megadim, Eshel Avraham*, 156.

[4] *Chofetz Chaim, Hilchos Lashon Hara*, first note in *klal* 2. See *Sfas Emes.*

[5] *Pri Megadim, Teivas Gomeh, chakira* 5.

[6] According to Rambam (*Hilchos Teshuva* 3:14), this punishment only applies to one who repeatedly embarrasses people. *Dvar Moshe* shows that *Tosafos* in *Sota* 10b ד"ה נוח לו disagree and hold that one can lose his share in the World to Come for embarrassing someone even once. Chofetz Chaim, *Shemiras Halashon* 2:§17, assumes the former opinion.

[7] *Bereishis* 38:24. See Rashi with *Sifsei Chachamim.*

[8] *Bereishis* 38:25.

[9] *Sota* 10b. *Tosafos* (*Sota* 10b ד"ה נוח לו) and Rabbeinu Yona (*Sha'arei Teshuva* 3:§139) understand this Chazal literally: one must actually give up one's life rather than embarrass another person. Meiri, on the other hand (*Berachos* 43b and *Sota* 10b), understands it figuratively, as an aphorism for people to remember. We have followed the former opinion, since *Pri Chadash* (*Mayim Chaim, Hilchos Yesodei HaTorah* 5:2) and *Pri Megadim* (*Teivas Gomeh, chakira* 5) rule this way.

[10] *Milei D'Avos.*

[11] *Bereishis* 45:1.

[12] *Midrash Tanchuma, Vayigash* 5.

[13] Ibid. with *Eitz Yosef.* Cf. *Bereishis Rabba* 93:9.

[14] *Tanna D'vei Eliyahu Rabba*, chap. 25.

[15] One is allowed to publicly embarrass someone who is committing an injustice if that is the only way to stop him (*Kovetz He'aros* §70). For example, one would be allowed to publicize that a certain man is a thief or is unfairly withholding a divorce from his wife if more diplomatic methods did not help. This is called embarrassing someone for a positive purpose (*leto'eles*) and is permitted, albeit with certain prerequisites (see *Lerei'acha Kamocha* 3:200).

[16] See Rambam (*Hilchos Chovel U'mazik* 3:7); *Tiferes Yisrael* (*Avos* 3:14).

[17] *Binyan Tzion*, §172, writes that according to *Tosafos, Bava Metzia* 59a ד"ה דכתיב, Tamar was standing so close to the fire that had Yehuda not admitted his responsibility right away, she would have died before managing to send another message. With this thesis, *Binyan Tzion* explains how we can learn from Tamar that one should give up his life rather than embarrass another person. After all, perhaps she was trying to save herself first through a subtle message, but had that failed, she would have named him explicitly. The reason we learn from Tamar can only be that she was so close to the fire that there wouldn't have been time for another message.

[18] See Rashi to *Sota* 10b ד"ה והיא שלחה.

[19] Menachem Mendel, *Pillar of Fire*, trans. Shaindel Weinbach (New York: Mesorah, 1992), 110.

The Power of the
Unwritten Word

פרק ג׳ משנה י״ז: רַבִּי עֲקִיבָא אוֹמֵר, שְׂחוֹק וְקַלּוּת רֹאשׁ מַרְגִּילִין לְעֶרְוָה. מָסוֹרֶת סְיָג לַתּוֹרָה. מַעְשְׂרוֹת סְיָג לָעֹשֶׁר. נְדָרִים סְיָג לַפְּרִישׁוּת. סְיָג לַחָכְמָה שְׁתִיקָה.

Chapter 3, Mishnah 17: *Rabbi Akiva said: Frivolity and light-heartedness lead a person to immorality. Masores is a protective fence around the Torah. Tithes are a fence for riches. Vows are a fence for abstinence. A fence for wisdom is silence.*

Today's technology has provided the religious world with new and more efficient ways of spreading Torah. Devices such as DVDs and MP3s store massive amounts of information and are increasingly being used to record and retain Torah *shiurim*. Obviously, Chazal never had such equipment, so you won't find any explicit mention of it anywhere in their writings. As we will see in this Mishnah, however, Chazal did deal with principles that relate directly to the use of such technology.

Committed to Memory

Rabbi Akiva says, "*Masores seyag laTorah — Masores* is a protective fence around the Torah." *Masores* means something that is passed down verbally from one generation to the next, and refers to the Oral Law. One would have thought that the way to ensure that the Oral Law never be forgotten by the Jewish people is to write it down, thereby preserving it forever. Rabbi Akiva informs us that the opposite is true. The best way to guard the Oral Law is not to write it down.

By keeping it unwritten, people feel responsible to remember it. Knowing that the weight of remembering rests solely on their shoulders, they will work day and night to ensure that no law escapes them. They will not go to sleep until they are certain they have memorized it completely. By writing the *Masores* down, though, that tension is lost. Feeling secure that the information is on paper, people breathe a sigh of relief and relax, knowing that the information can always be verified.[1] Transmitting the Torah by word of mouth as opposed to recording it is, therefore, the surest protection against forgetting Torah.

The idea that writing down the Oral Law weakens the impression it makes on one's being is stated by the *Mabit*[2] and *Midrash Shmuel*. The question one could ask on their principle is that G-d *did* command us to write down parts of Torah, namely the Written Law. If writing something down really weakens the impression it makes on a person, where does the Written Law fit into the scheme of things?

One could answer, however, that the Written Law itself was never written in such a manner that it could be understood on its own. If not for the oral interpretations, we would have no way of understanding what the Written Law is teaching us. For example, we would have no idea that *pri eitz hadar* refers to an esrog, that *totafos* is translated to be the tefillin on one's head, or which *melachos* are forbidden on Shabbos. Thus, the fact that the Written Law is written down does not obviate the responsibility of remembering it.

Rabbi Shimshon Raphael Hirsch compares the Written Law to shorthand notes.[3] Unless one heard the original lecture, the shorthand notes themselves are meaningless and look like nothing more than scribble. To the student who heard the lecture, however, the notes enable him to repeat the entire lecture verbatim. Every word jogs his memory and reminds him of what the lecturer said. Thus, one could argue that not only does the existence of the Written Law fail to contradict the idea that writing something down weakens the impression it makes on a person, but it actually strengthens the idea. After all, G-d specifically chose to have it written in an ambiguous form, thus making it necessary for man to remember the details.

In our Mishnah, Rabbi Akiva is making a profound point about human nature: Knowing that something is recorded elsewhere removes the burden of embedding it in one's mind.

G-d wants the Torah to be alive in every Jew's heart. Thus, writing it down would be detrimental, as it would deny people the feeling that they are playing a vital role in its transmission. Only when people feel that they alone carry the burden of storing its information does it occupy all their thoughts, becoming the air they breathe. People then identify with the Torah so closely that they will never forget it, just as they will never forget their own identity.

Lost in Notes

That is not to say that today we should not write down any Torah. Rabbi Yehuda Hanasi, who lived after Rabbi Akiva, saw that with the passage of time, the generations were growing weaker, and therefore he wrote down the Mishnah so that it would not be forgotten.[4] But even Rabbi Yehuda Hanasi made sure to write the Torah in such a manner that the teacher-student link would not be lost.[5] For example, although Rabbi Yehuda Hanasi was known for his clear language,[6] his Mishnayos do not always follow a chronological order,[7] and at times even have sections missing,[8] such that they still require the explanation of a teacher. In this way, although the Oral Law was committed to writing, it still retained its oral nature.[9] Thus, there is no contradiction between the writing down of the Oral Law and Rabbi Akiva's point.

The Chazon Ish and the Steipler strongly encouraged students to write down every insight they had.[10] The Maharsha even went as far as to say that the main benefit of learning comes from that which one writes down.[11] Writing helps crystallize one's learning. One often thinks he understands an idea clearly, but when he tries to write it down, he realizes it needs further clarification. But at the same time, one needs to be aware of Rabbi Akiva's warning — namely, that the writing not become a substitute for the Torah's residing in the person himself. Listening, learning, absorbing, and integrating the knowledge must precede writing, lest these be displaced by writing.

Erich Fromm, a German-born psychoanalyst and professor of psychiatry at New York University in the 1960s, noted this negative aspect of writing. He comments, "Teachers can observe that the students who carefully write down every sentence of the lecture will, in all likelihood, understand and remember less than the students who trusted their capacity to understand and, hence, remember at least the essentials."[12]

The main purpose of a Torah lecture is the impression it makes on the listener, not on his notebook. If the notes just sit on the shelf gathering dust, then of what use are they? A student who comes away from a *shiur* having understood only one point, but who was deeply touched by it to the extent that it became a part of him for the rest of his life, is a thousand times better off than a student who understood the whole *shiur* but fails to internalize any of it.

In the words of Fromm, "...the content does not become part of their own individual system of thought, enriching and widening it. Instead, they transform the words they hear into fixed clusters of thought, or whole theories, which they store up. The students and the content of the lectures remain strangers to each other, except that each student has become the owner of a collection of statements made by somebody else."[13] G-d doesn't want robots who can regurgitate a lecture word for word. He wants people who take the information to heart.

The same is true not only of writing, but of owning *sefarim*. It is not how big your library is, but how much of a living Torah you are. Take the Shaagas Aryeh, for example. He was so poor that he only had one Gemara. If he wanted to learn a new Gemara he had to exchange it for another volume.[14] Yet his lack of *sefarim* did not hinder his learning; it pushed him harder to learn. When he came across a new *sefer*, he committed it to memory, knowing that that was the only way he would have access to its contents. He once stayed with a wealthy *talmid chacham* who had a large collection of *sefarim* and was amazed that his host was so knowledgeable — despite his having so many books! Chazal say: Take heed of the poor, for from them Torah will come forth.[15] Said Rabbi Chaim Ozer Grodzensky, "Do you know why Torah will come forth from the poor? Because they have no *sefarim!*"[16]

So Close and Yet So Far Away

In our generation, Rabbi Akiva's message is even more poignant. Technology has opened new ways to record information. For a small price, you can buy the whole Tanach, Midrash, and Talmud, as well as every other *sefer* you are likely to need, on one compact disc. That so much Torah is available at our fingertips and can be accessed easily is a wonderful thing. But let us never allow this surge of information to prevent us from internalizing the Torah.

It is easy to fall into a false sense of security, feeling that one knows Torah when really it's the computer that "knows." G-d wants us, not our computers, to become living *sifrei Torah*. He wants us to think about Torah constantly, making it the center of our lives and the longing of our souls. If Rabbi Akiva said that writing could detract from identifying with Torah, how much more so can the knowledge that one has the whole Torah available at the click of a mouse lessen one's attachment to Torah. Technology is meant to *help* us further our Torah knowledge, not *substitute* for it. When the Heavenly Court tests a person's Torah knowledge at the end of his life, laptops will not be admitted.

Another application of Rabbi Akiva's principle in today's world is photography.

Like many others in Jerusalem, I prefer to do *kapparos* on *erev Yom Kippur* with a real chicken. It is a powerful experience. Being only a few hours away from the holiest day of the year, and knowing that this animal will soon be slaughtered as atonement for me, never fails to move me. Last year, though, I saw someone taking pictures of his children holding the chicken over their heads. This kills any feelings of holiness one might have drawn from the event.

We are no longer able to savor the moment without reaching for our cameras. When going to the Kosel, some tourists see everything through their viewfinders instead of focusing on the intensity of their prayers. Even when visiting tragic places such as Auschwitz and other death camps, one will find people busy taking photos instead of using the heartrending moment for deep thought and reflection.

On numerous occasions, Rabbi Shlomo Wolbe told his students who were about to go on an outing that photographing a scenic view comes at the expense of "living the experience." By turning every event into a photo op, we are becoming numb to what it means to be alive. Instead of being a living, feeling, thinking person, our character is becoming as thin and shallow as a digital memory card. What started as an aid is quickly turning into a handicap, preventing us from being affected by the power of the moment.

This does not mean one should never take pictures. Photos provide mementos of special occasions. They also enable those who could not be there to join in the event. Photographing is no worse than writing down, which, as we mentioned earlier, Rabbi Yehuda Hanasi saw was a necessary memory aid for the weaker generations. It is just important to be aware of a potential danger — namely, not to destroy an event's impact because we know that it's being recorded and can always be seen later.

Rabbi Akiva's message about the significance of an oral tradition has not faded with time. If anything, it is even more relevant in our day. Knowing that something is recorded elsewhere weakens its effect. Our challenge is to see and hear everything with open eyes and ears, and — most importantly — with an open heart.

---

[1] *Midrash Shmuel.*

[2] Introduction to *Kiryat Sefer.*

[3] *Shemos* 21:2.

[4] Rambam, introduction to *Mishneh Torah*.

[5] *Pachad Yitzchak, Chanuka*, first topic. See p. 180 for his source.

[6] Rambam, introduction to commentary to the Mishnah.

[7] *Ein seder laMishnah*.

[8] *Chisurei michsera*.

[9] *Pachad Yitzchak*, loc. cit.

[10] *Igros Chazon Ish* 1:§4; *Karyana D'igarta* 1:§5. *Pele Yo'etz*, s.v. כתיבה, also mentions the importance of writing.

[11] *Bava Basra* 10b.

[12] Erich Fromm, *To Have or To Be?* (New York: Continuum, 1976), 32.

[13] Fromm, op. cit., 29.

[14] See *Pe'er Hador* 4:61 where the same is said about the Chazon Ish.

[15] *Nedarim* 81a.

[16] R' Shimon Finkelman, *Reb Chaim Ozer* (New York: Mesorah, 1987), 111.

Rooted in the Past, Branching Out to the Future

פרק ג' משנה כ"ב: הוּא הָיָה אוֹמֵר, כֹּל שֶׁחָכְמָתוֹ מְרֻבָּה מִמַּעֲשָׂיו, לְמָה הוּא דוֹמֶה, לְאִילָן שֶׁעֲנָפָיו מְרֻבִּין וְשָׁרָשָׁיו מֻעָטִין, וְהָרוּחַ בָּאָה וְעוֹקַרְתּוֹ וְהוֹפַכְתּוֹ עַל פָּנָיו, שֶׁנֶּאֱמַר (ירמיה י"ז), וְהָיָה כְּעַרְעָר בָּעֲרָבָה וְלֹא יִרְאֶה כִּי יָבוֹא טוֹב וְשָׁכַן חֲרֵרִים בַּמִּדְבָּר אֶרֶץ מְלֵחָה וְלֹא תֵשֵׁב. אֲבָל כֹּל שֶׁמַּעֲשָׂיו מְרֻבִּין מֵחָכְמָתוֹ, לְמָה הוּא דוֹמֶה, לְאִילָן שֶׁעֲנָפָיו מֻעָטִין וְשָׁרָשָׁיו מְרֻבִּין, שֶׁאֲפִלּוּ כָּל הָרוּחוֹת שֶׁבָּעוֹלָם בָּאוֹת וְנוֹשְׁבוֹת בּוֹ אֵין מְזִיזִין אוֹתוֹ מִמְּקוֹמוֹ, שֶׁנֶּאֱמַר (שם), וְהָיָה כְּעֵץ שָׁתוּל עַל מַיִם וְעַל יוּבַל יְשַׁלַּח שָׁרָשָׁיו וְלֹא יִרְאֶה כִּי יָבֹא חֹם, וְהָיָה עָלֵהוּ רַעֲנָן, וּבִשְׁנַת בַּצֹּרֶת לֹא יִדְאָג, וְלֹא יָמִישׁ מֵעֲשׂוֹת פֶּרִי.

Chapter 3, Mishnah 22: *He [Rabbi Elazar ben Azaria] used to say: Anyone whose wisdom outweighs his deeds is like a tree with many branches but few roots, which is uprooted and turned upside down by the oncoming wind. As it says (Yirmiya 17), "He will be like a lone tree in the desert and will not see when the good comes; he dwells on parched soil in the wilderness, a salty and uninhabited land." But anyone whose deeds outweigh his wisdom is like a tree with few branches and many roots, which is not budged from its place even by all the winds of the world. As it says (ibid.), "He will be like a tree planted near water, which spreads its roots out to the stream of water; he will not notice when the heat comes, his leaves will remain fresh and will not be troubled in a year of drought, or cease bearing fruit."*

T he Mishnah appears to be speaking about one whose wisdom outweighs his deeds, yet the metaphor from *Yirmiya* about a tree with many branches and few roots

actually refers to something else entirely — those who place their
trust in man as opposed to those who place their trust in G-d:

> Cursed is the man who trusts in people and makes flesh [and
> blood] his strength, turning his heart from G-d. He will be like
> a lone tree in the desert...
> Blessed is the man who trusts in G-d; then G-d will be his
> security. He will be like a tree planted near water...[1]

How can the author of our Mishnah apply the above verses to
one whose wisdom outweighs his deeds when they were said in a
different context altogether?[2]

Deeds vs. Wisdom

This difficulty may have brought some of the commentators to
explain the word "wisdom" in the Mishnah as referring to intellectual
analysis of mitzvos, and "deeds" as referring to the performance of
mitzvos. One whose wisdom outweighs his deeds puts too much
emphasis on the reasons for mitzvos, keeping only those mitzvos
that he understands with his own logic. Such a person places his
trust in man and in man's power of reason. What sounds right to
him, he keeps; what seems outdated or illogical, he does not. Such
a person is like a tree with many branches but few roots. When the
wind blows — that is, when a new philosophy disproves his logic
— he falls. He no longer has any reason to perform those mitzvos,
and so he stops.[3]

The correct approach is that of the person whose deeds outweigh
his wisdom. Such a person performs mitzvos independent of his
understanding them. He places his trust in G-d, recognizing that
man's puny intellect cannot possibly fathom G-d's reasons for
wanting us to do certain things. Like a tree with many roots, he
stands strong, keeping the mitzvos whether or not he comprehends
their reasons.

One might conclude from the above comments that it is incorrect
to try to discern the reasons for the mitzvos. Such a conclusion,

though, is wrong.[4] Dovid Hamelech beseeched G-d to teach him the reasons behind the mitzvos.[5] The Rambam states clearly that it is proper to delve into the mitzvos and give reasons for them wherever possible.[6] Indeed, the *Sefer Hachinuch* offered reasons for virtually every mitzvah. Rabbi Shimshon Raphael Hirsch even went a step further, offering reasons not only for each mitzvah in general but for its details as well.[7]

What Chazal forbade, though, is using one's intellectual understanding of a mitzvah to decide whether or not to perform it.[8] We keep mitzvos not because they make sense to us, but because G-d in His infinite wisdom commanded us to do so. Yes, Dovid Hamelech asked G-d to show him the underlying reasons for the mitzvos, but in the very same breath he stated that he would keep them whether or not he understood them.[9]

This was what the Jewish people meant when they said, "*Na'aseh v'nishma* — We will do and [then] we will listen."[10] Why didn't they say it in the logical order: "We will listen and then we will do"? After all, it is impossible to do something until one has heard what it is. The phrase "we will listen," therefore, could not have meant we will listen with our ears to what we need to do. That was included in their assertion that "we will do." The phrase "we will listen" meant we will listen with our hearts; we will delve into the reasons behind the mitzvos, trying to understand their deeper meaning. But this declaration came only *after* they had already accepted the mitzvos. We will do first, and only later will we try to understand.[11]

The Essence of Mitzvos

When one considers that the mitzvos are the will of an Infinite Being, it becomes obvious that any attempt to delve into their meaning has to be made with submission. G-d's motivation for commanding us to do specific mitzvos is totally beyond our understanding. What we perceive as the reason for a mitzvah, therefore, is not the definitive reason, but only the lowest level, an outer shell, so to speak.[12]

This is alluded to in the Hebrew word *ta'am* (taste), which is used when giving a reason for a mitzvah, as in the phrase *ta'amei hamitzvos*. Every food has a taste, but it's not the taste that provides the nourishment — it's the nutrients contained in the food. The taste just makes the food more appetizing. After all, those unable to digest food normally can be sustained via intravenous injections, which have no taste. The reasons (*ta'amim*) offered for mitzvos are also just a "taste." They serve to make the mitzvos more palatable to us, to help us appreciate their value, and to do them with enthusiasm. But like the spice in a food, they are not what provides the nourishment. It is the mitzvah alone — the act of doing G-d's will independent of our understanding why — that provides spiritual nourishment to our souls.[13]

Thus, Rabbi Hirsch writes:

> Even...if every Divine precept were a riddle to us and presented us with a thousand unsolved and insoluble problems, the obligatory character of the commandments would not in the slightest degree be impaired by this. Whatever command or prohibition of G-d it may be that prompts one to ask why one should do this and not do that, there is but one and the same answer: Because it is the will of G-d, and it is your duty to be the servant of G-d with all your powers and resources and with every breath of your life.[14]

Rabbi Hirsch was responding to the Reform Jews of his day, who rejected everything that they could not justify intellectually and morally. The "enlightened" German Jew of the nineteenth century ascribed supremacy to man's power of intellectual reason. As Moses Mendelssohn wrote, "I recognize no eternal verities but those that can be grasped by human reason and demonstrated as well as validated by the human intellect."[15]

Reform Judaism is built on the doctrine of investigating the historical circumstances that resulted in a particular law in order to confront it with the present reality.

Conservative Judaism also tries to interpret Jewish law to suit present-day conditions. Thus, they believe that while the *Shulchan Aruch* is "certainly an important halachic source...it should not be viewed as the ultimate authority," because it "was written four hundred years ago and much has changed since then in the halacha, in society, and in our outlook on life."[16]

So, for example, regarding driving on Shabbos they write, "Refraining from the use of a motor vehicle is an important aid in the maintenance of the Sabbath spirit of repose.... However, where a family resides beyond reasonable walking distance from the synagogue, the use of a motor vehicle for the purpose of synagogue attendance shall in no way be construed as a violation of the Sabbath but, on the contrary, such attendance shall be deemed an expression of loyalty to our faith."[17]

Regarding *korbanos*, they state that those congregations that have a hard time mentioning the restoration of sacrifices in the Mussaf service because it doesn't agree with their "conscientious scruples" are granted permission to change any references to *korbanos* into historical reminiscences instead of prayers for the future.[18]

In his explanation of the need to introduce mixed seating in shuls, the president of one Conservative congregation wrote, "Under modern conditions, it is extremely important to make it possible for parents, during religious services, to assist their children, and for husband and wife to assist each other in the comprehension and appreciation of the prayers...."[19]

It is exactly this kind of toying with the mitzvos that our Mishnah is referring to when it speaks of those whose wisdom outweighs their deeds. They readily discard the binding authority of Jewish law that has been the hallmark of Judaism for centuries. This approach to Jewish law is the precise opposite of the attitude encapsulated by *"Na'aseh v'nishma."*

Truth Endures

The unfortunate consequence of those who place their wisdom before their deeds is spelled out in the Mishnah. Like the tree with many branches and few roots, they will be blown away and knocked down by the winds of time. Those who adhere to G-d's law, however, placing their deeds before their wisdom, will endure forever. Like the tree with strong roots, they will withstand the changing seasons and will produce many branches, bearing abundant fruit. The religious Jew with his unbending commitment to Torah survives, while the modern thinkers waving their flag of emancipation come and go, but do not endure.

How can this enigma be explained? How is it that the Orthodox Jew poring over ancient Talmudic folios and observing 2,000-year-old laws outlives all the rest? One would have expected precisely the opposite. Those who place their wisdom before their deeds, preaching reform and adapting their Judaism to fit in with modern trends, should be the ones to withstand the test of time.

Perhaps the reason is that the human intellect, no matter how advanced and sophisticated it might be, will never be able to escape the one limitation that is its very essence — that it is no more than a human intellect, subject to all its finite and mortal restrictions. Man's thoughts may climb the highest peaks of academic genius, his insights may pierce the depths of the earth, but he will never break loose from the world of time and space. G-d, on the other hand, is the Creator of time and space and transcends them. His commandments, therefore, also transcend time. As soon as man begins to poke around with halacha, trimming it here and there to suit his own ideals, he is left with a set of man-made laws. Even if his intentions are pure and the changes he makes only minor, it makes no difference. The result is still a man-made religion unable to survive eternally.

There is a fundamental difference between the ways these two groups approach Torah. The first group, "progressive" Jewry, approaches Torah from without, holding as sacred truth the beliefs with which they have been raised. If after opening the Torah they find a contradiction between what they perceive as truth and what the Torah actually says, then it is the Torah that has to be realigned to accommodate their beliefs. The second group, Orthodox Jewry, however, approaches Torah from the opposite end. They open the Torah with the attitude that it is the sacred truth. Any discrepancy between what the Torah teaches and what they previously believed to be true means that there is something wrong with their way of thinking that must be changed. It means that without realizing it, the values of the non-Jewish society that surrounds them have crept into their consciousness, and they immediately work to discard them.

The Torah is able to stand on its own two feet. It doesn't need us to "help it along" by adapting it to match modern values. That would be the biggest insult to Torah. Torah isn't some relic from a long-buried past that needs the "enlightened" man to fix it up a little so that it works better and runs more smoothly.

Those who try to modify the Torah to meet the needs of the times are forgetting that from the very beginning Torah values never conformed to those of contemporary culture.

In the eloquent statement of Rabbi Hirsch, whose words, though written in 1854, still reverberate today:

> *Was Abraham's Judaism suited to the times when the ruler of his fatherland cast him into the Chaldean fiery furnace because he broke in pieces the idols of his contemporaries? Was the Judaism of our ancestors suited to the times when, loathed by the Egyptians, they had for centuries to bow their neck under the yoke of slavery and to let their infants be swept away by the waves of the Nile? Was the Judaism of Hanania, Mishael and Azaria suited to the times when they entered the burning furnace rather than obey the command of the ruler to bend the knee before his statue? Was the Judaism of the Maccabees suited to the times when with heroic courage they resisted the*

introduction of the latest Grecian customs and culture? ...
And without doubt, the "modern" wisdom of that time preached
that it was now at last [time] to abandon the old Judaism... which
[was] only a source of mockery to their conquerors, now it was
surely impossible to remain Jews and Jewesses any longer. They
themselves, however, with true greatness of soul looked beyond
this period of downfall, they drew the bond of faith even tighter,
they taught even more passionately the holiness of the law and
of Jewish customs... in order that no thread of Jewish holiness
should be lost in the subjection and dispersion....

In all these centuries was Judaism suited to the times, did
it conform to the views of the dominant society... was it ever
convenient and easy to be a Jew or a Jewess? And yet we are told
[by so-called enlightened Jews] that it is the duty of Judaism to
be at every period suited to the times![20]

---

[1] *Yirmiya* 17:5–8.

[2] *Nachalas Avos, Midrash Shmuel.*

[3] *Tiferes Yisrael, Tiferes Tzion.* See *Nachalas Avos,* which also interprets the Mishnah along these lines, although in a much broader sense. *Ksav Sofer (parashas Eikev)* and *Beis Avos* give the same explanation to *Avos* 3:12, which also discusses the concept of a person's wisdom outweighing his deeds and which, according to Rambam, Rabbeinu Yona, and *Magen Avos,* parallels our Mishnah.

The Mishnah is thus expounding the passage in *Yirmiya,* "Cursed is the man who trusts in people...," as referring to one who places too much emphasis on his understanding of the mitzvos (*Nachalas Avos, Tiferes Yisrael*).

[4] *Pesachim* 118b–119a speaks of the great reward that awaits those who reveal *"ta'amei Torah."* According to Ramban on *Devarim* 22:6, the phrase *ta'amei Torah* refers to the reasons for the mitzvos, so we see that not only is it permitted to look into the reasons of mitzvos, it is even praiseworthy. (Cf. Rashash and Maharsha [second explanation], who understand the phrase *ta'amei Torah* differently.)

In *Bava Metzia* 115a, R' Shimon holds דרשינן טעמא דקרא, that we may give reasons for the mitzvos. For example, he explains that the reason the Torah prohibits taking a garment from a widow as a pledge (*Devarim* 24:17) is so that she will not come into ill repute with the neighbors when they see a creditor returning the garment to her house at night. R' Shimon therefore rules that the prohibition only applies to a poor widow who needs her garment returned daily. We, however, follow the opinion of R' Yehuda, who holds אין דורשין טעמא דקרא, and therefore rules that the prohibition applies to all widows, wealthy or poor. This is no contradiction, though, to what we stated above, namely, that one should give reasons for the mitzvos. That is because R' Shimon and R' Yehuda only argue when one tries to change the parameters of the mitzvah based on its reasoning. All agree, however, that one may offer rationales for mitzvos when there are no halachic consequences in doing so (*Tosafos, Sota* 14a ד"ה כדי; *Sedei Chemed* 3:22–24).

[5] טוב טעם ודעת למדני (*Tehillim* 119:66 with Meiri).

[6] *Hilchos Temura* 4:13. Although *Berachos* 33b cites one opinion that seems to frown on rationalizing mitzvos, Rambam, in *Moreh Nevuchim* 3:§48, says that we don't follow that opinion. See also Ramban, *Devarim* 22:6.

[7] In this regard, R' Hirsch differed from Rambam, who held that we are unable to know the reasons for the details of the mitzvos (*Moreh Nevuchim* 3:§26).

[8] With this principle, we can explain *Sanhedrin* 21b, which seems to disapprove of trying to offer reasons for mitzvos. The Gemara there asks why G-d did not reveal the reasons for the mitzvos and answers that in the two cases in which He did, Shlomo Hamelech rationalized that the reasons did not apply to him and ended up sinning. This Gemara implies that it is better not to look into the Torah's reasons but to leave them unknown. Maharsha (*Pesachim* 119a ד"ה טעמי, first explanation), however, explains that the Gemara is only saying why it is better that G-d Himself didn't give explanations for mitzvos. Where G-d reveals the reasons, people will take those reasons as absolute and use them to argue that they don't apply to them. Whereas when people offer reasons, all will realize that they aren't the definitive reasons but mere speculation. They, therefore, will not act upon their interpretation and will not change the parameters of the mitzvah based on their theories.

[9] טוב טעם ודעת למדני כי במצוותיך האמנתי (*Tehillim* 119:66 with Meiri).

[10] *Shemos* 24:7. *Avos D'Rebbi Nasan* 22:1 cites this verse in support of *Avos* 3:12, and *Ksav Sofer* (*parashas Eikev*), *Beis Avos* (Mishnah 12), and *Tiferes Tzion* (on our Mishnah) explain the connection to the verse as we have explained above.

[11] *Beis HaLevi, parashas Ki Sisa.* R' Hirsch (*Devarim* 6:8) writes that this is alluded to in the halachic requirement that the *tefillin shel yad*, which represents action, be put on before the *tefillin shel rosh*, which represents thought.

[12] Even when the Torah explicitly offers a reason, as it does, for example, with

the prohibition of a king taking too many wives, it is the simple, basic reason, but not the only reason. There are other deep and mystical reasons that we are not aware of. This is true not only of Torah commandments, but even of Rabbinic decrees. In other words, Chazal had other reasons for enacting their laws besides the ones they gave (*Peninim Mishulchan HaGra*, 228). See also *Michtav Me'Eliyahu* 4:355.

[13] R' Mordechai Gifter (*Pirkei Emuna*, 232), quoting R' Yerucham Levovitz. See also R' Avrohom Chaim Feuer, *Tehillim*, 1446.

[14] R' Hirsch, foreword to *Horeb*, clv.

[15] Quoted by R' Shimon Schwab in *Selected Writings*, 97.

[16] David Golinkin, *Halakhah for Our Time: A Conservative Approach to Jewish Law* (New York: United Synagogue of America, 1991), 30.

[17] *The Proceedings of the Committee on Jewish Law and Standards of the Conservative Movement 1927–1970* (New York: The Rabbinical Assembly, 1997), 1120.

[18] *The Responsa of Professor Louis Ginzberg* (New York: Jewish Theological Seminary of America, 1996), 53.

[19] See ibid., 95–96.

[20] R' Hirsch, *Judaism Eternal* 2:214–215.

The American Dream...
or Nightmare?

פרק ד' משנה א': בֶּן זוֹמָא אוֹמֵר, אֵיזֶהוּ חָכָם, הַלּוֹמֵד
מִכָּל אָדָם, שֶׁנֶּאֱמַר (תהלים קי"ט), מִכָּל מְלַמְּדַי
הִשְׂכַּלְתִּי. אֵיזֶהוּ גִבּוֹר, הַכּוֹבֵשׁ אֶת יִצְרוֹ, שֶׁנֶּאֱמַר (משלי
ט"ז), טוֹב אֶרֶךְ אַפַּיִם מִגִּבּוֹר וּמֹשֵׁל בְּרוּחוֹ מִלֹּכֵד עִיר.
אֵיזֶהוּ עָשִׁיר הַשָּׂמֵחַ בְּחֶלְקוֹ, שֶׁנֶּאֱמַר (תהלים קכ"ח),
יְגִיעַ כַּפֶּיךָ כִּי תֹאכֵל אַשְׁרֶיךָ וְטוֹב לָךְ. אַשְׁרֶיךָ, בָּעוֹלָם
הַזֶּה. וְטוֹב לָךְ, לָעוֹלָם הַבָּא. אֵיזֶהוּ מְכֻבָּד, הַמְכַבֵּד אֶת
הַבְּרִיּוֹת, שֶׁנֶּאֱמַר (שמואל א' ב'), כִּי מְכַבְּדַי אֲכַבֵּד וּבֹזַי
יֵקָלּוּ.

Chapter 4, Mishnah 1: *Ben Zoma says: Who is
wise? The one who learns from every person, as it
says (Tehillim 119), "From all my teachers I gained
wisdom." Who is strong? The one who controls his
desires, as it says (Mishlei 16), "One who is slow to
anger is better than a mighty warrior, and one who
rules over his will is better than one who conquers
a city." Who is rich? The one who is happy with
his lot, as it says (Tehillim 128), "When you eat
the fruits of your labor, you are fortunate and it
is good for you." "You are fortunate" — in this
world; "and it is good for you" — in the World
to Come. Who is honored? The one who honors
others, as it says (I Shmuel 2), "...for those who
honor Me I will honor, and those who scorn Me I
will degrade."*

T he last several decades have witnessed an unprecedented
increase in materialism. The size of today's houses is double
what it was fifty years ago,[1] with the average American
spending somewhere between 30 and 70 percent more than he did
twenty years ago.[2] In 1968, more than three-quarters of American
college students said "developing a meaningful philosophy of life"
was "very important" to them, while only 43 percent said the same

about "being financially well off." By 1996, those figures were reversed.[3]

Shopping has become a national pastime, with more and more people buying things because of the "therapeutic effect." In one poll, 93 percent of teenage girls rated store-hopping as their favorite activity, while fewer than 5 percent listed "helping others."[4] The average American spends six hours a week shopping and only forty minutes playing with his or her children.[5]

In light of this frenzied situation, it is more important than ever that we learn what our Sages had to teach us about wealth and the accumulation of goods, so that we can integrate their teachings into our lives. In our Mishnah, Ben Zoma tells us, "*Eizehu ashir? Hasamei'ach b'chelko* — Who is rich? The one who is happy with his lot." A careful analysis of each word reveals a crucial depth of wisdom in a world obsessed with acquiring and spending.

Acquiring True Wealth

Ben Zoma's statement teaches us that wealth is actually a character trait. Usually we measure wealth according to how much money and how many possessions a person has. But this kind of wealth is external — it exists outside of a person and can easily be lost. The wealth a person has due to his state of mind, however, is an integral part of his personality. It is an internal quality emanating from the core of his being, causing him to rejoice in whatever he possesses. It is this trait, and not a quantification of the material, that deems a person wealthy.[6]

There is, however, a basic difficulty with developing this character trait, which is that people have an inherent urge to expand and feel larger than they are at present. Chazal recognized this urge, stating that one who has one hundred desires two hundred.[7] People naturally want to own more, to grow beyond their current limitations and increase their holdings in this world. This being the case, Ben Zoma's advice, to be happy with one's lot, seems to contradict human nature. It may sound like a lofty ideal — to be sure, it would be a wonderful trait to have — but since it goes against our grain, it doesn't seem possible to attain.

Had Ben Zoma said to *make do* with one's lot (*mistapek b'chelko*), then his instruction would be going against a basic human urge. People have a drive to expand, and Ben Zoma would be suppressing that drive, telling them to deny their desires and not want more. But Ben Zoma does not say to *make do* with what one has — he says to be *happy* with what one has (*samei'ach b'chelko*). He wants us to actively enjoy what we own and take pleasure in our possessions.[8]

Happiness causes one to be expansive. The joy in a person's heart makes him want to increase his circle of influence, reaching out to more people. When a person is happy, he feels like jumping up in the air. The very act of smiling causes one's mouth to stretch, taking up more room on his face. Indeed, Chazal describe two kinds of measurements, a "sad handbreadth" (*tefach atzeiv*) and a "happy handbreadth" (*tefach socheik*). The latter one is slightly larger than the former, reflecting the inherent expansive quality of happiness.[9]

Ben Zoma is not stunting our desire to expand. He is telling us to channel it so that it will increase the good feelings we have about our belongings. Instead of expanding outwardly, he wants us to expand inwardly by taking the time to appreciate what we have. Try contemplating your possessions. Think of their form, their design, their beauty. Fill your heart with the joy and the benefit they provide you — their usefulness, their efficiency, their convenience. Don't think about how to increase them or obtain more of them. Just take pleasure in owning them, delighting in your good fortune. This is what Ben Zoma instructed: to be *samei'ach b'chelko*.

Being Happy With What You Have

With worldly possessions there will always be newer, fancier models, improved versions of what you already have. But Ben Zoma chose his words carefully, telling us to be happy with our *chelek*. A *chelek* means a part or a portion of something. However much you have, it will always only be a *chelek* — a portion — and there will always be more to buy out there.[10]

Try telling a collector of vintage cars who has had a particular car for years and takes great pride in it that there are faster cars available. He will laugh at you: "What do I want a new car for? I like *this* one." He cherishes his car and would not swap it for anything. Similarly, when you take pleasure in what you have, you don't care about what else is available. You are happy with yours.

The item may be small but — with happiness' power to inflate — it becomes large. Consider someone with a huge house and acres of land all around. If he is not happy with his lot, the mansion will feel small. Ask him to host a guest for the night and he will excuse himself, saying he has no space. "That room is for the computer; that one is for the gym. The basement is for my wine collection. There's simply not enough space!" On the other hand, consider someone who has a tiny apartment, but whose heart is bursting with happiness. "Room? Of course, there's room. We'll just move the couch into the kitchen and put the table in the corner and there'll be enough room on the living room floor to host a whole family!"

Yes, we have a need to expand and take up more room, but there are two ways to channel that need. Most people satisfy it by trying to expand outwardly, owning more and more possessions. But Chazal teach us that we can also satisfy it by expanding inwardly, increasing the impression our possessions make on our being. The happier we become with them, the more room they will occupy in our hearts and the less urge we will feel to buy whatever else is available.[11]

The other way of trying to achieve happiness, by increasing one's possessions, does not work. As Chazal explain, one will never be satisfied because the more one has, the more one wants.[12] Before founding Silicon Graphics, Jim Clark, founder of several computer companies, said a fortune of $10 million would make him happy; before Netscape, $100 million; before Healtheon, $1 billion. Now he says, "Once I have more than Larry Ellison, I'll be satisfied." Ellison, founder of the software company Oracle, has $13 billion.[13]

Shlomo Hamelech describes this unending love of money as *hevel*,[14] which literally means heat and vapor.[15] Vapor distorts reality, making things appear different than they really are. Take, for example, the hot air rising from desert sands, which creates the mirage of water up ahead. But when one approaches the "oasis," one finds that there is nothing there, and that what appeared as water was just an optical illusion, which now appears as far away as it did the first time. One imagines that having a certain item or earning a certain amount of money will bring happiness, but after reaching his goal, he realizes that it was just an illusion, and the happiness now appears to be waiting ahead at the next stage, like the oasis in the desert mirage.[16]

Besides being an impossible goal to reach, increasing one's possessions also prevents one from enjoying the here and now. This is because anticipating a future event removes some of the joy from the present. Consider a child eagerly counting down the days until a vacation, or an adult anxiously waiting to hear an important decision. Neither of them can fully enjoy the present moment because their minds are caught up with the upcoming event. In fact, the more one is caught up with the future, the less one enjoys the present, to the extent that, sometimes, when the matter weighs heavily on one's mind, a person cannot even enjoy his food.

One who is caught up in trying to attain certain financial aspirations overlooks the present, causing him to miss many of life's most precious moments. Awaiting the next stage precludes living in the present. What makes this particularly sad is that in the case of materialistic goals the much anticipated stage never materializes, and like the man chasing the mirage in the desert, one's life is spent in a perpetual state of frustration, always neglecting and ignoring the present to reach a future that never arrives.[17]

Unattainable goals aside, increasing one's possessions will never bring happiness because happiness depends on having one's emotional needs fulfilled, and material objects cannot satisfy emotional needs. Happiness depends on feeling connected to other people and enjoying close relationships with them, feeling a strong sense of self-worth, and deriving meaning and lasting enjoyment from life. None of these emotional needs can fully be satisfied by pursuing wealth or purchasing objects.

In his book, *The High Price of Materialism*, Tim Kasser, associate professor of psychology at Knox College, cites experiments done with lottery winners and others, which measure how one's well-being improves as a result of having his physical desires met. Psychologists found that beyond having enough money to meet basic needs for food, shelter, and the like, attaining wealth, possessions, and status does not yield long-term enhancement of a person's happiness and well-being. This led Kasser to conclude that "when people follow materialistic values and organize their lives around attaining wealth and possessions, they are essentially wasting their time as far as well-being is concerned."[18]

The Eye: Origin of Desire

One of the most formidable obstacles to being content with one's lot is the eye.

Chazal note that the eye is the origin of all desire. One first sees an object and then yearns for it.[19] Serve a child a piece of chocolate cake, and he will be delighted, but let him catch a glimpse of his sister's larger portion and he will no longer be happy. Until he sees her portion, he is perfectly content, but once he notices she has more, he becomes miserable.

It is the same with adults. We are only happy with what we have until we see someone has better. Take a tour of your friend's newly decorated home, and you will soon become dissatisfied with your own house — despite the fact that moments earlier you were perfectly content.

One who desires to be happy with his lot, therefore, would do well to keep his eyes only on his own things and not on what exists around him. Indeed, Chazal explicitly state: Do not cast your eyes on things that are not yours.[20]

When a person's body is at rest, his mind begins roaming and will tend to think back over everything it has seen that it is unaccustomed to seeing.[21] Thus, a person who wishes to develop the *midda* of being happy with his lot should minimize the amount of time he spends looking at other people's possessions. While there may be nothing strictly wrong with looking at these things,[22] doing so fills his mind with images of things he does not have, which then swirl around in his head, preventing him from being happy with what he actually has.

The challenge of not looking at that which we don't own is particularly difficult today with the lures of the advertising industry boldly emblazoned on every imaginable surface.

Advertisements have become pervasive, appearing on bananas, at the bottom of golf-course holes, and inside math textbooks. ("If Joe has thirty Oreo™ cookies and eats fifteen, how many does he have left?" Of course, there is a huge picture of Oreos on the page.)[23] The challenge posed by ads is thus bigger today than ever before. In the words of one economist, "Advertising separates our era from all earlier ones as little else does."[24]

Looking at ads can truly be destructive. If one realized the depth of research that goes into producing ads, one would approach them with great caution. Advertisers team up with psychologists, sociologists, and neuroscientists to analyze the human mind, understanding how we make decisions and how we can be manipulated. Calling their work *the psychology of consumer behavior*, they place hidden cameras behind shelves to measure the number of times a person's eye blinks per minute (a good index of inner tension), and analyze the effects of various colors (red and yellow create a hypnotic effect).[25] These experts have probed every sphere of the human psyche, learning about the way we think to such an extent that they know more about motivating us than we do. They also fool us into trying to satisfy emotional needs with products: Want more friends? Use this perfume. Worried you will die young? Eat this cereal.

Advertisements may look harmless, but they breed dissatisfaction, spreading discontent and even altering the way we think. As one scholar maintained, advertising "manufactures a product of its own: the consumer, perpetually unsatisfied, restless, anxious, and bored. Advertising serves not so much to advertise products as to promote consumption as a way of life."[26]

Happiness comes from concentrating on what one *has*, but looking at ads and other people's possessions causes one to focus on what he *does not have*, destroying any vestige of contentment he may have been able to develop. Indeed, Kasser cites studies that suggest that the more ads one sees, the lower one's life satisfaction and overall morale will be.[27]

As the heirs to a great spiritual legacy, we are fortunate to have ancestors who guide us and teach us to delight and take pleasure in what we own, while controlling our eyes from gazing at that which is not ours. If we want to be truly rich, we should follow the sage advice of Ben Zoma and learn to be happy with our lot. Beyond the basic necessities of life, the only acquisition we really "must have" is the acquisition of wisdom.

---

[1] The average size of a new house in America in the 1940s was 1,100 ft² (100 m²) compared to 2,340 ft² (217 m²) in 2002. See Alex Wilson and Jessica Boehland, "Small Is Beautiful: U.S. House Size, Resource Use, and the Environment," *Journal of Industrial Ecology* 9, nos. 1–2 (Winter–Spring 2005):277–287.

[2] Juliet B. Schor, *The Overspent American* (New York: HarperCollins, 1998), 11–12.

[3] David C. Korten, *The Post-Corporate World* (San Francisco: Berrett-Koehler, 1999), 33.

[4] Michelle R. Nelson and Laurie Ellis McLeod, "Adolescent Brand Consciousness and Product Placements: Awareness, Liking and Perceived Effects on Self and Others," *International Journal of Consumer Studies* 29, no. 6 (2005):515–528.

[5] Betsy Morris, "Big Spenders: As a Favored Pastime, Shopping Ranks High With Most Americans," *Wall Street Journal*, July 30, 1987, eastern edition. When Stillerman Jones & Co., a marketing-research firm, asked 34,300 mall shoppers across the country the primary reason for their visit, only 25 percent had come in pursuit of a specific item (ibid.).

[6] *Derech Chaim*; *Da'as Torah* 1:206. See also Rabbeinu Bachya. In total, Ben Zoma defines four traits in the Mishnah – wisdom, strength, wealth, and honor. The idea that he is revealing inner strengths as opposed to external ones applies to all four parts of the Mishnah (see *Derech Chaim*).

[7] *Koheles Rabba* 1:13.

[8] That *samei'ach b'chelko* means taking pleasure in one's physical possessions is clear from *Shabbos* 25b, "*Eizeh ashir? Kol sheyeish lo nachas ruach b'oshro,*" which Rashi equates with *samei'ach b'chelko*. This is also the approach taken by *Menoras Hama'or* (Abuhav, p. 54) and Rabbeinu Yisrael (quoted in *Peirushei Rabbeinu Yitzchak ben Harav Shlomo MiToledo*). Rabbeinu Yona and R' Eliyhau E. Dessler (*Michtav Me'Eliyahu* 1:1–3) take a more spiritual approach, teaching that the way to be happy with one's material wealth is by downplaying its importance, realizing that all wealth is nothing more than a means of spiritual growth. By setting his sights on spiritual attainments, a person automatically becomes happy with his possessions as he realizes that whatever G-d has allotted him is exactly what he needs to fulfill his mission in life.

[9] See *Eiruvin* 3b and *Sukka* 7a.

[10] See *Ruach Chaim*.

[11] The idea of resolving the seeming contradiction between our Mishnah and the rule of "one who has a hundred desires two hundred," by picking up on the word *simcha*, is from R' Reuven Leuchter. According to Rabbeinu Yona (quoted in note 8) the resolution lies in the fact that one who is *samei'ach b'chelko* never desires the "one hundred" in the first place. What he really wants is to learn Torah and do mitzvos, and the money is just a means to get there (*Dvar Moshe*).

[12] *Koheles Rabba* 1:13.

[13] Kurt Andersen, "Valley Guy," review of *The New New Thing: A Silicon Valley Story*, by Michael Lewis, *New York Times*, October 31, 1999, late edition.

[14] *Koheles* 5:9 with Ibn Ezra.

[15] *Sefer Ha'aruch*, s.v. הבל. Essentially, the word *hevel* means nothingness and is used to refer to vapor and heat because they are extremely transient, quickly dissipating into nothing (*Sefer Hashorashim*, s.v. הבל).

[16] *Yalkut Me'am Lo'ez* (*Koheles* 5:9) quotes this metaphor, but doesn't explain the word *hevel*. The idea of *hevel* connoting "misleading" is clear from the verse in *Yirmiya* 23:16, which says that the false prophets would *mahbil* (from the root *hevel*) the people, meaning they would mislead them (Radak, loc. cit., and R' Saadia Gaon, *Emunos V'de'os* §10).

[17] See *Michtav Me'Eliyahu* 1:2.

[18] Tim Kasser, *The High Price of Materialism* (Cambridge, MA: MIT Press, 2002), 43–47.

[19] Rashi, *Bamidbar* 15:39.

[20] *Midrash Zuta, Koheles* (Buber ed., Vilna, 5685) 7:19. See also *Maseches Derech Eretz* (Higger ed., New York, 5731) 3:6; *Maseches Derech Eretz Zuta* (Vilna Shas ed.), chap. 4.

[21] *Orach Yesharim* in *Orchos Chaim LehaRosh Hamevo'ar* §20, s.v. כוונת.

[22] Assuming he doesn't stare at them in a way that creates an *ayin hara*, and that he doesn't look inside other people's property.

[23] John de Graaf, David Wann, and Thomas H. Naylor, *Affluenza: The All-Consuming Epidemic* (San Francisco: Berrett-Koehler, 2002), 150.

[24] Wilhelm Röpke (1899–1966).

[25] More recently, they have begun using MRI scans to monitor exactly what goes on inside a viewer's head as he watches an ad (Wendy Melillo, "Inside the Consumer Mind: What Neuroscience Can Tell Us About Marketing," *Adweek*, January, 16, 2006).

[26] Christopher Lasch, *The Culture of Narcissism* (New York: Warner Books, 1979), 72.

[27] Kasser, *High Price*, 54–56.

The Hidden Giant
Among Us

פֶּרֶק ד' מִשְׁנָה ד': רַבִּי לְוִיטַס אִישׁ יַבְנֶה אוֹמֵר, מְאֹד
מְאֹד הֱוֵה שְׁפַל רוּחַ, שֶׁתִּקְוַת אֱנוֹשׁ רִמָּה.

Chapter 4, Mishnah 4: *Rabbi Levitas of Yavneh says: Be very, very humble, for the hope of earthly man is decay.*

T he Mishnah cautions us to be humble, using a double expression — *me'od me'od.* This is because unlike other character traits, in which the middle path is desirable, regarding humility, one should aim to be completely humble, without even a trace of pride. Haughtiness, which is the opposite of humility, is compared to idol worship, and is so despicable that one cannot afford to have any amount of it, no matter how small.[1] In fact, the only type of person about whom G-d says, "He and I cannot dwell [together] in the world," is a haughty person.[2] One must, therefore, go to the other extreme and do as the Mishnah advises, striving to become "very, very humble."

An Oft-Misunderstood *Midda*

Humility is often misunderstood as a feeling of inadequacy or worthlessness. According to this logic, the more a person feels himself to be nothing, the humbler he is. The *Chovos Halevavos*, however, says that such "humility" is found among fools who do not recognize their self-worth, and is not true humility at all. On the contrary, only *after* one appreciates his real value can he become truly humble.[3]

This is clear from Moshe Rabbeinu, the humblest man who ever lived. He spoke to G-d face-to-face, took the Jews out of Egypt, split the Red Sea, and went up to Heaven to receive the Torah at Har Sinai. To say he was not aware of his greatness is unlikely and borders on the absurd.

Furthermore, if being humble is interpreted to mean walking with head bowed and going through life feeling insignificant, how can we comprehend Moshe Rabbeinu killing the Egyptian taskmaster? Such behavior would hardly be expected from a self-effacing, "worthless" individual. And what about Moshe's entering the palace and demanding that Pharaoh let the Jews out of Egypt? Even the Jewish elders were frightened of this and dropped out one by one, leaving Moshe and Aharon to accomplish this daunting task alone.[4] Such behavior shatters the common image of humility.

True Humility

Humility, rather, is the recognition that all one's capabilities are Divine gifts and should be used appropriately. An artistic genius is not being humble when he denies his creative flair, saying that his work is inferior or that he lacks talent. He is being dishonest. He should recognize his abilities, but rather than become vain, he should contemplate G-d's purpose in endowing him with these skills and should ask himself about the implications that accompany such a gift.

A person doesn't have to be a future Van Gogh to recognize that his talents and abilities, no matter how commonplace they may seem, are actually gifts from G-d. One Jerusalem hostess is an excellent cook, and her Shabbos guests always profusely compliment her culinary creations. Rather than deny that the food is good, she always points upward and says, "*Baruch Hashem*! I couldn't do it without Him." It would be easy for this woman to take the credit or to wave her hand, saying, "Oh, it's nothing." Instead, she recognizes that even the smallest things a person does, which are often taken for granted, are actually dependent on His goodness.

In a sense, the more a person truly appreciates his talents the more humble he can become, because his feelings of responsibility increase proportionately. As Rabbi Yisrael Salanter once said, "I know that I have the mental capacity of a thousand men, but because of that, my obligation to serve G-d is also that of a thousand men."⁵ This is the authentic Torah approach to understanding and appreciating the Divine gifts of great talent and personal ability.

Rabbi Shlomo Zalman Auerbach was once walking along the streets of Jerusalem when a trash collector jumped off the back of the garbage truck, kissed his hand, and returned to his work.

"Who knows if he should be kissing me, or I should be kissing him?" said Reb Shlomo Zalman to his students, who were surrounding him. "Look at my life. I was born to a scholarly father, my parents encouraged me to learn Torah from the day I could read, my in-laws are extraordinary people. Look what intelligence G-d blessed me with and what a supportive wife I have. Who knows how much is expected of me? I should be changing the world. This man, however, was probably born to a different kind of parents. He very likely never had the opportunities I did, the education I had, or the upbringing I was given. And yet look at how much he has grown. He is the great one. It is I who should be kissing him."⁶

Reb Shlomo Zalman's comment encapsulates the way a humble person looks at the world. On one hand, he recognizes his accomplishments. But at the same time, he recognizes that all his successes and achievements are simply gifts that G-d has granted him in His kindness, and that this good fortune obligates him to serve G-d that much more devotedly.

-----

¹ Rambam.

² *Sota* 5a.

³ *Chovos Halevavos, Sha'ar Hakenia,* chap. 2.

⁴ Rashi, *Shemos* 5:1.

⁵ *Da'as Chochma U'mussar* 1:347.

⁶ Heard from R' Hillel Copperman.

A Jew
Is a Jew
Is a Jew

פרק ד' משנה ה': רַבִּי יוֹחָנָן בֶּן בְּרוֹקָא אוֹמֵר, כָּל
הַמְחַלֵּל שֵׁם שָׁמַיִם בַּסֵּתֶר, נִפְרָעִין מִמֶּנּוּ בְּגָלוּי. אֶחָד
שׁוֹגֵג וְאֶחָד מֵזִיד בְּחִלּוּל הַשֵּׁם.

Chapter 4, Mishnah 5: *Rabbi Yochanan ben Beroka
says: Whoever desecrates the Name of Heaven in
private will be punished in public. Acting without
intent is the same as acting purposely with regard
to chillul Hashem.*

The Mishnah mentions two aspects in which *chillul Hashem*
is worse than other sins.
Elsewhere, Chazal actually refer to *chillul Hashem* as
the worst of all sins.[1] Usually, one can atone for a transgression
through the process of *teshuva*. Some sins, however, are so grave
that *teshuva* alone is not enough and forgiveness is not attained
until Yom Kippur. Other sins are even more reprehensible, and
even *teshuva* and Yom Kippur do not suffice; atonement for such
offenses is only achieved after the person suffers as well.

Chillul Hashem, however, is in a category of its own. *Teshuva*,
Yom Kippur, and suffering combined cannot rid a person of this
transgression. Only his death is able to cleanse him of *chillul
Hashem*.[2] The reason is that the person's very existence recalls
the *chillul Hashem* he made. Whenever people see him, they are
reminded of what he did, and so complete atonement cannot be
achieved until he dies and leaves this world.[3]

Before we try to understand why *chillul Hashem* is treated so
severely, let us first understand what *chillul Hashem* really is.

Defining *Chillul Hashem*

In defining *chillul Hashem*, the Gemara quotes the statement of Rav
that if he were to buy meat without paying for it immediately, it
would be a *chillul Hashem*.[4] Rav intended to pay eventually, so there
would be nothing wrong with his buying on credit. Nevertheless,

because Rav was known for his Torah scholarship and piety, even the slightest act that could be construed as stealing would make people think less of Torah.[5]

Thus it emerges from the Gemara that any action that puts Torah in an unfavorable light is a *chillul Hashem*, even if no specific sin is involved.[6]

The Chofetz Chaim was once rushing to catch a train when he was asked to be the tenth man for a minyan in a mourner's home. Even though he had already davened and completing the minyan would have meant missing his train, he agreed to help so as not to create a *chillul Hashem*.[7]

Had the Chofetz Chaim refused to help, it certainly would not have been a transgression. Nevertheless, since the people may not have understood why he refused, he felt it would have been a *chillul Hashem* to do so. Again we see that a *chillul Hashem* depends on the *perception* of a behavior rather than on the behavior itself.

This is also clear from Chazal's remarkable statement that a *talmid chacham* who has a stain on his clothes is liable for the death penalty.[8] Now, nowhere does the Torah say, "Thou shall not walk around with a stain on thy clothes." How, then, can this warrant such a severe penalty? The reason is that a *talmid chacham* is G-d's representative in this world. When people see him wearing dirty clothes they will say, "Look how unkempt Torah scholars are." By causing people to have less respect for G-d and His Torah, he becomes guilty of desecrating G-d's Name.[9]

Chillul Hashem is relative to the status of the person doing the act. What is considered a *chillul Hashem* for one person is not necessarily a *chillul Hashem* for another. This is because the more learned a person is, the greater the level of refinement people expect of him and the more they will scrutinize his every deed. Thus, for Rav, who was exceptionally pious, not paying immediately constituted a *chillul Hashem*, whereas for most of us it would not.[10]

Nevertheless, since *chillul Hashem* depends on the way people perceive us, our true status may not be relevant.[11] For example, an ordinary *yeshiva bachur* may not think of himself as being a *talmid chacham* and so might not feel that Chazal's sharp comment about an unkempt *talmid chacham* applies to him. But his humility would be out of place, because to the outside world he appears like a *talmid chacham*. Whether he has studied for years in the world's top yeshiva and is well versed in the entire Talmud, or whether he is newly religious and still has doubts concerning the basic tenets of Judaism, is irrelevant. To the man on the street, he personifies a *talmid chacham* and must therefore act like one.[12]

If our appearance or behavior creates a negative impression, an onlooker will not limit his criticism to us alone, but will generalize it as applying to all religious Jews, saying how they're *all* disheveled and rude. This places a great responsibility on our shoulders. We should never think, "What does it matter what I do? I'm just one individual." We must realize that our every action will affect the way millions of other Jews throughout the world are perceived.[13]

This is the reason why one who desecrates G-d's Name in private is punished in public.[14] After all, why should a person who causes a small-scale *chillul Hashem* be punished publicly? It doesn't seem fair. The reason is to demonstrate that there are no boundaries between the individual and the group in regard to *chillul Hashem*. A negative image created by an individual will reflect badly not only on him but on all Jews everywhere. The corresponding punishment, therefore, is administered in public, without distinguishing between the few and the many.[15]

There are many types of religious Jews, each with his own code of dress. One religious Jew can usually identify which "group" another religious Jew belongs to merely by glancing at his head covering. But to the outside world we are all the same. Non-Jews don't distinguish between one type of religious Jew and another based on subtle differences in clothing. The shade and size of one's yarmulke, or the type of snood or *sheitel* one wears, is beside the point and makes no difference. The crime of a single Jew is placed at the door of the entire Jewry. A Jew is a Jew is a Jew. We are all part of one body, so to speak, and each of us affects the way every other Jew will be perceived. We must always be conscious of this collective responsibility and act accordingly.

For example, our behavior on the roads will shape not only *our* image, but also the images of *all* Jews. When one Orthodox Jew got into a cab in New York, the Chinese driver asked him, "You a rabbi? Let me ask you a question. Why rabbis who drive bus always cut me off?" The cab driver had probably seen just one or two Jews, yet he applied what he saw to all Jews, forming a negative impression of every Jew everywhere.

On the positive side, when we are polite and considerate, people will think better not only of us, but of all Jews. A story is told of a young man who lived in Brooklyn and often took cabs to Manhattan where he worked. One day, as he exited the taxi a block away from his office, another Orthodox Jew entered the cab. The driver turned to his new passenger and said, "See that fellow who just left my cab? You know what he told me? He works a block away from here, but he gets out here because it's right by the subway — this way, I'm sure to get a new customer as soon as he gets out of the cab. So he walks a whole avenue block, just to help me out! I see why G-d made you the Chosen People."[16]

With today's technology and news coverage, the concept of a private act becoming public takes on new meaning. When a Jew is found committing fraud, for example, his sin is recounted in newspaper, radio, Internet, and TV reports around the world. Thus, what began as a "private" act of *chillul Hashem* ends up being revealed to millions of people.

This information explosion can also work to our advantage. Take, for instance, this excerpt from an article that appeared in a non-Jewish newspaper that has a readership numbering in the tens of thousands. It reports on the yeshiva in Waterbury, Connecticut, and is a classic example of how today's press can turn a small-scale *kiddush Hashem* into a large one.

Republican-American

Author: Mandy Ruggeri   August 22, 2004

HOW A JEWISH SCHOOL IS RESHAPING A NEIGHBORHOOD

...Police see drop in crime

And it's not just Orthodox Jews who have been drawn to the city by the yeshiva. Several non-Jewish families have told Broder (a local resident) they plan to move in, saying they know the Orthodox Jewish residents are "educated, quiet, family-oriented, and make good neighbors," he said.

Ken Schwartz, a 60-year Farmington Avenue resident and Bnai Shalom congregant, said he knows of four non-Jewish families who already have moved onto his street. "It's a more desirable place at this time," he said. "And it's more desirable for all types of people."

The additional "eyes on the street" also have made the neighborhood feel more secure and tight-knit, he said.

One time, he said, his car was broken into and his briefcase was stolen, along with important papers. He thought they were lost forever. But they were returned to him — by yeshiva students who had found them on Columbia Boulevard.

"I thought that was remarkable," he said.

Police Chief Neil O'Leary has reported a decrease in crime, especially near Fulton Park and around the yeshiva's temporary headquarters on Cooke Street. He attributes that, in part, to the young yeshiva men whose late hours of studying and tendency to walk in groups around the neighborhood create a block watch that deters crime.

Mike Veillette, who has lived on Columbia Boulevard all 18 years of his life, agreed.

"They're good people," he said. "If my sister is walking down the street at one in the morning I'm not worried; I might have been before they came."

Students from the yeshiva gedola school clean up an area around Fulton Park in Waterbury during a lunch break.

The Purpose of Creation

The second stringency of *chillul Hashem* that the Mishnah describes is that one who commits it unintentionally is liable to the same punishment as one who does so intentionally.[17]

There are many actions that one might do inadvertently, such as turning on a light or dropping a pen. Some deeds, however, are so serious that one cannot claim that they were done accidentally. For example, one cannot assert that he lashed out against the president of the United States by accident. In the same way, the sin of *chillul Hashem* is so grave that one cannot claim he did it by mistake.[18]

To better understand why *chillul Hashem* is so serious, let us explore how it fits into G-d's master plan.

G-d created the world to spread His glory.[19] To this end, He set aside the Jewish people to sanctify His Name and be a light unto the nations. Had we not sinned and been expelled from our Land, G-d's glory and existence would have been recognized throughout the world relatively quickly. The presence of the *Beis Hamikdash* and the open miracles that G-d would have done for us would have made it clear to the world that He alone runs and controls the universe. The nations would have seen G-d's Providence much as the Egyptians saw it when He split the Red Sea.[20]

Because of our sins, however, we were deemed unworthy of this supernatural existence. Yet G-d did not abandon us. Instead, He relates to us through hidden, natural ways. Since it takes much longer for the nations of the world to recognize G-d's existence by these means, it only becomes possible when we are dispersed amongst them and are actually living within their midst.[21]

Thus, the purpose of our exile among the nations is to strengthen belief in G-d and sanctify His Name — not by lecturing or proselytizing, but by deed and example. One who desecrates G-d's Name, even unintentionally, is therefore punished in the harshest manner, because he acts against the ultimate purpose of creation and, in particular, of the Jewish nation.

Our role in exile as a "light unto the nations" is disregarded by many people. We usually think of our exile only in the negative sense, namely, as a punishment for our sins. We forget that we also have a positive part to play — to be G-d's ambassadors to the world.[22]

The impression we make in our daily dealings with non-Jews must be in the forefront of our minds. Whenever we meet gentiles, we should ask ourselves, "What mark will I leave? Will his respect for G-d and His nation increase as a result of my coming into contact with him?"

And if this is true about our relationships with non-Jews, how much more so is it true when we interact with non-religious Jews, who are our own brothers and sisters.

This is particularly important in Israel, where there is such a sharp divide between secular and religious Jews. A secular Israeli, who was flying El Al to New York, writes of the time he was squeezing his way through a noisy crowd of religious Jews davening in front of the emergency exit, when a flight attendant caught his eye and, smiling slyly, whispered in Hebrew, "You open the door, I'll push."[23]

The secular media feeds Israelis with vile images of religious Jews, inciting intense hatred and creating a distorted image of what religious people are like. When a secular Israeli woman visited our home on Shabbos and saw me bouncing my children on my lap, singing, and laughing with them, she was surprised. "I never realized religious Jews have fun!" she later confided to my wife.

Against such a background, the need for impeccable behavior is that much greater. A smile, a kind word, a helping hand, or a courteous "good morning" is sometimes all it takes to shatter the distorted image secular people have of the religious.

Rabbi Yosef Shalom Elyashiv once commented that every generation possesses a mitzvah that is especially significant for its time. The mitzvah for our day, he said, is to "let the Name of Heaven become beloved through you."[24]

To let the Name of Heaven become beloved through you: what an awesome privilege! Consider: Mortal, finite man, filled with self-doubt and uncertainty, here today and gone tomorrow — this weak, mortal man, each one of us, is entrusted with the privilege of making the Name of Heaven, the King of kings Himself, become beloved through the way we live and conduct ourselves. This is the wondrous gift of the A-mighty to us, His children. To accept this gift and the responsibility that goes with it is to enhance not only the Name of G-d, but also to enrich our own lives.

---

[1] *Yerushalmi, Nedarim* 3:9; Rambam, *Hilchos Shevuos* 12:2.

[2] *Yoma* 86a. *Sha'arei Teshuva* (4:§5) and *Kad Hakemach* (s.v. חילול השם) point out, however, that one can attain forgiveness through bringing about a *kiddush Hashem*.

[3] *Michtav Me'Eliyahu* 4:88.

[4] *Yoma* 86a.

[5] In view of today's market practices, it would seem likely that regular credit card purchases would not fall into this category.

[6] *Kad Hakemach*, s.v. חילול השם. Cf. Rashi, *Yoma* 86a ד"ה ולא יהיבנא. The idea that a *chillul Hashem* can occur even where no actual sin is committed is also mentioned in Rambam (*Hilchos Yesodei HaTorah* 5:11) and *Sefer Hachinuch* §295.

[7] *Chofetz Chaim al HaTorah*, 167–168.

[8] *Shabbos* 114a.

[9] See *Sefer Hayira* ד"ה ואל תהרג.

[10] See *Mirkeves Hamishneh*; *Kad Hakemach*, s.v. חילול השם; *Mesillas Yesharim*, chap. 11.

[11] As R' Yisrael Salanter put it, "Even if in my own eyes I am nothing, when it comes to *chillul Hashem* I have to act like the spiritual leader of the generation if that's what people think I am." *Tnuas Hamussar* 1:283.

[12] Perhaps this is why the *Pele Yo'etz* (s.v. נקיות) says that, in regard to not walking around with a stain on one's clothes, everyone should consider himself a *talmid chacham*. *Leket Reshimos*, 38, records in the name of R' Nosson Wachtfogel that all *bnei Torah* in our generation have the status of *talmidei chachamim* regarding all laws of *chillul Hashem*. R' Mattisyahu Salomon made a similar remark (*Matnas*

Chaim, Yamim Nora'im, 89).

[13] *Horeb*, chap. 97.

[14] The Mishnah's mention of causing a *chillul Hashem* "in private" does not mean that there is no other person present at the time of the transgression. After all, the definition of a *chillul Hashem* is doing something in front of others that denigrates G-d or His Torah in their eyes. "Private," rather, means on a small scale compared to the punishment, which is carried out in front of many people (*Derech Chaim* and *Tosefos Yom Tov*).

[15] Cf. *Pirkei Moshe*.

[16] R' Shimon Finkelman, "*Middos* Instruction: Prerequisite for Torah," *Jewish Observer*, March 2001.

[17] That the Mishnah means to equate the punishment of a *chillul Hashem* done by accident with one done willfully is the interpretation of *Peirushei Rabbeinu Yosef ben Shoshan* (quoted in *Midrash Shmuel*); *Kad Hakemach*, s.v. חילול השם; *Hachassid Yaavetz*; *Derech Chaim*. However, Rambam, Rabbeinu Yona, and *Sefer Mussar* disagree with this interpretation, explaining that the Mishnah means only to equate an unintentional *chillul Hashem* with an intentional one in regard to their both being punished in public, but not in regard to the severity of their punishment. Equating the punishment of the two would be making G-d's system of justice unjust.

[18] Based on *Peirushei Rabbeinu Yosef ben Shoshan*, *Hachassid Yaavetz*.

[19] *Yeshaya* 43:7.

[20] See *Ha'amek Davar*, *Bamidbar* 14:21.

[21] See ibid.

[22] Had the exile been meant only as a punishment, G-d would have utilized other punishments (*Pesachim* 87b with Maharsha). *Kad Hakemach*, s.v. גאולה (1), also points out this dual purpose of *galus*.

[23] Noah J. Efron, *Real Jews* (New York: Basic Books, 2003), 4. See *Halichos Shlomo* 1:95–96, quoting R' Shlomo Zalman Auerbach as ruling that it is better to daven *Shemoneh Esrei* sitting down in one's seat than standing up in the aisle, both because of one's own intent and out of consideration for others.

[24] Heard from R' Asher Weiss. The directive to "let the Name of Heaven become beloved through you" is found in *Yoma* 86a.

Reach Out...
and Teach Someone

פרק ד' משנה ו': רַבִּי יִשְׁמָעֵאל בְּנוֹ אוֹמֵר, הַלּוֹמֵד תּוֹרָה עַל מְנָת לְלַמֵּד, מַסְפִּיקִין בְּיָדוֹ לִלְמוֹד וּלְלַמֵּד. וְהַלּוֹמֵד עַל מְנָת לַעֲשׂוֹת, מַסְפִּיקִין בְּיָדוֹ לִלְמוֹד וּלְלַמֵּד לִשְׁמוֹר וְלַעֲשׂוֹת.

Chapter 4, Mishnah 6: *Rabbi Yishmael, his son, says: One who learns in order to teach is given the ability to learn and to teach; but one who learns in order to practice is given the ability to learn and to teach, to keep and to practice.*

The Mishnah discusses two types of people — those who learn in order to teach and those who learn in order to keep the mitzvos.[1] There is, however, another group of people not mentioned in the Mishnah — those who learn for the sake of their own learning, people whose main concern is with their own growth.

While these people would certainly not withhold Torah knowledge from others, they hesitate to go out and teach, because doing so would mean having less time for their own learning. In the time it takes to prepare and give a *shiur*, they could be furthering their own Torah knowledge and covering new ground, and since their prime ambition is to become accomplished scholars themselves, they are averse to teaching. Certainly their intent is noble and G-d will surely help them to become *talmidei chachamim.*[2]

However, as the *Midrash Shmuel* points out, a higher level of learning is achieved by one who learns in order to teach.[3] Don't think, says Rabbi Yishmael, that by devoting time to teaching others you will end up knowing less yourself. G-d will see to it that your own learning will not suffer and that you will accomplish everything the one who learns for his own sake achieves. Thus, one who learns in order to teach is given the means *lilmod*, to learn as much as he would have had he devoted all his time to learning for himself,[4] and *lelamed*, to teach others.

Learning From Avraham

Chazal compare teaching others to lighting a flame.[5] Just as lighting another's candle with one's own doesn't diminish the original flame, so, too, teaching other people doesn't diminish one's own learning.[6] Quite the opposite — one who shares his wisdom with others is assured that "his wisdom will increase and deepen."[7]

G-d chose Avraham Avinu to found the Jewish nation. One might think that Avraham was chosen because he was the only righteous person of his time. But that wasn't the case. There were other righteous individuals before Avraham who also knew G-d and strove to learn His ways. Chanoch, for example, dedicated his entire life to serving G-d, reaching such levels of perfection that he ceased being human, and was transported to Heaven while still alive.[8] In fact, the Chasam Sofer writes that Chanoch reached *higher* levels of spiritual perfection than Avraham did. Besides Chanoch, there were Shem, Eiver, and others, who served G-d and became prophets. Yet none of them were chosen to start the Jewish nation. So what was unique about Avraham?[9]

G-d answers this question when He says that He loved Avraham "because he commands his children and his household after him that they keep G-d's way."[10] In other words, G-d chose Avraham because he taught others Torah and brought them closer to Him.[11]

Yes, there were other righteous people before Avraham, but they were all concerned with their *own* service of G-d, whereas Avraham reached out to others.[12] Chanoch may have attained the highest level of human perfection, but he did so while leaving the rest of his generation to perish as sinners. Had Avraham wanted to, he could have done the same, separating himself from the rest of the world and becoming an angel like Chanoch. But he didn't, because he realized that bringing others close to G-d was a greater way to sanctify His name. If the righteous people of every generation would concentrate on perfecting themselves alone, one in a thousand would be G-dly, while the majority of the world would be corrupt.[13]

Teaching as the Highest Goal

Rabbi Yerucham Levovitz writes that man's task in this world is to influence those around him and help them grow and develop spiritually, and not remain isolated in any way.[14]

This concept can be derived from contemplating why one's *neshama* had to come down to this world. After all, a *neshama* is an intrinsic aspect of G-d Himself, so to speak, and before it descends to this lowly earth it is exposed to things that are hidden from us. It is free to gaze upon everything in the Heavenly spheres, with a perspective not limited by physicality. Upon entering the human body, however, the *neshama* loses this blissful existence, and is blinded by the physical limitations of this world. For the *neshama*, being in this world is like being dragged in mud, and there is no guarantee that it will ever return to its original level of purity after it leaves this world. Why, then, must the *neshama* go through this suffering? What did it lack above that it had to be dragged down here?[15]

The answer is that despite its idyllic state in Heaven, the *neshama* was lacking one thing — the ability to give. The *neshama* could only receive Divine emanations from its Creator, but did not have the capacity to give of its light to others or influence them in any way. Since the greatest pleasure one can attain is to be like G-d, Who gives of Himself to others, the *neshama* had to come down to this world and constrict itself in order to become a giver.[16]

Man must follow the cue of his *neshama*, limiting his own development in order to share his knowledge with others.[17] For this reason, the Torah instructs us several times to educate and correct others.[18] These mitzvos teach us that the ultimate purpose of creation is not achieved by perfecting oneself alone, but by trying to perfect others as well.[19]

Obviously, a person can't teach others until he has first learned himself.[20] Even then, each individual needs to seek the advice of his teachers to help him choose the right time for him to begin teaching. When a young scholar came to ask the Chazon Ish whether he should leave the yeshiva for half a year in order to teach others, he was told that he should not go. "The spiritual success of the *klal* is dependent on the greatness of the individual. The more one learns Torah, the more he will be able to influence others."[21]

Whether a person has much more to learn, or simply is not ready to begin teaching, his purpose in everything he learns should be that he will ultimately be able to share his Torah knowledge with others.[22]

Someone who was not succeeding in *kollel* once asked the Steipler whether he should continue learning or look for a teaching job. The Steipler replied that there used to be a time when everyone's aspiration was to teach, and only those who could not find any available teaching position would continue to learn in *kollel*. Furthermore, he pointed out that every great Torah personality in history grew and became elevated by teaching others.[23]

The greatest prophet of the Jewish people, after all, is not known as Moshe our prophet, or Moshe our redeemer, but as Moshe Rabbeinu, Moshe our *teacher*.

Beginning with Avraham Avinu and continuing until the *Gedolim* of our time, we find that there is no nobler enterprise than teaching others.[24] And as the Mishnah says, one's own learning will not suffer as a result. On the contrary, G-d will help a person who is learning for the sake of others to grasp in one hour what had previously taken him several hours, and to reach levels of understanding far beyond his natural ability.[25]

---

[1] The Mishnah implies that those who learn in order to teach are not learning in order to keep mitzvos. This cannot be the Mishnah's intent, however, because, as Rabbeinu Yona points out, anyone who learns with no intention of practicing what he learns will have no success in learning or teaching. See Rabbeinu Yona and *Midrash Shmuel*.

[2] *Midrash Shmuel*. Cf. *Lechem Shamayim* cited in note 22.

[3] *Midrash Shmuel* is only discussing one who wants to teach for pure motives,

to further other people's Torah learning. One who wishes to teach for egotistical reasons — for example, to gain popularity or for financial gain — will still be helped to learn and teach but is not on the same level as the person discussed above.

[4] Ibid.

[5] See Rashi on *Bamidbar* 11:17.

[6] R' Elazar Simcha Wasserman, *Kovetz Ma'amarim V'igros* 3:239.

[7] *Tanna D'vei Eliyahu, Eliyahu Rabba,* chap. 27. Cf. *Makkos* 10a. *Midrash Shmuel* (6:7) writes that one who learns with the intent of teaching others will have the "gates of Torah opened before him."

[8] See *Maseches Derech Eretz,* chap. 1.

[9] Based on *Chofetz Chaim al HaTorah, parashas Vayeira* 18:19, and *Chasam Sofer,* introduction to responsa on *Yoreh De'ah.*

[10] *Bereishis* 18:19.

[11] *Chofetz Chaim* and *Chasam Sofer,* loc. cit. The Chasam Sofer says that it was for this reason that Avraham merited being called by G-d "My beloved," a term of endearment that was not used regarding any other ancestor.

[12] *Chofetz Chaim,* loc. cit.

[13] *Chasam Sofer,* loc. cit.

[14] *Da'as Torah* 1:11.

[15] *Chasam Sofer,* loc. cit.

[16] Ibid.

[17] Ibid. The Chasam Sofer writes there that the ideal Torah personality cares as much for other people's perfection as he does for his own.

The idea that a person must be prepared to cut his own growth short for the sake of others is elaborated on by R' Avraham Grodzenski in *Toras Avraham,* 229–230. He notes that this is the *midda* of G-d, Who constricted His essence for the good of the world, and that this is the task of every father when he teaches his son Torah, learning simple things with him at a time when he could be learning deeper, more complex ideas.

[18] *Devarim* 4:10 and 11:19; *Vayikra* 19:17.

[19] *Chasam Sofer*, loc. cit.

[20] See Rashi, *Berachos* 14b ד"ה וזה ללמד, and *Chiddushei HaRitva*, *Berachos* 14b ד"ה הוא דין הוא שיקדים וכו'.

[21] *Pe'er Hador* 2:207. The Chazon Ish had a young acquaintance who had a natural inclination to benefit others and serve the public. When the Chazon Ish noticed this man's inclination, he told him: "Chazal relate that R' Yochanan ben Zakkai learned forty years and then taught forty years. Now, during the forty years he learned, didn't he have anyone to teach? Rather, it seems that this is the proper order and this is the way to succeed more. Even the Chofetz Chaim toiled many years to become the 'Chofetz Chaim,' and afterward he changed the world in a short time" (ibid.).

[22] The Torah places the command to teach Torah ("*v'shinantam l'vanecha*") before the command to learn it ("*v'dibarta bam*") in *Devarim* 6:7. The Ksav Sofer writes that this order seems illogical, because one has to learn before one can teach. He answers that the Torah is teaching us that one's own learning must be done with the motivation of teaching others later (quoted in *Dvar Yerushalayim*, 181). R' Aharon Kotler cites the same principle (*Shiurei U'fninei Da'as*, 22). A source for this idea can be found in *Avos* 6:6 where "learning with the intent of teaching" is listed as one of the forty-eight tools essential for acquiring Torah. *Lechem Shamayim* writes that learning in order to teach others is the most basic intention one should have while learning and that anyone who does not do so will have no reward.

[23] *Mishel Ha'Avos* quoting *Ashkavtei D'Rebbi*.

[24] Also, see Meiri to *Sanhedrin* 24a, who describes teaching others as the *tachlis hasheleimus*, the greatest level of perfection one can reach. When Chazal say *talmud Torah* is greater than all other mitzvos (*Pe'ah* 1:1) they do not mean to imply that learning is greater than teaching, for the phrase *talmud Torah* refers to both learning and teaching, as is clear from the Rambam in *Sefer Hamitzvos*, Aseh 11. Indeed, the Rambam (loc. cit.) and *Sefer Hachinuch* (§419) define the very mitzvah of Torah study as learning *and* teaching, such that one who learns without teaching has not completely fulfilled his obligation. Moreover, Chazal say that one who learns but doesn't teach scorns the Torah (*Sanhedrin* 99a). R' Yerucham Levovitz, *Da'as Torah* 1:89, writes that learning and teaching are not two separate concepts: If the learning is complete, the teaching should follow automatically.

[25] *Chasam Sofer*, loc. cit. This, explains the Chasam Sofer, is the intent of *Bava Basra* 10a, which says that although prophecy no longer rests on the prophets, it is still found amongst *chachamim*. The prophecy of the *chachamim* is that of the hidden mysteries of Torah that G-d reveals to them in the merit of disseminating Torah.

Another Look
at Kollel

פרק ד׳ משנה ז׳: רַבִּי צָדוֹק אוֹמֵר, אַל תַּעֲשֵׂה עֲטָרָה
לְהִתְגַּדֵּל בָּה, וְלֹא קַרְדֹּם לַחְפֹּר בָּה. וְכָךְ הָיָה הִלֵּל אוֹמֵר,
וּדְאִשְׁתַּמֵּשׁ בְּתַגָּא, חֲלָף. הָא לָמַדְתָּ, כָּל הַנֶּהֱנֶה מִדִּבְרֵי
תוֹרָה נוֹטֵל חַיָּיו מִן הָעוֹלָם.

Chapter 4, Mishnah 7: *Rabbi Tzadok says: Do
not make the Torah into a crown for your own
aggrandizement, or a spade with which to dig. This
is what Hillel used to say: "He who uses the crown
[of Torah for personal benefit] shall fade away."
This teaches you that whoever derives personal
benefit from the words of Torah removes his life
from the world.*

The above Mishnah is one of the most well known
Mishnayos in *Pirkei Avos*, yet, in a way, also one of the least
understood.

The Mishnah warns us not to convert the Torah into a tool from
which one benefits materially. On the face of it, this would seem
to forbid rabbis from receiving a salary, and young scholars from
receiving stipends from their *kollelim*. In our society, however,
such conduct is normal. Obviously, therefore, we need to study
this Mishnah carefully and consider what exactly it means. Does
it really mean to preclude the acceptance of money for learning or
teaching Torah?

According to the Rambam, that is precisely what the Mishnah
means. Based on this Mishnah, he sharply criticizes Torah scholars
for demanding financial support from others in order to help them
learn, saying that there is no source anywhere in Chazal that justifies
such behavior. If we search the words of the Sages, we do not find
any of them asking people for money or collecting funds for their
yeshivos. On the contrary, we find that many of them worked to earn
their own living and, despite their poverty, never asked for charity.
Had they held out their hands and sought financial assistance they

would surely have amassed enough wealth to fill their houses with gold and jewels. But they didn't ask, because the idea of accepting gifts from others for studying Torah was anathema to them.[1]

The Rambam supports his point of view by pointing to Hillel, the leading Torah scholar of his time. Despite his greatness, Hillel was a woodchopper who earned just about enough money each day to pay the entrance fee for the *beis midrash*.[2] Had he requested financial support from others he would surely have received immediate help from the wealthy people of his generation. He refused, however, because to do so would have lessened people's respect for Torah, causing them to view it as just another job.[3]

The Rambam's position was quite controversial, and many Torah giants took issue with his view.

Some commentators systematically approach each of his proofs, challenging them one by one. They point out, for example, that Hillel only worked before he became a great Torah scholar, but once he was appointed *nasi* he accepted money for his position. Beyond refuting each of the Rambam's proofs, they cite many examples of rabbis who did in fact receive support from their communities.[4]

Others claim that the Rambam was critical only of those who irresponsibly throw themselves on the community, demanding that others sustain them. The Rambam never meant, however, to castigate a person who finds others who are willing to support him.[5] After all, the Torah itself sanctions such a partnership regarding Yissachar and Zevulun. Zevulun worked so that his brother Yissachar could devote his life to Torah. The Gemara even mentions a *Tanna*, Shimon Achi Azaria, who was called by his brother's name because the latter supported him.[6]

Still others point out that although earlier generations were able to work without having it affect their learning, nowadays the majority of people are not able to reach the levels of Torah scholarship needed to guide others while also holding down a job.[7]

Consider the Rambam himself. Most people would recognize

that his ability to learn with full concentration despite working all day was exceptional and that few people today would be able to do the same.[8] Anyone about whom it is written, "From Moshe to Moshe there was no one like Moshe," was obviously no ordinary genius, and if we insisted that Torah scholars today follow his example and support themselves, we would be left with no one to guide and teach the rest of the Jewish people.

For these as well as other reasons, the custom today is for Torah scholars and teachers to accept remuneration for their efforts.[9]

But according to those who argue with the Rambam, what is the Mishnah saying? If it does not mean to forbid rabbis from accepting money for their work, what *does* it mean?

Let's Call a Spade a Spade

In order to answer this question, we must take a closer look at the Mishnah's metaphor of a spade.

A spade is an instrument used for a specific purpose: to dig holes. Like other tools, its importance stems from what it can be used for, not from any intrinsic value of its own. Thus, when the Mishnah tells us not to make Torah into a tool, it is telling us not to view it as a means to an end, as a way of earning a livelihood.[10]

Yes, as mentioned above, the custom has developed that Torah scholars do accept money for their learning, and rabbis and other religious officials do receive a salary from their congregants. Nevertheless, one should never reduce Torah into a moneymaking instrument. Torah isn't just another job, one more way of earning a living. The Torah scholar doesn't learn so that he'll get paid. He gets paid so that he can learn. The difference between the two is immense. The first uses the Torah for his own selfish purposes, while the second uses material possessions to serve the Torah.[11]

This idea is true not only of receiving a stipend to learn, but also of receiving a salary to teach.

A lawyer practices law so that he will receive his paycheck at the end of the month. An accountant audits books so that he will be able to support his family. Although they may be providing an important service, their job is purely functional, a tool through which they can put bread on the table. The Torah teacher is different. His job is a holy one — to imbue his students with a love of Torah and fear of G-d. The money he earns is a means that enables him to continue his Divinely ordained role. If his goal is the paycheck and his teaching just a means to get it, he is in effect using the Torah as a mere tool, an act that our Mishnah says will cost him his place in the World to Come. On the other hand, if his paycheck is only a way for him to feed his family, while his primary interest is to impart Torah to others, then he is fulfilling his mission as a scholar and teacher.[12]

No Job Like Torah

Rabbi Moshe Feinstein wrote a letter of advice to Torah teachers in which he reminds them that their job is unlike any other. Although they have an employer as in other jobs, their ultimate obligation is not to their earthly employer, but to G-d Himself. As such, there may be times when teachers must put in extra hours of their own in order to help certain students who need extra attention. Instead of comparing their job to others and saying how hard it is, teachers should strengthen themselves in their holy work and act according to the needs of their pupils, not their wages. Once they have accepted the job they have a personal responsibility to G-d to teach His children to the best of their ability, even if it means working more hours than their salary warrants.[13]

When the suggestion was made to install a time clock in a certain yeshiva, Rabbi Yaakov Kaminetsky was "incensed."[14] A rebbe's devotion, he said, should go well beyond the time he spends teaching in the classroom and is not something that can be monitored by the precise number of minutes he spends in the yeshiva.

These observations about a rebbe's devotion to his job are both based on the same principle: teaching Torah is not an ordinary occupation, another way of earning a living, and should never be treated as such.

Sometimes a rabbi's role as teacher comes into conflict with his source of income and he is forced to make the difficult choice between the two. For example, his community may be acting in a way that is against Torah values, and, as their spiritual leader, it is his obligation to point this out to them. Since no one likes criticism, however, he knows that saying what needs to be said would make him very unpopular and could jeopardize his position. In order to protect his contract, he chooses to remain silent and feigns oblivion. In doing so, however, he bends the Torah to suit his needs, treating it like a paycheck, which he conveniently folds and slips into his wallet.

Rabbi Eliyahu E. Dessler describes people "who were great in Torah, extremely capable, meticulously observant of mitzvos, brilliant thinkers, who nevertheless never fully succeeded in imbuing their students with the spirit of a *ben Torah*. The reason is because they treated their [role in their] yeshivos as a 'position,' as a source of livelihood and prestige. This approach will never succeed in changing other people's basic attitudes."[15]

Rabbi Meir Shapiro (the famed founder of the *Daf Hayomi* movement) was a living example of the idealistic attitude a person should have toward teaching Torah if he is to be effective and make an impression.

Reb Meir was supported by his father-in-law, one of the wealthiest men in Austria-Hungary, with whom he lived for several years. When a community sent an invitation to Reb Meir offering him to become their spiritual leader, Reb Meir's father-in-law was against the idea. He tried to dissuade Reb Meir, but it was of no avail. In a desperate attempt, Reb Meir's mother-in-law took an enormous amount of money from her husband's safe. She placed it on the table in front of Reb Meir and told him it was all his on condition that he remain in their house.

The close friends present in the room stared in amazement at the amount of money she was offering him. Although it was more than he would be able to earn during his whole lifetime, Reb Meir remained unruffled and unimpressed.

In moving words, laden with emotion, he said, "Heaven is my witness that I don't want to become a practicing rabbi so that I can make a career for myself; nor do I want it for the honor and prestige I can gain. My only craving is to study Torah and share it with others; and I am completely convinced that the only way I can really attain my goal is with a rabbinic position.... Believe me: if I didn't feel a revulsion for money, if I didn't detest unearned income, I would never put on a rabbi's garb."[16]

As we know, Reb Meir went on to attain greatness. Today, his *Daf Hayomi* program is the most widespread framework for Gemara learning throughout the world. At the last *Siyum HaShas* I was struck by the awesome thought of tens of thousands of Jews gathered together in various cities and towns around the world. I couldn't help but wonder about Reb Meir's merit in establishing such an historic program. What was it about him, what teaching power did he have, that his brainchild should still be having such a major impact today, seventy years after he passed away?

Perhaps the answer lies in the above story. There he mentions two points, both of which are taught in our Mishnah. His statement that he didn't "want to become a practicing rabbi so that I can make a career for myself" echoes the warning not to make the Torah into a spade with which to dig. And his second statement — that he didn't "want it for the honor and prestige I can gain" — echoes the words "Do not make the Torah into a crown for your own aggrandizement."

The Mishnah concludes by saying that one who uses the Torah for personal gain will fade away. Little wonder, then, that the Torah of Rabbi Meir Shapiro should still be alive today. A man who took Heaven as his witness and testified that he had no desire for personal gain but longed only "to study Torah and share it with others," a man who despised unearned income and accepted it only so that he could spread G-d's word, such a man is worthy of having his teachings live on eternally. He understood that the warning against taking money for Torah isn't an outdated ideal, but a proper frame of mind for every Torah scholar.

In today's society, because it has become the norm to accept money for Torah-related pursuits, there is a tendency to view the warning of our Mishnah as irrelevant. Nothing could be further from the truth. The Mishnah is as timely today as it was 2,000 years ago when it was written, and provides each one of us with the proper attitude toward the role of Torah in our lives. The Torah is its own kind of "spade": a Heavenly implement with which we can build a life of purpose and fulfillment in this world, and a life of eternity in the World to Come.

---

[1] Rambam, commentary to this Mishnah.

[2] *Yoma* 35b.

[3] Rambam, commentary to this Mishnah.

[4] See *Tashbatz* 1:§142–148; *Nachalas Avos*; R' Yosef ibn Aknin (the Rambam's student and the one for whom he wrote *Moreh Nevuchim*), *Sefer Mussar*; *Kesef Mishneh, Hilchos Talmud Torah* 3:10.

[5] *Rishon L'tzion, Yoreh De'ah* 246:21; *Aruch Hashulchan, Yoreh De'ah* 246:39–40.

[6] *Sota* 21a with Rashi.

[7] See *Kesef Mishneh, Hilchos Talmud Torah* 3:10; *Dvar Shmuel*, §138, quoted in *Be'ur Halacha* 231:1.

[8] See his letter to Shmuel ben Yehuda ibn Tibbon, where he describes his hectic schedule (*Igros HaRambam*, Shilat ed., §35, 550–551).

[9] Rema (*Yoreh De'ah* 246:21). After citing both opinions, he concludes that one who has the means to learn and support himself is practicing a *middas chassidus* and is truly blessed with a G-d-given gift. R' Moshe Feinstein (*Igros Moshe, Yoreh De'ah* 2:§116) writes that those who refuse to accept money for studying Torah solely based on the Rambam's words are driven by their evil inclination, which

wishes for them to busy themselves with earning a living and to neglect their Torah studies. The Chofetz Chaim (*Shem Olam, Sha'ar Hachzakas HaTorah*, last note of chap. 11) makes a similar point. Being self-sufficient is no more than a *midda tova b'alma*, a worthwhile thing. But is one willing to forsake his entire share in Torah in order to achieve a praiseworthy *midda*? Indeed, the Chofetz Chaim (*Be'ur Halacha* 231:1), R' Moshe Feinstein (loc. cit.), and R' Ovadia Yosef (*Yabia Omer* 7, *Yoreh De'ah* §17) all rule that it is better for someone to learn all day and be supported than to learn less but be self-supportive.

[10] That the Mishnah is not actually forbidding the taking of money, but merely defining what a person's intent should be, is clear from the Seforno on this Mishnah and the Shelah in *Maseches Shevuos, Perek Ner Mitzvah* §40.

[11] Consequently, *Nachalas Avos* says that someone who has other income and still takes money for learning Torah is indeed using the Torah as a tool. See also *Yam Shel Shlomo, Chullin* 3:9, who says that someone who takes money for learning when he has no need for it is sinful.

[12] Perhaps the test of whether a person is taking money in order to teach, or teaching in order to make money, is when he is asked on the odd occasion to teach without payment. If he refuses, it shows that his motivation in teaching all along was to earn money, thus using Torah as a tool (R' Zev Leff).

[13] *Igros Moshe, Yoreh De'ah* 3:§71.

[14] R' Nisson Wolpin, ed., *The Torah Profile*, 170.

[15] *Strive for Truth* 2:126.

[16] R' Yehoshua Baumol, *A Blaze in the Darkening Gloom: The Life of Rav Meir Shapiro* (Jerusalem: Feldheim, 1994), 54–59.

Head Like
a Rock

פרק ד' משנה י"א: רַבִּי יוֹנָתָן אוֹמֵר, כָּל הַמְקַיֵּם אֶת
הַתּוֹרָה מֵעֹנִי, סוֹפוֹ לְקַיְמָהּ מֵעֹשֶׁר. וְכָל הַמְבַטֵּל אֶת
הַתּוֹרָה מֵעֹשֶׁר, סוֹפוֹ לְבַטְּלָהּ מֵעֹנִי.

Chapter 4, Mishnah 11: *Rabbi Yonasan says: Whoever fulfills the Torah in poverty will ultimately fulfill it in wealth, and whoever neglects the Torah in wealth will ultimately neglect it in poverty.*

We have presented above the straightforward translation of the Mishnah: that one who keeps the Torah in poverty will be blessed with wealth.[1] The difficulty with such a reading is that many righteous people, who dedicate their lives to Torah despite abject poverty, die without a penny to their name.[2] Examples of such people abound; how, then, is the Mishnah to be understood?

Some commentaries explain that the Mishnah is not referring to financial poverty, but rather to ignorance and weak learning skills. Accordingly, the Mishnah is to be read as follows: Anyone who keeps the Torah despite his ignorance or weak intelligence will ultimately be blessed with greater knowledge and intelligence. He will thus be able to observe the Torah's precepts with a deep and profound understanding.[3]

The person of poor intelligence may find it hard to believe that his mind can so improve that even he could turn into an erudite Torah scholar. He may have become so accustomed to seeing those around him grasp Torah concepts at lightning speed while he remains in the dark, that the Mishnah's promise may seem to him like nothing more than a pipe dream.

However, the truth is that everything is in the hands of Heaven, and the brilliant student only understands the Torah because G-d enables him to do so. That being the case, the person of weak intelligence and the person of great genius depend equally on G-d for insight, and there is no essential difference between their potential abilities to mine the depths of Torah. If G-d desires that a person understand, he will understand, regardless of his native intelligence.

Thus, a person should never think, "What chance do I have of succeeding in Torah study with my mental limitations and poor memory?" For if he tries his best and genuinely wants to grow, he can, in time, be granted from Above a level of wisdom and intelligence far superior to that with which he was born.

Rising Above Limitations

This potential to rise above one's natural limitations has been demonstrated time and again throughout history.[4]

Consider the prophet Shmuel. His mother, Chana, prayed for a child who would be "average amongst men...neither brilliant nor foolish."[5] From her words "This is the child that I prayed for,"[6] it is clear that her request was granted. Thus we see that Shmuel — who became the greatest of all the biblical judges and a prophet equal in stature to Moshe and Aharon combined — started out with average capabilities.[7]

Consider, also, the great *Tanna'im* Rabbi Akiva and Ben Azai. The Midrash says that their abilities to understand Torah were initially "like that of barren rock." Due to their immense exertion, however, G-d opened the floodgates of wisdom for them. Rabbi Akiva revealed hidden aspects of the Torah to the world, and Ben Azai explained laws that were beyond the comprehension of even Beis Shammai and Beis Hillel.[8] In fact, Ben Azai became so brilliant and profound that later generations held him up as the symbol of mental sharpness and acuity.[9]

But one doesn't have to look as far back as the prophets or *Tanna'im* to find examples of people rising above their limitations and becoming Torah luminaries. Rabbi Naftali Tzvi Yehuda Berlin, better known as the Netziv, was an average child. As a youngster, he was shunned by his peers for not being as bright or intelligent as they were. Yet he was determined to learn. It is told of him that he would even place his feet in ice-cold water to prevent himself from dozing off at his *shtender*.[10] His yearning to learn was so overpowering that when he reached the prayer of *Ahava Rabba* and recited the words "Merciful Father, have mercy upon us and put it into our hearts to understand, to learn, and to teach Your Torah," tears would roll down his cheeks. By the end of his life he had become the head of the renowned Volozhin Yeshiva and the author of many classic works.

Desire and Determination

A delegation of *Roshei Yeshiva* once came to ask the Chazon Ish for his blessing on a new venture they were planning. They wanted to open a *kollel* geared exclusively toward talented young scholars, people they felt would become the future leaders of Torah Jewry. The Chazon Ish refused. "If we only concentrate on the geniuses," he exclaimed, "from where will we get the Yitzchok Elchonon Spectors of the world?"[11] Reb Yitzchok Elchonon was born with average mental abilities but worked incredibly hard, ultimately becoming an acknowledged halachic authority throughout the world.

Rabbi Elazar Shach expressed the same sentiments when asked about opening a yeshiva exclusively for gifted boys. Basing himself on fifty years of experience in working with yeshivos, he said that it is impossible to know beforehand who will grow in Torah knowledge and who will not, and that all boys should therefore be given equal opportunities.[12]

When children were brought to him for a blessing that they grow in Torah learning, he would tell them, "If you want to learn, you will become a *gadol baTorah*." With this one sentence he was instilling in them the recognition that success in Torah does not depend on a person's intelligence or any outside factor, but on one thing alone — his desire to learn.[13]

Chazal say that one's intelligence is determined at the time of conception.[14] But what is apparent from our Mishnah, as well as from several other sources,[15] is that with the right desire and determination a person can transcend any natural mental limitations and reach heights of knowledge and understanding far beyond his dreams.

---

[1] Although the word *mekayem* literally refers to keeping the Torah, it can also refer to learning Torah. See Rabbeinu Yona; *Milei D'Avos* (first interpretation); *Be'er Ha'Avos*.

[2] For various solutions to this difficulty, see *Nachalas Avos*, *Midrash Shmuel*, *Ruach Chaim* and *Tiferes Yisrael*.

[3] *Milei D'Avos* (second interpretation); *Midrash Shmuel* (second interpretation); *Be'er Ha'Avos*; R' Yitzchak Hutner (*Sefer Hazikaron*, 89), in the name of R' Yehoshua Leib Diskin. Accordingly, the latter half of the Mishnah is to be interpreted along the same theme: One who has intelligence and knowledge but misuses them will ultimately lose them (*Milei D'Avos, Midrash Shmuel, Be'er Ha'Avos*).

Lest one consider this interpretation to be contrived, it should be noted that the Gemara in *Kesubos* 68a, explaining a halachic Mishnah, interprets the terms *oni* and *osher* (the same terms used in our Mishnah) as referring to intellectual poverty and wealth. See *Milei D'Avos*, which cites a different Gemara to support this interpretation. (The Vilna Shas, however, has a different reading of that Gemara text.)

[4] See Meiri, *Mishlei* 13:11.

[5] *Berachos* 31b.

[6] I *Shmuel* 1:27.

[7] *Sichos Mussar* 5731:§18. Cf. *Hagahos Yaavetz* to *Berachos* 31b.

[8] *Midrash Hallel* cited in *Otzar Midrashim* (New York: Eisenstein, 1915) 1:131.

[9] See *Eiruvin* 29a.

[10] Told by his nephew R' Baruch Epstein (author of *Torah Temima*) in *Makor Baruch* 4:1678–1683.

[11] Heard from R' Isaac Bernstein. See *Pe'er Hador* 2:242. *Nitzotzei Eish*, 289, quotes the Chazon Ish as saying that most *Gedolei Yisrael* were not born with exceptional intelligence but became great through hard work alone. R' Chaim

Kanievsky (*Orchos Yosher*, 90) writes, "It is well known that generally it is not the brilliant ones who succeed in Torah learning, but the diligent and industrious ones." See also *Chayei Olam* 2:§12; *She'ifos*, 8.

[12] *Masores Hachinuch*, 89.

[13] Ibid.

[14] *Nidda* 16b.

[15] *Chovos Halevavos, Sha'ar Cheshbon Hanefesh*, chap. 3 (*cheshbon* 21); Maharsha, *Nidda* 69b; *Midrash Shmuel* 4:1; Chida, *Tziporen Shamir*, §218, quoted in *Binyan Olam*, 35. The sons of the Vilna Gaon write in their introduction to their father's commentary on *Yoreh De'ah* that this is the meaning of the verse *eidus Hashem ne'emana machkimas pesi* (*Tehillim* 19:8): The Torah can be trusted to make the simple one wise.

The Workaholic Within Us

פרק ד' משנה י"ב: רַבִּי מֵאִיר אוֹמֵר, הֱוֵי מְמַעֵט בְּעֵסֶק,
וַעֲסוֹק בַּתּוֹרָה. וֶהֱוֵה שְׁפַל רוּחַ בִּפְנֵי כָל אָדָם. וְאִם
בָּטַלְתָּ מִן הַתּוֹרָה, יֶשׁ לְךָ בְּטֵלִים הַרְבֵּה כְּנֶגְדֶּךָ. וְאִם
עָמַלְתָּ בַּתּוֹרָה, יֶשׁ לוֹ שָׂכָר הַרְבֵּה לִתֶּן לָךְ.

Chapter 4, Mishnah 12: *Rabbi Meir says: Reduce*
work and occupy yourself in Torah, and be humble
before others. If you neglect the Torah, there will be
many causes of neglect in your way, but if you toil
in Torah, G-d has abundant reward to give you.

When Dr. Wayne E. Oates coined the term "workaholism" in 1968 to describe a disturbing psychological obsession he noticed around him,[1] he could not have imagined how common a phenomenon this would become. Workaholism has been termed "one of the fastest-growing diseases of modern life,"[2] with over 13 percent of Americans affected. According to Professor Yitzhak Harpaz of Haifa University's School of Business, Israelis have the third-highest rate of workaholism in the world, with 8 percent of the population hooked on work.[3]

Bryan Robinson, professor of counseling at North Carolina University and author of *Chained to the Desk: A Guidebook for Workaholics*, states that workaholism is not defined by how long you work. "It's the preoccupation with work. Workaholics can be lying on a beach and obsessing about work. It's the inability to turn it off."[4] One executive, wanting to test his middle managers' devotion to work, sent them an e-mail on Saturday at 2 a.m. and received an immediate reply from every one of them![5]

If ever there was a generation that needed to heed Chazal's instruction to "reduce work," it is ours. Let us explore the wisdom of our Sages.

Making a Schedule

At its most basic level, the Mishnah is teaching us to reduce working time in order to free time to learn Torah. Chazal obligate us to set aside fixed times to study Torah every day,[6] explaining that at the end of our life, this is one of the first things about which the Heavenly Court will inquire.[7] The reason Chazal required designating specific times to learn is because they recognized that unless a person creates a fixed schedule, he will be consumed by work and never get around to learning.[8]

Work has the unbelievable power of self-generation — no matter how much one does, there always seems to be more. One hour turns into two, which eventually becomes three, and so on, until a person is left with no time to learn. Because Chazal were aware of this phenomenon, they required us to reserve specific times for learning.

Many non-Jews have also come to recognize work's tendency to dominate their lives and have therefore tried to set limits on their careers.

Robert Gilbertson, 48, is an accomplished non-workaholic. He has created distinct borders between his professional and personal lives. The CEO of DataSwitch, a Connecticut electronics company with annual sales of around $114 million, he works from 8 a.m. to 7 p.m. and no longer. He leaves his briefcase behind at the office and discourages colleagues from calling him at home, to the extent that he once fired an employee who disregarded his warnings and called him three times in one evening. Says Gilbertson: "I can't think of any business we've lost, or any customer who has been aggravated."[9]

Setting "work limits" isn't just a luxury of the big executives. Aline Kaplan, 42, who works in marketing at Wang Laboratories, also does it. "I set up boundaries in every job I ever interviewed for, telling the company at the outset that I had children and that I couldn't work more than eight or nine hours a day. I've never been turned down for a job," she says. Once hired, she always maintained those boundaries: "I haven't missed any promotions because of them."[10]

We can learn from people like Gilbertson and Kaplan, who have disciplined themselves to maintain their schedules. Like them, we can make fixed times in which to work and other times in which to learn.

Simply understood, Chazal are telling us to work less and learn more. But, as with everything in Torah, there is always a deeper explanation and a more complete understanding beneath the surface waiting to be discovered. When we examine Chazal's words in more depth, we see that their choice of words, *hevei mema'et b'esek, va'asok baTorah*, teaches us more than setting times for working and learning.

An Occupied Mind

Chazal's use of the word *esek* is of particular interest. There are several words for "work" in Hebrew besides *esek*, such as *melacha*, *sechora*, and *derech eretz*. In choosing the word *esek*, the Mishnah focuses on one aspect of work, namely, the great mental and emotional effort that work requires.[11]

Work consists of more than simply going into an office, carrying out a particular procedure, and returning home. It usually involves a whole framework of things: people to deal with, deadlines to meet, calls to make, problems to resolve. New issues constantly arise, and as soon as a person completes one task, something new pops up. Work demands a great deal of energy and attention, and can easily take over a person's life and become the focus of his thoughts.

The Mishnah also uses the word *esek* when referring to Torah because Torah has the same ongoing, all-consuming element to it. Those who are immersed in their learning don't just finish learning a text, close their *sefarim*, and go home. The Torah is filled with never-ending insights, and as soon as one thought is uncovered, another surfaces. The Torah consumes their entire being, becoming the focus of their thoughts throughout the day — even when they are not in front of their *sefarim*. Thus, there is a parallel between the *esek* of work and the *esek* of Torah, which is why the Mishnah uses the same word to describe them both. Each possesses the same overpowering and all-encompassing quality, occupying the totality of one's mind and energies.

But there's a catch: involvement in one comes at the expense of the other. In presenting the reduction of work together with the increase of Torah, the Mishnah teaches us that the two are vying for our attention, and the more a person's heart is occupied with one, the less room will be left for the other.[12] It is like a house with limited space, where each new object that is brought in must displace another.

This is true not only of business matters, but of all worldly concerns. The more one is occupied with worldly affairs, the less room there is to concentrate on other aspects of life.[13]

When my wife and I were choosing floor tiles for our apartment, we spent a few hours going from shop to shop, trying to find the best tiles we could. On my way home, I found myself still thinking about floor tiles, and, for the next few days, whenever I walked into someone's home, the first thing I noticed was the floor tiles!

When your mind is really involved with something, it focuses on that thing to the exclusion of other matters. Of course, you can still take care of other things and think about them if you need to, but everything else blurs in comparison, and your mind inevitably returns to whatever it is you are so involved in.

So it is with work. When a person is very involved in his business matters, the *Tosafos* seems flat, and it is difficult to get excited over what it says or to concentrate deeply enough to understand it. His mind is too preoccupied with thoughts of work to delve into other matters properly and concentrate on anything else. His body may be in front of the Gemara, but his head will be far away in the office.

The opposite is also true. When a person is deeply involved in his learning, he still takes care of his physical needs, but his mind is on what he just learned. Physically, he may be in the fruit store buying fruit, but his head will be buried in his Gemara.

The Proper Perspective

How, then, can a person be involved in worldly endeavors without letting work become the center of his life, occupying all his thoughts? The solution is not to stop working and remove oneself entirely from worldly affairs, for as the Mishnah says: *Im ein derech eretz ein Torah* (*Avos* 3:21) — without worldly pursuits there can be no Torah.[14]

The key lies in keeping things in perspective — and this depends on the frame of mind with which one approaches physical endeavors. If one sets out to accomplish a goal realizing from the start that it is only a means to an end, then he will be able to carry out that task without it overtaking him. Having defined a clear understanding of the task's purpose from the outset, he will be able to maintain a balanced view.

Returning to my floor tiles, had I reminded myself from the start that my purpose in buying them was to have an aesthetically pleasing home to enhance my *avodas Hashem*, I would not have lost myself in the search, allowing it to consume my thoughts. I would have approached the search with a much more detached mindset, managing to look for an appropriate tile one minute and returning home unaffected the next. The reason it did overtake me is because I went into the search focused on buying the best tiles around, treating it like an end in itself.

The same principle can be applied to work. When one approaches his job realizing that it is just a way of earning a living and putting bread on the table, he will be able to enter the workplace, take care of business, and leave without letting it overtake his life and thoughts. It is when one forgets that work is only a means to an end and attaches more value to it than it deserves that it begins to sweep a person away, becoming his focal point.

One should not take this as license to minimize the quality of work he produces or slack off in any way. That would be stealing from the employer or the customer. One needs to do the work and do it well, but at the same time, he must see it as a tool of which he is in control. When a surgeon uses a scalpel in an operation, he holds it carefully and works with full precision, but he does not let himself become overwhelmed by it. It is he who controls the scalpel, not the other way around. Similarly, it should be the worker who is in control of the work, not the work that controls him.

Having good intentions from the outset is all well and good, but often one loses himself in the process, forgetting what is of primary and what is of secondary importance. Keeping the proper perspective is an ongoing battle, a daily struggle, and the Mishnah addresses this point in its careful choice of words. Although until now we have translated *hevei mema'et b'esek* as "reduce work," a more accurate translation would be *"continually* reduce work."[15] Chazal are instructing a person to reduce his emotional connection to work every day. This is a constant battle, requiring one to remember daily that work is only a means to an end and not an end in itself.

When someone finds himself loading his office with various creature comforts, beyond what he needs to function effectively, his office is no longer just the place where he earns a living, but a place in which he has invested something more. Of course, certain items may be necessary to enhance a workspace or to make it a more pleasant place. But when one finds himself looking for more ways to decorate his desk and thinking about which screensaver to use on his computer, that is a signal to take a serious look within himself and figure out why he's investing so much in this.

Business vs. Busyness

With this deeper understanding of the Mishnah in mind, we can now appreciate that the instruction to "continually reduce *esek*" applies to each one of us: working or learning, man or woman, young or old. Every person must strive to be *mema'et b'esek*.

One woman, who was expecting her first child, was surprised to find herself preoccupied with noticing other people's strollers. She had never before paid attention to a stroller, and suddenly she was so distracted by them that she sometimes couldn't concentrate on what other women were saying because she was busy looking at whether or not their carriages could lie flat, whether the handle was reversible, what size the basket was, and how far down the hood could be lowered!

If not put into the proper perspective, every incident that arises or arrangement that needs to be made expands until it occupies all of one's thoughts. *Hevei mema'et b'esek* doesn't just refer to reducing business, but to reducing all *busyness*. As necessary as our daily chores are, they are only chores — means to ends, and not ends in themselves. *Hevei mema'et b'esek, va'asok baTorah* instructs us to distinguish the busyness (*esek*) of daily life from the business (*esek*) of holiness. *Asok baTorah* means not to permit ordinariness to become anything more than what it is: ordinary. It means not permitting the mundane to dominate our days to such an extent that there is no space left for other concerns such as: Why am I here, what does the *Borei Olam* want from me, and how can I make the world a better place?

The term "workaholic" may apply to only 10 percent or so of our generation, but the "inability to turn it off" exists in all of us, causing us to become more and more involved with the pursuits of this world, until we become so preoccupied with them that we think of them and nothing else. *Hevei mema'et b'esek, va'asok baTorah* teaches us to allow sufficient holy space in our lives so that the true joy and meaning of life — studying and living by the ideals of Torah — can shine forth. The Mishnah challenges us to treat the ultimate purpose of life as the real *esek*, the real busyness of our days, and to view the mundane aspects of life as distractions — certainly necessary and important, but distractions nevertheless. To redirect our focus in this way is to unlock the secret of life.

---

[1] Christopher Clausen, "Against Work," *American Scholar*, September 22, 2004.

[2] "Are You a Workaholic? When Does Your Healthy Drive to Succeed Become a Neurotic Need for Power?" *Daily Mail* (London), June 11, 2001.

[3] "Many Israelis Work Too Hard," *Jerusalem Post*, October 19, 2003.

[4] Kathryn Tyler, "Spinning Wheels: Workaholism Causes Poor Productivity, Low Morale, and Hazardous Working Conditions," *HRMagazine*, September 1, 1999.

[5] Pietro Basso, *Modern Times, Ancient Hours: Working Lives in the Twenty-First Century*, trans. and ed. Giacomo Donis (London: Verso, 2003), 218–219.

[6] Rambam, *Hilchos Talmud Torah* 1:8; *Shulchan Aruch, Yoreh De'ah* 246:1 and *Orach Chaim* 155:1; *Mishnah Berurah* 155:4; *Shemiras Halashon, Sha'ar HaTorah*, end of chap. 3; *Igros Moshe, Yoreh De'ah* 4:§36, subsection 3. If for some reason one was unable to learn one's set quota for the day, one should treat it like an unpaid debt that needs to be made up during the night (*Eiruvin* 65a with Rashi; *Mishnah Berurah* 155:4). Rama MiFano mentions that the times should be set for the same time every day (quoted in *Kaf Hachaim* 155:13).

Based on the verse והגית בו יומם ולילה (*Yehoshua* 1:8), Rambam (*Hilchos Talmud Torah* 1:8) and *Shulchan Aruch* (*Yoreh De'ah* 246:1) state that one is obligated to fix two times to learn, one during the day and one during the night.

[7] *Shabbos* 31a: "קבעת עתים לתורה" — Did you set aside times for Torah?" Maharsha (*Shabbos* 31a ד"ה קבעת עתים) points out that the use of the plural (*times*) alludes to the obligation to set aside two times, one by day and one by night (see previous note).

The Vilna Gaon said that the inquiry *kavata itim laTorah* will be made even of *talmidei chachamim* whose chief involvement is Torah study. "Fixing times for Torah" means setting aside times exclusively for Torah, without interruption even for pressing matters (cited by R' Eliyahu Lopian in *Lev Eliyahu* 3:352). R' Lopian records that *Gedolim* of previous generations learned with a note by their side saying, "Sorry, I cannot be interrupted," and would not lift their heads from their Gemaras.

[8] Rashi, *Shabbos* 31a ד"ה קבעת עתים.

[9] Walter Kiechel, "Workaholics Anonymous," *Fortune*, August 14, 1989.

[10] Ibid.

[11] *Be'er Ha'Avos*. That *esek* refers to the great effort involved in work is based on the Taz (*Orach Chaim* 47:1), who says this idea regarding the *esek* of Torah.

[12] See *Lev Avos*.

[13] Indeed, Rashi interprets the *esek* of the Mishnah as referring to *derech eretz*, which includes all worldly involvements and pursuits (see *Encyclopedia Talmudit*, s.v. דרך ארץ).

[14] *Peirushei Rabbeinu Yitzchak ben Harav Shlomo MiToledo* on our Mishnah and Rashi to *Shabbos* 31a ד"ה קבעת עתים. As the commentators point out, R' Meir advises one only to reduce work, not to cut it out totally (*Peirushei Rabbeinu Yitzchak ben Harav Shlomo MiToledo*, *Mirkeves Hamishneh*, and *Nachalas Avos*).

[15] *Midrash Shmuel* and *Be'er Ha'Avos*.

Spending the Year in Israel

What Students and Their Parents Can Learn

פרק ד' משנה י"ח: רַבִּי נְהוֹרַאי אוֹמֵר, הֱוֵה גוֹלֶה
לִמְקוֹם תּוֹרָה וְאַל תֹּאמַר שֶׁהִיא תָבוֹא אַחֲרֶיךָ, שֶׁחֲבֵרֶיךָ
יְקַיְּמוּהָ בְּיָדֶךָ. וְאֶל בִּינָתְךָ אַל תִּשָּׁעֵן (משלי ג).

**Chapter 4, Mishnah 18: *Rabbi Nehorai says: Exile
yourself to a place of Torah and do not say that it
will come after you, for your friends will cause it
to remain with you; and "do not rely on your own
understanding" (Mishlei 3).***

E ach year, thousands of young people travel across the world
to study Torah in yeshivos and seminaries far from home. In
Israel alone there are over 8,300 single and 4,300 married
male foreign students learning in yeshivos,[1] and these numbers
exclude the estimated 3,000 female seminary students who come
to learn for a year. The source for this widespread practice is our
Mishnah. Let us see, therefore, what Chazal have to say about it.

Exile Whom?

The Mishnah's instruction to exile oneself to a place of Torah is
understood by some commentators as being directed at people
who lack a Torah environment. Whether because there is a lack
of Torah scholars where they live[2] or because they seek scholars
with greater breadth and depth in Torah knowledge,[3] such people
should move to a place of greater Torah learning.

Other commentators, however, explain that "Exile yourself to a
place of Torah" applies no matter where one lives.[4] Even if a person
lives in Torah surroundings, there is a definite benefit to learning
Torah away from home. Indeed, this was the accepted practice
throughout history. Yitzchak Avinu, for example, sent Yaakov to
learn in the yeshiva of Shem despite the fact that Yitzchak's home
was a tremendous *makom Torah*. Rabbi Yehuda Hanasi acted the
same way, sending his son away for twelve years even though he
himself headed a yeshiva.[5]

We see that even if your father is the *gadol hador* and your house is a hub of Torah learning, you should still exile yourself to a place of Torah.[6]

This practice of moving away from home to learn was not limited to a few individuals, but was the accepted custom of all the *Amora'im*. Those who lived in Bavel went to Eretz Yisrael to learn, while those who lived in Eretz Yisrael went to Bavel to learn.[7] Obviously, both countries were centers of Torah learning and each group could have learned where they were. But they didn't. Instead, they subjected themselves to journeys that in those days lasted for weeks and involved many hardships.

Why Leave?

The commentators give several practical reasons why someone who already lives in a Torah community should nevertheless travel away from home to learn. For example, they point out that when a person is away from home he has fewer disturbances and interruptions that interfere with his learning.[8]

They also point out that a child at home will always remain a child. In their great love for him, his parents will continue to smother him with affection as they did when he was young, thus preventing him from maturing into a man.[9]

Furthermore, the commentators note that the more effort a person invests in a project, the more he will try to make certain that it succeeds and bears fruit. Thus, having uprooted himself from his home and having put so much time and effort into going to yeshiva, a young adult will make much more of an effort to grow than he would have had he remained at home.[10]

But beyond the practical reasons, there is a more profound reason why a young adult should leave home to learn. Understanding it will hopefully change our whole perception of Torah study, thus affecting not only young adults spending their "year in Israel," but every one of us throughout our lives.

Transcending Our Reality

A person's reality is rooted in his father, mother, family, and friends. The way he thinks, the way he perceives the world, and his values are all shaped by them. By providing him with all his needs, his family makes him who he is. They mold his personality and identity, and therefore constitute his world.

Torah, however, exists on a plane higher than that of a person. Its Divine thought process is above man's way of thinking. In order to truly connect to Torah and experience its beauty a person must leave his present reality and go to another place where he is not bound by any of his previous roots.

If he remains where he is, expecting to understand Torah from his present position, he will never be able to penetrate its depths. Only when he leaves his home and his comfortable community and surroundings and tries to understand Torah on its own grounds will he create the new reality needed to comprehend Torah.

This idea is what the Mishnah is teaching us when it says, "and do not say that it [the Torah] will come after you." By exiling yourself from where you live, you attempt to understand Torah from where it is, from its own position. But by staying where you are, in the comfort of old friends and loved ones, you are like one who thinks Torah will come to him even if he does not search for it.[11]

It is human nature to try to categorize any new piece of knowledge together with what one already knows. Upon hearing new information, your mind links it with whatever it already understands about that subject, and stores it in the appropriate place. In computer jargon you could say that your head opens the relevant file, saves this new fact inside, and closes the file again.

That is the way we think when it comes to secular knowledge. But Torah is G-d's wisdom and must be approached differently. The Torah's conception transcends that of the human mind. Instead of bringing it down to our level, we need to reach up to it. When one of my teachers was a young man, he was stuck on what seemed to him to be a contradiction between two statements in Chazal. He went to Rabbi Yosef Shalom Elyashiv, who told him, "My dear child, let me tell you a rule for life. Whenever you come across a difficult Chazal, instead of trying to force their head into yours, try to force your head into theirs. It may take a day, maybe a week, possibly even a month or a year, but little by little your way of thinking will become aligned with theirs."[12]

Dealing in Diamonds

The following metaphor may help crystallize this rather obscure idea.

When a baby is given an object, the first thing he does is put it into his mouth. It makes no difference what it is, a priceless diamond or a piece of wood, he will immediately try to explore it with his mouth. The reason is that his lips and tongue are his primary means of discovering the world, and so when you present him with a valuable object, he has no way of appreciating its beauty other than by what it feels like in his mouth. The diamond's sparkle, or the fact that it is worth thousands of dollars, is irrelevant. From his perspective, the diamond's value is determined only by the way it feels and tastes.[13]

The characteristic of measuring everything according to our own preconceived notions is deeply rooted in human nature, and is present within us from the time we are born. Unless we make a conscious effort to change it, this attribute stays with us throughout our lives, and so when faced with a statement of Chazal, or any aspect of Torah, we instinctively categorize it into what we *already* know. Instead of making an effort to insert our minds, our way of thinking, into their minds, and reexamine what we believe to be true against what they are telling us, we do the opposite. By doing this, we strip the Torah of its beauty and value, much like the baby who thinks the diamond's real worth can be measured with his tongue.[14]

This idea is conveyed by the Mishnah in its last phrase, which is a quote from *Mishlei*: "Do not rely on your own understanding."[15]

The wise person realizes that every word of Chazal stems from a higher reality, and instead of pulling it down to his level, he tries to pull himself up to their level. When faced with a new concept from Chazal, he analyzes it for what *it* is, looking at it with open eyes. Rather than placing the diamond upon his tongue to check its taste, he makes the effort to develop new senses so that he can appreciate the true magnificence of what he beholds.

Obviously, since the Torah is above our way of thinking, it is impossible for us to grasp it on our own. By definition, we can't comprehend something that is beyond our comprehension. We can only succeed if we have help from outside, someone above us to pull us up.

For this, we must turn to our Torah teachers and mentors to help us reach beyond where we are. More importantly, we have to turn to the One Above — the Source of the Torah's wisdom — and beg for His help, asking that He open our minds and lift us up so that we may absorb His teachings. And that is exactly what the verse from *Mishlei* tells us: "*Trust in G-d with all your heart* and do not rely on your own understanding."[16] In other words, look to Him for help in understanding the secrets of the Torah.[17]

The importance of not relying on our own understanding is accentuated when we contemplate the vast chasm that exists between our own spiritual level and that of previous generations. Consider the Sages of the Gemara, for example. Several of them were so attuned to Heavenly ways that they were able to bring the dead back to life.[18] When Rabbi Eliezer and Rabbi Yehoshua studied Torah, a fire came down from Heaven and engulfed them.[19] When Rabbi Yonasan ben Uziel studied, the angels came to listen, causing any birds overhead to be burned.[20] Even the *Amora'im* felt that their level of understanding was only a fraction of that of the *Tanna'im*, comparing it to the difference in size between the entrance to a banquet hall and the eye of a needle.[21] And if that is what the *Amora'im* said of themselves over a thousand years ago, what can we say of ourselves today?

One who contemplates the holiness and purity of these people should approach their every word with awe and trepidation. Instead of learning their words with the attitude of "Yeah, sure. I knew that!" a person should pause to reflect on how the level of Chazal's thinking is far above one's own. And, if one doesn't understand something they said, instead of immediately casting it aside as a mistake, one should exert himself to comprehend its inner meaning.

The instruction to exile oneself to a place of Torah applies to all of us, even to those who live in thriving Torah communities. And the philosophy that underlies it — namely, that we approach Torah on its own original terms instead of trying to force it into our preconceived notions — is relevant to all of us throughout our lives whenever we hear new Torah ideas.

So whether we or our children are packing bags to leave for seminary and yeshiva, or our suitcases are buried away untouched in the attic, we can still take Chazal's words to heart by exiling ourselves to a place of Torah — even in our very own homes.

---

[1] Israel Ministry of Religious Affairs, 2005.

[2] *Bartenura.*

[3] See Meiri.

[4] *Tiferes Yisrael, Chelek Yaakov.*

[5] *Chasam Sofer, Choshen Mishpat* §9.

[6] Ibid.

[7] *Tosafos, Shabbos* 9b ד"ה הא לן. *Chasam Sofer* (loc. cit.) proves that this was the practice of *all* students of that time.

[8] *Pele Yo'etz* (s.v. גלות) based on *Tosafos, Shabbos* 9b ד"ה הא לן.

[9] *Tiferes Yisrael* (Boaz, note 2).

[10] *Midrash Shmuel* quoting *Lev Avos.*

[11] See ibid.

[12] Heard from R' Hillel Copperman.

[13] R' Yosef Yehuda Leib Bloch, *Shiurei Da'as* 2:132.

[14] Ibid.

[15] *Mishlei* 3:5 with Malbim.

[16] Ibid.

[17] As *Nidda* 70b states, learning a lot is not enough. One must also ask for Divine assistance from G-d.

[18] See *Avoda Zara* 10b, *Megilla* 7b, and *Kesubos* 62b.

[19] *Tosafos*, *Chagiga* 15a ד"ה שובו.

[20] *Sukka* 28a with Rashi ד"ה נשרף.

[21] *Eiruvin* 53a.

The Final Stroke

פֶּרֶק ד' מִשְׁנָה י"ט: רַבִּי יַנַּאי אוֹמֵר, אֵין בְּיָדֵינוּ לֹא
מִשַּׁלְוַת הָרְשָׁעִים וְאַף לֹא מִיִּסּוּרֵי הַצַּדִּיקִים.

Chapter 4, Mishnah 19: *Rabbi Yannai says: It is not in our power to explain either the tranquility of the wicked or the suffering of the righteous.*

The Mishnah addresses the age-old question of why the righteous suffer while the wicked prosper, informing us that it is beyond our understanding.[1]

When Moshe asked G-d to reveal His ways to him so that he might understand this ultimate of questions,[2] G-d replied that He would show Moshe His back, but not His face.[3] G-d was saying that man can only comprehend in retrospect why apparently bad things have happened, but not while they are still unfolding.[4]

Consider, for example, a person who applies for a job or school and is rejected. Initially, he feels disappointed. He may even be angry at the institution for not accepting him. But many years later, after having landed another job or having attended a different school, he may look back and be thankful that he wasn't accepted, recognizing that it was actually for his own good. This is symbolized by G-d's showing Moshe His "back," as if to say that man cannot expect to understand the purpose of his suffering until it has already passed.

Strokes in the Masterpiece

Chazal say that the verse "*Ein tzur k'Elokeinu* — There is no rock like our G-d" is to be read, "*Ein tzayar k'Elokeinu* — there is no painter like our G-d."[5]

This metaphor of G-d as the ultimate painter can be explained by looking at how a master artist creates his magnum opus. Leonardo da Vinci, for example, would often begin a work of art by painting a dark background and only later adding elements of light. Anyone watching him throw that first streak of black paint across the canvas would think him to be reckless, hardly a world-class artist. A layman would be convinced that Leonardo had ruined the canvas with the black paint and that he would need to start again.

Only months later, after the painting is complete, does the full picture become clear. One realizes that the black paint was no mistake, but rather a stroke of genius made to create a striking contrast of light and shadows. Similarly, some Divinely orchestrated events may seem dark and unpleasant. But at the End of Days, they will be recognized as having formed a majestic composition of beauty, carried out by the Master Painter of the world.[6]

The time it takes until we can appreciate G-d's intention is not always the same. While in some cases the understanding may come about relatively quickly — as in the example of the person who didn't get the position he wanted — there are other calamities that are so beyond comprehension that we may never come to fully understand them, even after many decades. The pain of losing a loved one, or the trauma of the terrorist attacks in our generation, leave wounds so painful and profound that we cannot hope to grasp their inner meaning until G-d reveals Himself to the world and ends our long exile. Until that time, we must hold on to our faith and accept that everything G-d does is for a purpose and for our ultimate good.

Ultimate Recognition

Over the last 2,000 years, the Jews have suffered many tragedies. The instinctive reaction is, *why*? Why the blood libels, the Inquisition, the pogroms, the Holocaust, and in our day, the unspeakable sadism of the Arabs?

One might imagine that when G-d finally reveals Himself and brings our exile to an end, it will take Him a long time to explain the reasons behind all the suffering. But from the story of Yosef and his brothers we learn that when the time comes, everything will be understood immediately.

When Yosef found his stolen cup in Binyamin's sack, he threatened to keep him in Egypt as a slave. Yehuda, who didn't know Yosef's true identity, was furious with him, for he knew that Yaakov would die of grief if Binyamin did not return. He offered himself as a slave in Binyamin's place, but the Egyptian ruler was not interested. As far as Yehuda was concerned, the situation was desperate and there were only two options available — either let Binyamin remain in Egypt as a slave, which would literally kill his father, or escape with Binyamin, which would mean going to battle.

Imagine Yehuda's inner turmoil. We read the story knowing that this cruel Egyptian leader was none other than Yosef, so we don't stop to think about how things must have appeared from Yehuda's perspective. But when we look at the events from Yehuda's point of view, we become aware of the confusion and utter despair that overcame him as he stood before the viceroy of Egypt.

Consider the questions that surely plagued his mind: Why had this Egyptian leader only cross-examined Yehuda and his brothers and not any of the other thousands of people who had come to buy grain? Why had he treated them so harshly, framing Binyamin as a thief? Why had he returned their money to their sacks? And why was he unwilling to accept Yehuda, who was much stronger than Binyamin, as a slave in place of his brother?

Yehuda felt trapped; his whole world was collapsing. He could not envision any way out of his suffering. He was so desperate that he was prepared to kill or be killed, and he even began to instruct his brothers as to who would wipe out which area of Egypt.[7]

But all it took was two short words — *Ani Yosef* (I am Yosef) — and everything fell into place. All of Yehuda's questions were answered in an instant. There was no need for lengthy discourses or drawn-out explanations. Two words brought about complete comprehension.

And so will it be on that long-awaited day when G-d reveals Himself to the world. All our questions and fears and doubts will

vanish with just two words — *Ani Hashem* (I am G-d).[8] The reasons
for the Holocaust and the bus bombings, the maimed and the
suffering, the childless and the sick, will instantly become apparent.
Just two words — *Ani Hashem* — and all will become clear.

But the analogy between Yehuda and the End of Days goes
beyond this.

Yehuda's salvation did not appear from some new, unanticipated
area, or from some hero galloping in at the last moment. It appeared
from the actual source of his troubles. The one who seemed to be a
sadistic, conniving Egyptian tyrant turned out to be his long-lost
brother. Thus, the very root of Yehuda's sorrows was transformed
into his greatest joy and exultation.

Similarly, at the End of Days we will recognize that our very
suffering was the source of our salvation. It is not that one day
the pain will suddenly end and the suffering disappear. Rather,
we will realize that *the pain itself was what made us complete.* G-d
will reveal to us that those events and experiences that gave us the
most anguish and torment, and that made the least sense, were
in actuality the stepping stones toward our spiritual perfection.
We will finally comprehend that the very obstacles that were our
greatest challenges were in reality pathways leading to our personal
growth, and that every drop of pain was but another brushstroke
by the Master Painter par excellence.[9]

---

[1] Rashi (first explanation); *Bartenura* (first explanation).

[2] *Shemos* 33:13 according to *Berachos* 7a.

[3] *Shemos* 33:23 with *Sifri* to *Bamidbar* 12:8 בחידות ולא ה"ד. See especially Vilna
Gaon's version and *Eimek HaNetziv* loc. cit. אחורייס מראה ה"ד (p. 316).

[4] See Chasam Sofer, *Toras Moshe, Shemos* 33:23.

[5] *Berachos* 10a.

[6] Heard from R' Zev Leff.

[7] *Midrash Tanchuma, Vayigash* 5.

[8] *Chofetz Chaim al HaTorah*, 79.

[9] The idea of the bad itself being in reality a cause of spiritual growth is mentioned in *Da'as Tevunos*, 26–27, 104, 118–119. See also *Da'as Chochma U'mussar* 1:7–8, 74. The application of this principle to Yehuda and Yosef is based on a lecture by R' Akiva Tatz.

Beyond the Sounds of Silence

פרק ד' משנה כ': רַבִּי מַתְיָא בֶּן חָרָשׁ אוֹמֵר, הֱוֵה
מַקְדִּים בִּשְׁלוֹם כָּל אָדָם. וֶהֱוֵה זָנָב לָאֲרָיוֹת, וְאַל תְּהִי
רֹאשׁ לַשׁוּעָלִים.

Chapter 4, Mishnah 20: *Rabbi Masya ben Charash says: Initiate a greeting to every person [you meet]; and be a tail to lions, and not a head to foxes.*

The Mishnah instructs us to initiate greetings rather than wait to be greeted. In other words, one shouldn't be content with merely responding to those who speak to him, but should inquire about their well-being first.[1]

The fact that the Mishnah needs to tell us to be the first to greet others demonstrates that people naturally resist doing so. This reluctance may stem from several sources. Firstly, there is pride. We feel it more dignified to be greeted rather than to greet. After all, why should I say hello to him if he hasn't said hello to me? Secondly, there may be a sense of vulnerability. We don't know how the person will react. He may not respond with the same warmth we accorded him, or, even worse, he may not respond at all.

The Mishnah tells us to disregard these concerns and greet others before they greet us.[2]

Greeting Others First

Resistance to making the first move is not limited to saying hello, but affects relationships in general. Each party in a relationship looks to the other to take the initial step and neither side wants to be the first one to do so. This is ironic considering that both parties secretly crave the other's closeness and wish the other side would make the first move.

The teacher waits for his pupils to approach him with their questions and concerns. Meanwhile, the students are waiting for their teacher to provide an opening so that they can draw closer to him. Similarly, the rabbi of a community wants his congregants to open up to him, while at the same time they are waiting for him to reach out to them. The same idea applies to friends, spouses, in-laws, and virtually every other relationship. Sometimes years can go by without either side moving closer to the other. This is particularly sad, for what is being lost is not just a "good morning" but a lifelong friendship.

How wise and perceptive are the words of Chazal, who penetrated the depths of human nature and encapsulated the key to building relationships in one short phrase: Be the *first* to greet other people.[3]

Greeting Every Person

But besides emphasizing *how* to greet others — namely, being the first — Chazal also emphasize *whom* to greet. They didn't say to greet just your friends or acquaintances, but to greet *every person*.[4] This includes the people we tend not to notice or who we may feel are not included in this instruction, like bus drivers, street cleaners, and security guards. We may feel too important — or perhaps too busy or self-absorbed — to stop and wish these people a good day. Instead, we pass them by as if they don't exist.

We would do well to learn from the example of Rabbi Yochanan ben Zakkai.

Rabbi Yochanan ben Zakkai was the preeminent Sage during the last years of the Second Temple. He was thoroughly versed in every area of Torah knowledge — Mishnah, Gemara, halacha — and even understood the speech of angels and demons.[5] He was the *nasi*, which was the highest-ranking position attainable amongst the Jewish people at that time, and was responsible for all the communal needs of his generation. When an emissary was needed to speak to the Roman authorities on behalf of the Jewish people, it was Rabbi Yochanan ben Zakkai who went.[6]

And yet, despite his high rank and prestige, the Gemara says that Rabbi Yochanan ben Zakkai never failed to greet other people first

— including the non-Jews in the marketplace.[7] Had the Gemara said that he always returned people's greetings — no matter who greeted him or how busy he was — that in itself would have been impressive. But the Gemara doesn't say that. It says that he greeted others *first*, and not only that, it says he *always* did so!

There must have been times when he was in a rush for an important meeting and didn't feel like stopping to wish passersby a good morning. Yet he never allowed his own concerns to prevent him from saying hello.[8] The Romans he passed in the marketplace were also probably not the kind of people he wanted to befriend. Thus, if anyone could ever have felt that he was too important a person to bother greeting others, it was Rabbi Yochanan ben Zakkai as he passed people well below his spiritual and intellectual level. Nevertheless, he still greeted them. We, too, should emulate him and greet everyone courteously, no matter how important or busy we think we are.

The Far-Reaching Effects of a Hello

If Rabbi Yochanan ben Zakkai made such an effort to greet people, it was because he realized the significance of this seemingly minor act. Wishing someone a good morning shows that you acknowledge who he or she is. In a world where people are often not appreciated enough, you are giving the message that you recognize the other person's existence and see it as something of worth.[9] This simple message can be very powerful.

Consider the following story about an Eastern European rabbi:

> *During his morning walks it was the rabbi's custom to greet every man, woman, and child whom he met on his way with a warm smile and a cordial "Good morning." Over the years, the rabbi became acquainted with many of his fellow townspeople this way and would always greet them by their proper title and name.*

Near the outskirts of town, in the fields, he would exchange greetings with Herr Müller, a Polish Volksdeutsche (ethnic German). "Good morning, Herr Müller!" the rabbi would hasten to greet the man who worked in the fields. "Good morning, Herr Rabbiner!" would come the response with a good-natured smile.

Then the war began. The rabbi's strolls stopped abruptly. Herr Müller donned an SS uniform and disappeared from the fields. The fate of the rabbi was like that of much of the rest of Polish Jewry. He lost his family in the death camp of Treblinka and, after great suffering, was deported to Auschwitz.

One day, during a selection at Auschwitz, the rabbi stood on line with hundreds of other Jews awaiting the moment when their fates would be decided, for life or death. Dressed in a striped camp uniform, head and beard shaven and eyes feverish from starvation and disease, the rabbi looked like a walking skeleton. "Right! Left, left, left!" The voice in the distance drew nearer. Suddenly the rabbi had a great urge to see the face of the man with the snow-white gloves, small baton, and steely voice who played G-d and decided who should live and who should die. He lifted his eyes and heard his own voice speaking: "Good morning, Herr Müller!"

"Good morning, Herr Rabbiner!" responded a human voice beneath the SS cap adorned with skull and bones. "What are you doing here?" A faint smile appeared on the rabbi's lips. The baton moved to the right — to life. The following day, the rabbi was transferred to a safer camp.[10]

We see that a simple act of saying good morning can make such a deep impression on another person as to even turn a sadistic monster into a human being. After all, this man was an SS guard, a Nazi murderer. He had no qualms about sentencing Jews to death with the flick of his finger. Had any of them erupted in tears, begging to be spared, he probably would not have flinched at sending them to their deaths. Yet the recognition that the rabbi had accorded him made such a powerful impression that it cut through the coldest of hearts, bringing out a trace of humanity.

And if that is the effect a simple "good morning" can have on a heart of stone, just think what it does and how much pleasure it can bring to a heart of flesh and blood.

---

[1] *Midrash Shmuel.*

[2] See *Ethics from Sinai*, 587. The first reason, pride, is mentioned in *Derech Chaim.*

[3] Based on *Alei Shur* 1:191.

[4] See *Seforno.* Cf. *Piskei Tosafos, Nedarim* §18 with *nuschaos kisvei yad.*

[5] *Sukka* 28a.

[6] *Gittin* 56a.

[7] *Berachos* 17a. *Toldos Yehoshua* comments that the need to greet non-Jews is particularly important during our exile, when we rely on their kindness to let us live amongst them. Indeed, as *Lechem Shamayim* points out from the Mishnah in *Gittin* 61a, there is a specific obligation to greet non-Jews for the sake of peace, such that there is more of an obligation to greet non-Jews than there is to greet Jews.

[8] See *Michtav Me'Eliyahu* 4:246.

[9] Conversely, someone who does not respond to another person's greeting is considered a thief (*Berachos* 6b) because he robs the individual of his dignity (*Michtav Me'Eliyahu* 4:247).

[10] Yaffa Eliach, *Hasidic Tales of the Holocaust* (New York: Vintage Books, 1982), 109–110.

Living Other
People's Lives

פרק ד' משנה כ"ח: רַבִּי אֶלְעָזָר הַקַּפָּר אוֹמֵר, הַקִּנְאָה וְהַתַּאֲוָה וְהַכָּבוֹד מוֹצִיאִין אֶת הָאָדָם מִן הָעוֹלָם.

Chapter 4, Mishnah 28: *Rabbi Elazar HaKappar says: Jealousy, desire, and honor remove a person from the world.*

A number of years ago, a woman in my shul was diagnosed with leukemia. She was pregnant at the time, and in order to increase her chances of survival, she was forced to undergo an abortion. Even after the abortion, she remained in critical condition.

After she had recovered, her husband went to share the good news with Rabbi Chaim Kanievsky, who had been involved with the family throughout the illness. He mentioned to Reb Chaim that he and his wife intended to make a *seudas hoda'a.* Reb Chaim advised them against it.

"Take the money you were going to use for the *seuda*," said Reb Chaim, "and distribute it amongst the needy. And then, instead of making a large *seuda* for many people, make one only for your children. People today find it hard to rejoice in other people's good fortune, and by making a large commotion you will just be bringing an *ayin hara* upon yourselves."

Reb Chaim's comment is a sad reflection on our generation, underscoring our inability to share in other people's joy and truly revel in their happiness. This inability is the root cause of jealousy. If it is difficult for people to wholeheartedly celebrate with a woman who has just recovered from a potentially fatal illness, how much more so are people hard-pressed to feel genuinely happy when they see neighbors building an addition onto their homes or driving a new car. Unfortunately, far too often we resent them and the good things in their lives.

By understanding the root causes of jealousy and why it is that we begrudge other people their good, we will hopefully be able to uproot this insidious trait from within ourselves.

The desire to obtain other people's good for ourselves is an inescapable drive in man.[1] It caused the first murder in the world, led to the split between Yosef and his brothers, and drove Korach to rebel against Moshe. The homes and families it has torn apart are beyond enumeration.

But jealousy has been placed within us for a reason. G-d is Infinite and wants us to enjoy the infinite reward of the next world. To this end, He created us with the desire to reach the highest level of spiritual good. Thus, when we see others enjoying any type of good we don't have, whether it be spiritual or material, we naturally want it for ourselves.[2]

Though it may be hard to believe, jealousy has actually been planted within us for reasons of kedusha, to keep us striving for ever-higher levels of holiness. The trouble is that we misuse this trait for negative reasons, begrudging other people their joys and good fortune. Instead of using this attribute to acquire more for ourselves, we use it to withhold good from others.[3]

How, then, can the destructive side of jealousy be avoided? As with any obstacle, in order to overcome it, we first need to understand the cause of it.

Worthwhile or Worthless?

Shlomo Hamelech writes: "u'rekav atzamos kina," which literally means, "jealousy is the rotting of bones."[4] On one level, the verse is describing the aftermath of jealousy, namely, that it has the effect of making a person's bones rot.[5] Indeed, the Gemara relates that the bones of a certain corpse had remained intact for years after the person had died, and explains that the reason for this was that the person had not harbored jealousy during his lifetime.[6] However, on another level, the verse can be understood as explaining the reason behind jealousy, namely, that jealousy occurs when a person considers his own bones as rotten.[7] That is to say, the jealous person fails to recognize his own talents and considers his own self worthless. He is so preoccupied with his friends' achievements and possessions that he pays little or no attention to his own faculties and assets, regarding his inner self, his "bones," as valueless and filled with rot.[8]

Thus, the way to avoid jealousy is by focusing on the positive qualities one has.[9] The more a person recognizes his own worth and the more secure a person feels about himself, the less jealous he will be of others. The reason one becomes jealous of other people's qualities and possessions is that the object of his envy is perceived as having an advantage over himself. But when a person is filled with an appreciation of who he is and what he already possesses, he feels complete within himself and does not feel diminished when seeing the good others enjoy.

In connection with this, it is crucial to bear in mind that G-d has created each of us with exactly what we need to complete our own unique work in this world.

Imagine a father asking his two sons to draw a picture for him of what each draws best: the first, a drawing of the sea; the second, of the forest. The father then gives each child the necessary colors to complete his work — to the first he gives shades of blue, and to the second he presents greens and browns.

Both children withdraw to their rooms, fretting about their assignments. "Why must I do the sea?" wonders the first child. "I would much rather do a forest like my brother." The second child is also upset with his subject and decides to do a sketch of the sea, which he feels is more exciting.

The result is that neither son will end up with anything meaningful. Having drawn the sea in green and brown, the first will not present a good rendering of it, nor will he have done the forest. The second son will suffer the same fate. By trying to switch roles, each child will be left with nothing.

The same applies to our existence in this world. G-d places each of us in this world to accomplish a certain mission, and gives us all the necessary tools to accomplish that mission. Like an artist who has been given the precise materials required to create his particular masterpiece, we have each been given exactly the right circumstances and opportunities necessary to fulfill our calling. But by looking at other people and wishing we had their tools, we end up fulfilling neither our mission nor theirs. We fritter away our lives, concentrating on trying to be like others instead of using our own tools to develop ourselves.

The masterpiece of our life is one that only we can create. It has the potential to be one of profound beauty, but it can only be completed by investing all our energies into the task at hand. Looking at others and fretting over why we don't have the same things they have debilitates our potential. It is like the son who has been given a sea to draw but wishes he could make a forest. Instead of viewing the world from his own standpoint, he views the world from the stance of other people and their missions. By so doing, he removes himself from his own unique and authentic world. Thus, when the Mishnah says that "jealousy removes a person from the world," it means from *his* world.[10]

Look in the Mirror

Sometimes a person concentrates on the advantages of others to such an extent that he fails to realize that the very people he envies are actually jealous of him! Indeed, quite often the people who seem to "have it all" are in reality struggling with issues that we don't have to deal with, and from their vantage point, *our* lives appear to be the perfect picture of serenity.

The *mashgiach* of a yeshiva was once approached by two *bachurim*. The first boy indicated that he wanted to discuss something very personal and asked if they could stand to the side so that his friend wouldn't be able to hear them talking. Once out of earshot, the boy began to speak:

"My friend and I are *chavrusas* and we very much enjoy learning together. Yet, despite our close friendship, I am plagued with jealousy. He has an encyclopedic knowledge of virtually every topic we discuss, and this breadth of wisdom gives me no rest."

The *mashgiach* told the boy that the matter required a lengthier discussion and that he should return later when he would have more time to speak with him in depth. The boy left, and the second boy, who had been waiting, stepped forward to discuss his problem. He related the same story as the first, describing how much he enjoyed learning with the first boy and how they got along so well. "What irks me, however, is his phenomenal depth of understanding. His analytical skills are way beyond mine, and I find myself consumed with jealousy."

The *mashgiach* immediately called the first boy back and asked him to repeat in front of his friend what he had confided just moments before. With his head bowed and his eyes downcast, the boy uncomfortably repeated his story. The second boy then recounted his version, and when the two realized what had transpired they burst out laughing. Their mutual jealousy had vanished.[11]

We look at others and what they possess and wish we had the same. But we don't realize that the very people we look at with envy are often looking at us and wishing they had what we possess. Instead of wasting all this energy looking into other people's lives, we need to focus on our own, realizing that there are aspects of our lives that other people dream of having.

Weaknesses Become Strengths

Jealousy strikes hardest when a person who is undergoing difficulties sees other people who appear to be having it easy in the very area in which he is challenged. A person who is struggling to make ends meet, for example, is almost sure to envy a friend who tells him he just got a high-paying job. It takes great strength of character to rejoice for the friend and feel happy for him, without comparing oneself to him and thinking, "What about me?"

Such an individual can draw strength from G-d's words to Kayin.

When Kayin felt intense jealousy toward Hevel because Hevel's offering was accepted while his own was rejected, G-d told him, "*Im teitiv se'eis* — If you work to improve, you will become uplifted."[12] Had Kayin used his situation constructively instead of letting himself be consumed by jealousy, he could have grown from the ordeal and become uplifted.

The same applies to all challenges. Instead of wishing them away and resenting one's friends who seem to have it easy, one can use these trials positively to become a more fulfilled — and more contented — person.

Thomas Edison, famed inventor of over 1,000 ingenious instruments and devices (including the electric light, the phonograph, and the motion-picture camera), was partially deaf. He once wrote that he was "unable to hear a bird sing since he was twelve years old." Yet, rather than become bitter over his loss of hearing and begrudge other people their ability to hear, Edison thought about how he could use his handicap to his advantage.

"When in a telegraph office, I could hear only the instrument directly on the table at which I sat, and unlike the other operators I was not bothered by the other instruments." Edison insisted that being deaf set him apart from the masses and gave him an excuse to turn away from tiresome social involvements, making him a far more productive thinker. In fact, when people pleaded with him to use his creative genius to invent an apparatus that would become the ultimate hearing aid, he declined, refusing to surrender what was essentially his passport to the inner world.[13]

The difficulties we face in life are not the result of an unfortunate stroke of luck, but the result of Divine Providence that prods us to move forward and improve in specific areas.

The words *im teitiv se'eis* teach us that rather than bow to jealousy, we should use every challenge as an opportunity to grow, just as Edison used his hearing loss to his advantage. Very often it is precisely the areas that give us the most difficulty that will ultimately push us to develop and perfect our nature.

Blessings Lead to More Blessings

One of the most effective ways of overcoming jealousy is to concentrate on the immense reward that awaits anyone who does so successfully.

Let us return to Shlomo Hamelech. In *Mishlei* he writes that "*nefesh bracha sedushan* — a soul that blesses will become fat."[14] When a person hears good news, his bones are said to "grow fat."[15] Thus, the fatness referred to is the glad tidings that the person who blesses others will bring upon himself. One who desires the best for others, showering them with nothing but blessings and good wishes, fills their hearts with joy and happiness, and thereby makes their bones fat. In this merit, G-d will shower blessings upon him, thereby making his own bones fat. This is in contrast to the jealous person, whose bones rot with jealousy.[16]

About ten years ago, there was a family in Bnei Brak with eight sons, the oldest of whom was having difficulty finding a *shidduch*. When the next boy in line was old enough to begin the *shidduch* process, the oldest brother encouraged him to find the right person and to get married, and not be concerned about the fact that his older brother was still single. One by one, the younger brothers got married, leaving the oldest still unmarried.

The youngest brother was particularly close with the oldest brother, and when it was time for him to start dating, he refused, not wishing to cause his older brother pain. The oldest brother, however, insisted that his youngest brother proceed with *shidduchim*, and even went out of his way to help him find his match.

In time, the youngest brother was duly married. At the last *sheva brachos*, the oldest boy stood up to speak. It was the first time the older brother was to speak publicly, and everyone was silent, waiting to hear what he would say.

"I don't know if I am reading your thoughts correctly, but you are all probably thinking how sad I must be feeling, left alone, with even my youngest and closest brother now married. Let me tell you one thing: My youngest brother is a part of me; all my brothers are a part of me, and I rejoice in their *simcha*. They are not to blame for my being single and there is no reason why they should suffer because of me. I wish you, my dear brother, happiness and success in your marriage and in everything you do. I harbor no jealousy or ill feelings against you or any of the others. On the contrary, I am happy that none of you had to suffer on my behalf. May you have many children, and may none of them remain single like me!"

A month later, the oldest boy became a *chasan* himself.[17]

The *Mesillas Yesharim* writes that there will come a day when people will no longer be jealous of one another, and when it will no longer be necessary to hide one's good fortune from others in order to prevent jealousy.[18] If we take the holy words of Chazal to heart, and focus on who we are and what we already possess, rather than on what others have; and if we view every challenge as a potential path for personal growth and inner strength, then that blessed, jealousy-free world will not be far off. It will be a truly joy-filled time, for then all of us will be able to function with that most blessed quality: to view the joys of others as if they were our own, and by so doing, to become happy and fulfilled members of *Am Yisrael*.

---

[1] *Orchos Tzaddikim, Sha'ar Hakina.*

[2] *Ohr Yechezkel* in *Orchos Chaim LehaRosh Hamevo'ar* §113.

[3] See ibid.

[4] *Mishlei* 14:30.

[5] *Metzudas Dovid, Mishlei* 14:30.

⁶ *Shabbos* 152b.

⁷ *Alei Shur* 1:37 and 2:83.

⁸ Note that the Hebrew word *etzem* means both "bone" and "self."

⁹ The method of overcoming jealousy by appreciating what you have is mentioned in *Peirushei Rabbeinu Yitzchak ben Harav Shlomo MiToledo* (2:9), *Milei D'Avos* (2:11), and *Alei Shur* 1:36–37. *Bava Kama* 82a says that garlic takes away jealousy and Rashi there explains that the reason is because it makes one happy. See also *Mesillas Yesharim* (chap. 11), which says that there is no jealousy between angels because they rejoice in the good that they have and are *samei'ach b'chelkam*.

¹⁰ The Mishnah says that jealousy "removes a person from the world," but does not state which world it refers to. That it refers to the person's own world is stated by R' Shlomo Wolbe, *Alei Shur* 2:83. Cf. Meiri, *Midrash Dovid*, *Menoras Hama'or* (Abuhav, p. 21), and *Baruch She'amar*, which explain it to refer to this world; Rabbeinu Yona (*Berachos*, commentary on *Rif*, 3a) and *Sefer Mussar*, which explain it to refer to the next world; and *Avos D'Rebbi Nasan* (*nusach acher*) 34, *Hachassid Yaavetz*, and *Tiferes Yisrael*, which explain it as referring to both this world and the next.

¹¹ *Yalkut Lekach Tov*, *Chaim Shel Torah* 3:70.

¹² *Bereishis* 4:7. In translating *se'eis* as "will be lifted up," I have followed Ibn Ezra. Cf. Rashi and Ramban.

¹³ Carol Cramer, ed., *Thomas Edison* (San Diego: Greenhaven Press, 2001), 32, 38.

¹⁴ *Mishlei* 11:25.

¹⁵ Ibid. 15:30.

¹⁶ Vilna Gaon to *Mishlei* 11:25.

¹⁷ Heard from Rabbi Dovid Breverman, who was present at the *sheva brachos*.

¹⁸ *Mesillas Yesharim*, chap. 11.

Conversation 101
Lessons from Chazal

פֶּרֶק ה' מִשְׁנָה ט': שִׁבְעָה דְבָרִים בְּגֹלֶם וְשִׁבְעָה בֶּחָכָם.
חָכָם אֵינוֹ מְדַבֵּר לִפְנֵי מִי שֶׁהוּא גָדוֹל מִמֶּנּוּ בְּחָכְמָה
וּבְמִנְיָן, וְאֵינוֹ נִכְנָס לְתוֹךְ דִּבְרֵי חֲבֵרוֹ, וְאֵינוֹ נִבְהָל
לְהָשִׁיב, שׁוֹאֵל כָּעִנְיָן וּמֵשִׁיב כַּהֲלָכָה, וְאוֹמֵר עַל רִאשׁוֹן
רִאשׁוֹן וְעַל אַחֲרוֹן אַחֲרוֹן, וְעַל מַה שֶׁלֹא שָׁמַע אוֹמֵר
לֹא שָׁמַעְתִּי, וּמוֹדֶה עַל הָאֱמֶת. וְחִלּוּפֵיהֶן בְּגֹלֶם.

Chapter 5, Mishnah 9: *There are seven characteristics of an uncultivated person,*[1] *and seven of a wise person: (1) A wise person does not speak in front of one who is wiser or older than he, (2) he does not interrupt his friend, (3) he is not hasty to answer, (4) he asks to the point and answers accurately, (5) he discusses the first point first and the last point last, (6) concerning that which he has not heard he says, "I have not heard," (7) and he acknowledges the truth. The uncultivated person has the opposite traits.*

The traits listed in the Mishnah follow the chronological order of the way people speak: how to behave before the conversation begins, how to act while the other person is talking, and what to do once he has finished. We will discuss the first three traits.

Remaining Silent

The first characteristic of a wise person is that he remains silent in the presence of those wiser or older than he. This does not mean that he remains totally quiet without saying a word. The intent, rather, is that he is more concerned with listening to what others have to say than with telling them what *he* has to say. Thus, he may engage wiser and older people in conversation and ask them questions, but his purpose in doing so is to encourage them to speak and share their knowledge, so that he may learn and grow wiser.[2]

The Mishnah mentions two categories of people before whom a wise person does not speak: those who are wiser and those who are older. This is because he has much to learn from both types of people. Those who are older will have something to share from their years of experience, even if they are not wise, while those who are more knowledgeable will have something to teach from their stores of wisdom, even if they are young. Thus, the wise person remains silent before people who are wiser or older than he.[3]

We derive the characteristic of remaining quiet before others from Elihu, one of Iyov's friends.[4] After Iyov lost his children and wealth, he was visited by four friends, each of whom tried to comfort him. They sat on the floor while Iyov complained about his lot, saying that G-d had treated him unfairly and had afflicted him unjustly. The first friend, Elifaz, tried to explain to Iyov why G-d had acted properly, but Iyov refuted each of his arguments. The second friend, Bildad, also tried to respond to Iyov's allegations, but again without success. The third friend, Tzofar, fared no better.[5]

Elihu, meanwhile, sat quietly and listened.

After this first round of discussion, Elifaz, Bildad, and Tzofar each tried a second line of reasoning, but Iyov once again refuted their arguments. The dialogue between Iyov and his three friends continued back and forth — but still, Elihu simply sat and listened.[6]

Finally, when the three friends had exhausted all their arguments and got up to leave, Elihu began to speak.[7] He explained that the reason he had remained quiet until then was because his friends were older than he, and he therefore wanted to hear what they had to say first. He then offered a solid explanation for Iyov's suffering, one to which Iyov had no response.[8]

Considering the length of the text, as well as the depth of thought and serious nature of the discussion, the dialogue between Iyov and his friends must have lasted hours, if not days.[9] That means that Elihu sat quietly for many hours, listening to his friends without voicing any opinion. One might have thought that the reason for his silence was that he had nothing to say. Or one might wonder if he only thought of his argument while his friends were talking, and that is why he had not spoken up earlier. But it is clear from the verse and the commentators that Elihu was prepared with his argument from the moment Iyov began speaking, and that his silence was a result of restraint rather than a loss for words.[10]

Listening Respectfully — Not Interrupting

The second characteristic of a wise person, that of not interrupting others, is also derived from Iyov's discussion with his friends.[11] The text presents each friend's words in a very clear and distinct manner, to teach us that they listened respectfully to one another without interrupting.

In this regard, there is a great contrast between the way people carry on conversations today and the way they did generations ago. Nowadays, it is normal to interrupt someone in mid-sentence with a comment, question, or idea of one's own. If the phone rings while talking to a friend, it is understood that you stop the conversation and answer the phone. Interrupting one another has become so commonplace that phone companies provide the ability to accept phone calls from other people in mid-conversation.

In previous generations, however, such behavior was abnormal. In fact, one of the early commentators on the Mishnah refuses to accept that the Mishnah refers to interrupting another person, because this is something that "even children don't do," let alone wise people.[12] How times have changed! According to some of the commentators, interrupting another person is not simply a question of bad manners — it is a Torah prohibition.[13] It is thus evident that there is an enormous difference between the way we speak to one another and the way the Torah would have us speak to one another.[14]

Thinking Before Responding

The third quality of a wise person is that he is not hasty to answer. Instead of blurting out a response without hesitation, he pauses to consider what has been said.

A group of people once approached Rabbi Shlomo Wolbe for advice on a *chinuch* issue. After listening to their question, Rabbi Wolbe lowered his head and closed his eyes. Thinking that Rabbi Wolbe had nodded off, the questioners offered more information in the hope of regaining his attention. Rabbi Wolbe looked up and listened, and when they finished talking, closed his eyes again. Once again the people began to speak, and once again Rabbi Wolbe "woke up." This scenario repeated itself several times until Rabbi Wolbe's student, who had been standing in the background, could no longer contain himself and shouted: "Unless you give the Rav a chance to think, you will never get a response!"[15]

Rabbi Wolbe had not been dozing, but was thinking about what the people had asked, forming a picture of their situation and analyzing their predicament from all sides. Each time new information was added, however, Rabbi Wolbe had to begin weighing the situation anew, considering how the latest details altered the picture. Without time to think he would never have had an opportunity to reach a conclusion and the exchange would have continued all day.

Rabbi Wolbe's behavior is a classic example of not replying hastily. *Eino nivhal lehashiv* means more than merely waiting a certain amount of time before responding. It requires *thinking* about what the other person has said, and not responding until you have taken the time to reflect on his words.[16]

This quality of taking a few moments to digest what one has heard before replying is not so common today. People expect immediate responses the moment they finish posing their question or presenting their argument, and should the listener fall silent for a few moments to contemplate, he would be considered strange.

If we stopped to consider this manner of speech, we would realize how empty it is. After all, what value is a comment made with no forethought? If you pour your heart out to a friend, sharing with him the troubles and problems you're facing, do you really want him to respond quickly with a hollow "That must be terrible," or would you prefer that he take a moment to put himself in your shoes, trying to imagine what you must be going through, before attempting to console you?

Three Elements of Good Conversation

We have looked at the first three traits of the wise person, analyzing each one independently. If we put the three together, considering them in their broader sense, we form a model of how Chazal perceived conversation — a model vastly different from the one to which we are accustomed.

Most of our discussions are just opportunities to swap information. A tells B something about her vacation or her family, perhaps a story or *dvar Torah*, and B responds with some relevant bit of information she has gleaned on that topic. After the conversation ends, A and B have essentially just switched data banks, with A now knowing what B previously knew about the subject and B now knowing what A knew about it. No new ideas have been formed.

While there is nothing wrong with such exchanges, a higher level of conversation is where the two parties arrive at new insights based on their talking together, forming ideas that did not previously exist in either of their minds.

Each person contains an array of memories and experiences, thoughts and beliefs, which form the entirety of his being and set him apart from everyone else, making him a world unto himself. If instead of merely regurgitating what they already know, A and B take the time to let the other person's words resonate, original ideas will result. Seen in this light, a conversation is a unique event: the colliding of one person's experiences and life situation with another person's personality, giving birth to new thoughts and ideas. They are like two musicians performing together, with each side contributing half the melody, and the duet only coming together from the union.

In order to reach this higher form of conversation we need three ingredients:

The first is that we approach conversations eager to listen to what the other person has to say. When we speak with someone, whose words do we consider more important: ours or theirs? The Mishnah teaches us that we should be far more interested in hearing what the other person will say than we are in what we have to say.

As we discussed earlier, this does not mean remaining silent. To be sure, the wise person shares incidents about his personal life and relates stories or *divrei Torah* he may have heard, but his primary intent in doing so is to elicit a response and hear what his friend has to say, not to give voice to his own thoughts.

The next ingredient is that we not interrupt one another.[17]

When the other person is speaking, clear your mind of what you know about the topic and give him your full attention. If you think about your response while he is speaking, planning what you will say next, you will never reach the higher level of conversation, which demands setting aside your own opinions and preconceived ideas. Be spontaneous and let the conversation come alive on its own. Free yourself from set replies and become absorbed in what the other person is saying, letting your response emanate from within your own personality and trusting in who you *are* rather than in what you *know*.

The reason we find it so hard not to interrupt one another may be because most of our conversations are of the information-swapping variety. If the other person's words are just a trigger for us to respond with a prerecorded idea, then as soon as he brings up a topic about which we have something to say, waiting becomes a challenge. Why wait till the other person finishes his sentence when we already have our response ready now? The wise person doesn't find this a challenge because he doesn't know what he is going to say until after the other person has finished speaking.

This leads to the final ingredient of good conversation: not being hasty to respond.[18] Having cleared your mind for your friend to speak, look into the depths of your personality to see what lies inside. Don't go for speed. Go for quality: the sincerity and degree to which your answer reflects your true feelings on the matter. In a sense, this is the climax of the conversation — the moment when you let the other person's thoughts intertwine with your own to arrive at new ideas. It requires peace of mind and strength of character to overcome the urge to respond before having looked inside your own personality and thought the matter through, but it is this trait — together with the others — that makes this mode of talking the most pleasurable, as well as the most meaningful.

---

[1] This translation of the word *golem*, which is taken from the ArtScroll siddur, is the best I could find. The English language, however, does not contain a precise term for a *golem*. Rambam, Rabbeinu Yona, and others explain that a *golem* — a word which literally refers to an unformed substance — possesses both intellectual and moral virtues, but in an incomplete and disorderly way, much like an unfinished utensil.

[2] *Nachalas Avos* and *Peirush Maseches Avos L'Rebbi Mattisyah HaYitzhari.* Cf. Rabbeinu Bachya.

[3] *Midrash Shmuel.*

[4] *Seforno* based on *Iyov* 32:6–7. See also *Avos D'Rebbi Nasan* 37:13.

[5] *Iyov* 3–14.

[6] Ibid. 15–31.

[7] Malbim, *Iyov* 32:16.

[8] *Iyov* 32–37.

[9] I could not locate any early sources regarding the time span of the debate between Iyov and his friends. In a preface to the book of *Iyov* (*Machon Hama'or* ed., Jerusalem, 2001), the writer claims that the debate spanned twelve months.

However, while the Mishnah in *Eduyos* 2:10 cites twelve months as the duration of Iyov's tribulations, I found no indication that the debate lasted that long. (It should be noted that in deriving a lesson from Elihu's behavior, the commentators seem to be following the opinions that the story of Iyov and his friends actually transpired and is not just a parable. See *Bava Basra* 15a.)

[10] *Iyov* 32:4 and 6 with *Metzudas Dovid*.

[11] *Avos D'Rebbi Nasan* 37:13. The idea of not interrupting another person is also derived from Avraham's pleading with G-d on behalf of Sodom, where G-d waited for Avraham to finish his argument before responding (ibid. 37:12). From this incident we derive that one should not interrupt another person even if that person is well below one's own level, such as a student (see *Dvar Moshe*). We also derive that even when one knows what the other person is about to say, one should still not interrupt him. After all, G-d not only knew the end of Avraham's sentences, He even knew the beginning. Moreover, He knew that Avraham's entire argument was for naught as there were not enough righteous people in Sodom for it to be saved. Nevertheless, He still did not interrupt (see *Avos D'Rebbi Nasan* 37:12 and *Machzor Vitri*).

[12] *Magen Avos*. He therefore explains that the Mishnah is warning us not to begin a conversation with one's teacher while the teacher is still involved in a discussion with someone else.

[13] *Nachalas Avos* and *Peirushei Rabbeinu Yosef ben Shoshan* write that it is included in the prohibition of *ona'as devarim* (*Vayikra* 25:17). Cf. *Tiferes Yisrael*, which simply states that it is not *derech eretz* to interrupt.

The attribute of not interrupting another person is hard enough to attain in casual, everyday conversation. It is clear from Chazal, however, that one is not meant to interrupt another person even during an argument, when the other person is expressing views that are opposed to one's own. See *Avos D'Rebbi Nasan* 37:13 and *Tiferes Yisrael*. This is also borne out from *Nachalas Avos*, which says that the trait of not interrupting others is derived from Moshe Rabbeinu, who listened patiently while Korach attacked him and ridiculed him and his authority. Only after Korach had finished everything he had to say did Moshe reply (*Bamidbar* 16:3–4).

[14] *Nachalas Avos* and *Peirush Maseches Avos L'Rebbi Mattisyah HaYitzhari* write that the attribute of not interrupting another person also includes pausing for a moment after the person finishes speaking.

[15] Heard from the student.

[16] Rabbeinu Yona, Meiri, and *Nachalas Avos*. Cf. Rambam.

[17] This second condition is a natural progression from the first. After all, if your whole intent in speaking to the other person is to listen to what he has to say, why would you then go ahead and cut him off in mid-sentence?

[18] The word *nivhal*, which we have translated as "haste," also has a second meaning: "to be afraid of an outside threat" (see Malbim, *Ya'ir Ohr, Beis* §7). The connection between these two meanings might be that *nivhal* in the sense of haste refers specifically to the rapidity of movement caused by fear of some external danger. In the context of speaking with people, one may reply hastily out of fear of what the other person may think of one's response or its timing.

A Note from
the Boss

פֶּרֶק ה' מִשְׁנָה י"א: אַרְבַּע מִדּוֹת בְּדֵעוֹת. נוֹחַ לִכְעוֹס
וְנוֹחַ לִרְצוֹת, יָצָא שְׂכָרוֹ בְּהֶפְסֵדוֹ. קָשֶׁה לִכְעוֹס וְקָשֶׁה
לִרְצוֹת, יָצָא הֶפְסֵדוֹ בִּשְׂכָרוֹ. קָשֶׁה לִכְעוֹס וְנוֹחַ לִרְצוֹת,
חָסִיד. נוֹחַ לִכְעוֹס וְקָשֶׁה לִרְצוֹת, רָשָׁע.

Chapter 5, Mishnah 11: *There are four types of dispositions:*

- *One who is quick to anger and quick to calm down — his gain is offset by his loss.*
- *One who is slow to anger and slow to calm down — his loss is offset by his gain.*
- *One who is slow to anger and quick to calm down is pious.*
- *One who is quick to anger and slow to calm down is wicked.*

I n 1986, scientists at the Harvard Medical School tested the psychological well-being of 1,305 men. Using the Minnesota Multiphasic Personality Inventory (MMPI-2), which includes a section designed to quantify anger, the scientists gave each participant a score that indicated his level of anger and hostility. The men returned for comprehensive medical examinations every seven years, at which time they were checked for heart disease.

When the study began, all the participants were healthy; but during the seven years of observation, 110 of them developed heart disease. The men with the highest anger scores were at the greatest risk for developing heart disease. And the risk was substantial: heart disease was diagnosed three times more often in the most angry men than in the least angry men.[1]

These statistics are frightening, but our Mishnah makes it clear that anger can be overcome.

The Mishnah describes four types of people, each personality with its own set of character traits. There is a fundamental difference, however, between the descriptions of the first two personality types and the second two. Regarding the first two cases — those who are either quick or slow to become angry as well as to calm down — the Mishnah does not label these people, but rather describes their relative gains or losses. But in the last two cases — those who are quick to one and slow to the other — the Mishnah actually labels these people, describing them as either pious or wicked. What is the distinction between the first and last two categories that leads the Mishnah to address them differently?

Understanding Inborn Traits

We must examine the personality types more closely to answer this question.

People naturally retain the character traits they are born with. Someone with a slower temperament may not anger quickly, but he will also take longer to calm down after he has been provoked. On the other hand, a person who is excitable may get angry quickly, but, having fleeting emotions, he will also calm down more easily and find it less difficult to get over the incident.[2]

That being the case, the first two groups in our Mishnah — those who are quick or slow to both — describe people whose temperaments have been fairly constant since birth. Not having altered their character traits one way or the other, these people cannot be assigned labels such as "good," "bad," or "average," because their dispositions are inborn. The Mishnah says about these people only that the very traits that make them strong in some areas also form their weaknesses in other areas.

However, someone who is easily angered but is not easily pacified has clearly changed his nature. Because a person is born to be one way or another, someone who is slow to one and quick to another must have changed his disposition. If he is now quick to anger and slow to calm down, it can only be because he has destroyed one of his naturally good qualities. Hence the Mishnah labels this person wicked.

Conversely, someone who is slow to anger and quick to calm down must have worked on himself to overcome one of his innate characteristics. This person is therefore described as pious.[3]

We see that even a person whose tendency is to become angry quickly *can* change his temperament and become slow to anger.[4] The Mishnah teaches us how.

Changing Our Natures

It opens with the phrase: *Arba middos b'de'os*, which we have translated as "There are four types of dispositions." Literally, *de'os* means that which one knows, thinks, or maintains. By using this word to describe character traits, the Mishnah teaches that we can change our character by changing our way of thinking.[5]

What new thought patterns can we adopt to raise our anger threshold?

Nearly all anger is rooted in the thought that "I can control the situation." This thought leads us to form mental images of what *should* be happening to us and how other people *ought* to treat us. When these expectations are not fulfilled, we become angry.

This concept is clearly illustrated by parent-child relationships. Perhaps one of the reasons people so frequently find themselves angered by their children is that parents have such profound feelings of control over them. Having brought them into the world and having provided them with everything they need — clothes, food, schooling — a parent feels he "owns" his children, just as he owns a piece of property. Since he has mental images of how they should behave, he becomes frustrated when they act up.

Of course, it is a parent's responsibility to educate his children and make certain that they behave properly, but at the end of the day, children have their own free will. If they disobey, the correct response is not unrestrained anger, but another attempt to calmly teach them better. Even when the best way to teach them is through showing anger, it is meant to be an external, premeditated show of anger, never a real, inner, spur-of-the-moment anger.[6]

Besides persuading himself that he controls other people, a person also imagines that he controls his time. That is why nothing rattles a person more than when his meticulously planned schedule goes awry. We can all relate to the frustration of missing a plane or watching the clock tick by as we wait for a friend, knowing that our time for lunch together is getting shorter and shorter. Convinced that one has some kind of ownership over his time, he becomes irritated when faced with the stark reality that he is not really in charge after all.

Who's Really in Charge?

Since anger is often rooted in issues of control, one way to overcome anger is to come to terms with the reality that we are not in control of our lives — G-d is. As Shlomo Hamelech said, "Man makes many detailed plans, but the counsel of G-d alone prevails."[7] Life demands flexibility; to be able to adjust easily from one's envisaged plans to those of the Master Planner is a key element in conquering anger and calmly dealing with the unexpected. One needs to be able to easily say, "I thought I should be doing _____ now, but if my attention is needed elsewhere, that means that G-d has different designs, and I will happily follow His will."

Once a person understands and accepts that G-d is in control, a large amount of anger can be eliminated from his life. But this knowledge also helps overcome anger in another way, namely, by changing the focal point. Instead of focusing solely on the outcome — that things didn't turn out as expected — one thinks more about the intermediate steps.

Take, for example, being late for a meeting or a wedding: When running behind schedule, the reason a person finds himself angry with anyone who gets in his way is that he is concentrating exclusively on the end result of being on time. He views the preceding steps — the process of getting there — as inconsequential, and therefore he is frustrated when they don't go as planned.

When one bears in mind that G-d is in control, his perspective changes, for he realizes that the end result is not in his own hands, but in G-d's. One who is late no longer gets annoyed, as he understands that what matters most is not whether he arrives on time, but whether he is the best person he can be along the way.

We can all benefit from this change in perspective on *erev Shabbos*.[8] When there is only one hour left until candle-lighting and the house is still in chaos, people tend to be short-tempered. They're focusing on the end result — a clean house, a set table, being dressed for Shabbos, getting to davening on time — and are frustrated by anything that stands in their way. Of course it would have been better had they allowed more preparation time, but it doesn't occur to most people that, under the circumstances, G-d much prefers a house that is disorderly but serene to a clean one filled with discord.

Imagine that you found this letter under your pillow on Thursday night:

Dear (your name here),

Tomorrow, an hour before Shabbos, you will have a difficult ordeal. Everyone will want to shower at the same time, and I just wanted to write and let you know that I will be watching.

Love, G-d

You would find the bathroom occupied, but instead of being annoyed, you would sing with joy, thanking G-d for the challenge and the opportunity to grow. People would get in your way, but instead of shouting, you would smile and speak calmly, knowing that G-d is watching.

The same person who is usually enraged over mishaps on *erev Shabbos* becomes a model of serenity when he knows G-d is testing him and observing his reactions. This demonstrates that when a person expects frustrations and mentally prepares himself for them, he is capable of managing almost any challenge. The reason people are so frequently frustrated is that they are not expecting the test. They think only of the end result — getting to the meeting on time or being ready for Shabbos — and view any obstacle along the way as a nuisance. Had they received a note like ours, they would have realized that the "obstacle" is not an obstacle at all, but the main point of the event.

The idea that the purpose of our lives is to face challenges and meet them in a way that pleases G-d is one of the fundamentals of Jewish belief. As Chazal teach us, the point of our being placed in this world is to conquer our undesirable character traits and cleave to G-d, thereby earning ourselves a share in the World to Come.[9]

We don't have to wait to find such a letter under our pillows before reacting calmly in aggravating situations. We already have such a letter in our possession. It is called the Torah. We merely need to carry its teachings around with us, and pull its message out whenever we find ourselves in trying circumstances.

---

[1] Harvey B. Simon, "Can Work Kill?" *Scientific American Presents* 10, no. 2 (Summer 1999):45–46.

[2] *Derech Chaim.*

[3] Based on *Derech Chaim.*

[4] Note that the highest level mentioned in the Mishnah, the pious person, is not someone who never gets angry, but only one who is slow to anger. According to the commentators, if you never get angry you're not human — you're an angel! (See *Midrash Shmuel; Yalkut Me'am Lo'ez.* Cf. *Hachassid Yaavetz.*) Even the most righteous people had to work hard to overcome their anger. R' Moshe Feinstein was extremely mild-mannered and did not show a trace of anger even

in provocative situations. Yet he once remarked, "Do you think I was always like this? By nature, I have a fierce temper, but I have worked to overcome it." Shimon Finkelman, *Reb Moshe* (New York: Mesorah, 1986), 228.

R' Moshe Gershon Movshovitz, who studied in Radin and later became the Rav of Sidra, relates how on a couple of occasions he noticed the Chofetz Chaim entering the *beis midrash* in the middle of the night and remaining there for a little while. Curious to know what the Chofetz Chaim was doing, R' Movshovitz hid beneath one of the benches. When midnight arrived, the Chofetz Chaim appeared, opened the *aron kodesh*, and began begging G-d for help in overcoming his *midda* of anger that plagued him (*Tnuas Hamussar* 4:70). As physical beings, we are susceptible to anger (*Nachalas Avos*). We are not expected to be perfect, but we must try our utmost to avoid anger.

[5] *Dvar Yerushalayim.*

[6] Rambam, *Hilchos De'os* 2:3; *Mesillas Yesharim*, chap. 11. R' Eliyahu Lopian said that someone who still has internal anger cannot use external, pretend anger (*My Disciple, My Child*, 148).

[7] *Mishlei* 19:21.

[8] The evil inclination tries particularly hard to cause disagreements on *erev Shabbos* (see *Gittin* 52a and *Aruch Hashulchan, Orach Chaim* 262:5).

[9] *Mesillas Yesharim*, chap. 1

Crossing the
Finish Line

פֶּרֶק ה' מִשְׁנָה כ"ג: יְהוּדָה בֶן תֵּימָא אוֹמֵר, הֱוֵי עַז
כַּנָּמֵר וְקַל כַּנֶּשֶׁר וְרָץ כַּצְּבִי וְגִבּוֹר כָּאֲרִי לַעֲשׂוֹת רְצוֹן
אָבִיךָ שֶׁבַּשָּׁמַיִם.

Chapter 5, Mishnah 23: *Rabbi Yehuda ben Teima says: Be bold as a leopard, light as an eagle, swift as a gazelle, and mighty as a lion to do the will of your Father in Heaven.*

T he Mishnah delineates four stages that are crucial to completing an act.[1]

Bold as a Leopard

The first step in any action is to decide to do it. For this, one needs boldness — the ability to face up to the challenge without being overwhelmed by the magnitude of the task or being deterred by apparent barriers.[2] The leopard exhibits both these aspects of boldness.[3] Firstly, it isn't frightened away by the magnitude of its quarry; it attacks animals up to four times its size.[4] And secondly, it hunts in all types of climates, allowing neither scorching heat nor extreme cold to stand in its way.[5]

Indeed, one wildlife researcher said of leopards, "One thing is certain: just when you think you understand them, they do something utterly surprising." Leopards are known for their innovative hunting techniques, which seem to break the rules, and they aren't put off by obstacles.[6] To quote one zoologist, the leopard is an "opportunist," taking advantage of potential kills wherever and however they present themselves.[7]

Thus, when the Mishnah instructs us to be "bold as a leopard," it is telling us to be defiant and daring in our service of G-d. When a new challenge presents itself, we should undertake it with energy and vitality, instead of shying away from it, hesitating and wondering whether or not we are suited for the job.[8]

When approached to organize *chesed* projects or say *divrei Torah*, people often decline, preferring to leave the challenge to someone else. "Who am I to accept such a task? Projects like that are meant for people much greater than I am."[9]

The leopard isn't the strongest of creatures, yet it fearlessly attacks animals many times its size. Similarly, we should not be deterred by our perceived limitations, but should push forward and accept spiritual challenges without deliberation.[10]

Light as an Eagle

Having accepted the challenge, we need to be "light as an eagle" in order to follow it through to completion.[11]

Seeing as eagles are one of the heaviest types of birds, what is the "lightness" to which the Mishnah refers?

The word "light" doesn't refer to physical weight, but rather, to the ability to do something without tiring.[12] Indeed, among the dictionary definitions of "light" are "exerting a minimum of force or pressure" and "requiring little effort."[13]

The eagle's flight is effortless.[14] Should it decide to travel to a particular place, it does not set out in that direction at once. Weather permitting, it first flies upward in circles, spiraling increasingly higher until it reaches a height from which it will be able to fly toward its destination *in one continuous glide*. By first climbing up — sometimes reaching heights of 8,000 feet and disappearing into a cloud — it can then glide through the air without having to move its wings even once.[15]

Seton Gordon, an ornithologist who observed a pair of eagles for eight years, noted that the eagle travels "without effort," reaching its hunting ground "in one long glide," which is "on occasion more than 20 miles" away. "Utilizing its mastery in gliding, the golden eagle arrives at its destination after a journey on which no energy has been expended; one can almost say that distance means nothing to this bird."[16]

The verse notes this aspect of an eagle's flight when it writes that those who put their hope in G-d will "...grow wings like eagles; run without tiring, and walk without growing weary."[17] Thus, the eagle is used as a metaphor for traveling without exhaustion, which supports the idea that the "lightness" of the eagle is its effortlessness in flight.[18]

Being light as an eagle, then, means meeting challenges in such a way so as not to wear oneself out and quit in the middle. By analyzing how the eagle is able to travel long distances effortlessly, we can try to learn from its example and do the same.

The eagle easily covers great distances by riding the currents of the wind. Instead of generating all the energy itself, which would exhaust it very quickly, the eagle positions itself where it is able to harness an independent force of nature — the wind — to carry it along smoothly. Because the wind blows continually and the eagle is able to harness this force, it can travel great distances without using its own energy.

In order to complete a new challenge, then, we need to find some perpetual force that will carry us along, ensuring that we not lose hope and give up in the middle. Relying on willpower alone may seem like a viable option while one is still caught up in the initial excitement, but eventually that excitement wears off, and without a continuous source of energy to keep one stimulated, the chances are that one will grow weary in the middle. One may be able to push himself for a week, or a month, but eventually he loses enthusiasm and abandons the project.

The perpetual forces we need to employ are the character traits that are etched deep into our psyches, and are thus ever-present. Initial enthusiasm fades over time, but the traits with which a person is born are part of his being and continue to exist as long as he does. Examples of such characteristics are the desire for honor and recognition, or the tendency to conform to peer pressure, both of which lie at the core of a person's being and can be constructively used to motivate oneself. By linking our commitment to these basic characteristics, we connect ourselves to a permanent source of energy, avoiding the risk of losing steam before the mission is accomplished.[19]

Consider a teenager who regrets wasting time on the computer. It requires the boldness of a leopard to undertake to address the problem without being intimidated by the enormity of the task or by the number of failed past attempts. However, once he has committed himself to resolving the issue, he needs to be "light as an eagle" in order to persist with his goal through the inevitable highs and lows. He could, for example, use the quality of embarrassment to overcome his weakness by obligating a friend to report him to someone he greatly admires and before whom he would be embarrassed should he succumb in the future.

With the help of his friends, he will be able to control his bad habit for years to come, whereas, if he were to use determination alone, he may succeed in the short-term, but would probably lack the wherewithal to sustain his commitment for an extended time. This is the secret of "light as an eagle": the overwhelming force of personal embarrassment becomes the powerful wind that will carry him to his ultimate destination.

Swift as a Gazelle

Even after pinpointing and utilizing a character trait to provide momentum, a person will still encounter times of uncertainty, when he wonders if it was really wise to undertake the project in the first place. Doubts begin to surface: "Perhaps I was being too ambitious when I accepted this commitment? Maybe I was aiming too high and expected too much of myself?" At such times, one mustn't hesitate, but must push forward, running like a gazelle.[20]

The gazelle is hunted by several predators. In order to escape from a lion or leopard, it has to run swiftly, darting as fast as it can. It can't afford to stop and think, but must put all its energy into running. Even a moment's hesitation could mean death.

Thus, the instruction to run like a gazelle teaches us to keep projects going. Once you've accepted the challenge, do not hesitate or stop to question the wisdom of the decision, lest you lose momentum and place the whole project in danger of collapse.[21]

Consider a person who decides to complete a *masechta*. Having been "bold as a leopard" to undertake the task and "light as an eagle" to find a source of energy to fuel him, there will no doubt be moments of weakness when he wonders whether it was a good idea to begin with. At such times, he must run like a gazelle, not stopping to consider what he is doing. Sprinting at maximum speed demands clearing one's mind of all external thoughts, and focusing clearly on the finish line. Similarly, in the midst of a project, one must empty his head of all doubts and focus on nothing but the intended goal. Doubts and worries are the weapons of the evil inclination, which uses them to stall positive endeavors, filling a person's mind with reservations and afflicting him with uncertainties.

Mighty as a Lion

Having successfully undertaken and carried out an action, one reaches the final stage — the conclusion. The inherent danger in conclusions is that one will try to end the project before its proper time. No one likes unfinished business, and for the sake of "wrapping it up" there is a tendency to finish a project prematurely, just to have it behind you and no longer weighing on your mind.

Imagine that your mother asks you to pick up some things from the local grocery. Having completed the errand and walked into the kitchen, packages in hand, most people would place the shopping bags on the floor or plop them on the counter. The proper way to complete the mitzvah, however, would be to put everything where it belongs. The tendency to dump the packages on the floor instead of putting them away highlights the temptation to bring an action to its end just short of its rightful completion.

Another example is the tendency to leave shul moments before the end of the last *Kaddish*. Of course, people have all kinds of reasons why they have to leave early, but underlying all the reasons is also a deep desire to be rid of whatever one is busy with so that one can move on to the next thing.

The lion teaches us to bring matters to their proper completion.

The Torah says that the lion "…does not lie down until it eats its prey, and drinks the blood of the slain."[22] The Torah uses the lion as the metaphor for completing a task and not resting until a mission is fulfilled, which in the lion's case is capturing prey.[23] Although many animals hunt for food, and none of them would willingly go hungry and opt to lie down for the night without first eating their fill, the lion is unique. When food is scarce and there is nothing else to eat, other carnivores will make do with whatever they can get their paws on — some grass, shrubs, or maybe a few grasshoppers and insects. The lion, however, will not settle for anything other than real meat — even when something else is available.[24]

Kings always demand the best: the highest-quality furniture, the most refined china. A king won't settle for some little shack — he expects a royal palace. He won't make do with a measly meal — he expects a feast. In the same way, the lion, which is the king of the animal world,[25] is not satisfied with anything other than real meat. Filling up on grasshoppers or shrubbery would simply be beneath its dignity.[26]

Being "mighty as a lion," then, means completing an act with finality, bringing it to its proper end, and not contenting oneself with halfway measures. Just as the lion does not settle for food that is not fit for a king, we should not settle for any act that is not carried out to perfection.[27]

Having gone to the trouble of buying your mother her groceries, finish the act properly and put the items away.

Having spent a morning in shul, complete the mitzvah properly by staying until the very end.

Whatever it is you do in life, make sure you finish it off regally. Do not let it out of your hand until you have put all your energy into ensuring that it is the best you can possibly make it.

From Animals to Angels

We have discussed the four phrases of the Mishnah, showing how each one refers to a separate stage of performing an act. Let us conclude with the following thought.

The *Tanna D'vei Eliyahu* states that a Jew is capable of reaching levels of spirituality higher than those of the ministering angels or any other part of creation.[28] Because a Jew's *neshama* stems from G-d Himself, he is capable of accomplishing more than any other creature.[29]

After describing the unbelievable heights of success a Jew can achieve, the *Tanna D'vei Eliyahu* concludes by saying that it is for this reason that we are instructed to be "bold as a leopard, light as an eagle, swift as a gazelle, and mighty as a lion."[30]

On the surface, the *Tanna D'vei Eliyahu* is difficult to understand. What relevance does our Mishnah have to the great potential a Jew contains within himself?[31] However, when we bear in mind the explanation that the four phrases are the key to carrying out any act successfully, the matter becomes perfectly clear.

In order to actualize our potential and reach the lofty heights of which we are capable, we need to follow the four steps of the Mishnah, and incorporate its message into our daily lives. We must boldly grasp spiritual opportunities as they arise, execute them in ways that ensure their endurance, and carefully complete them down to their finest detail. Then there will be no limit to what we can achieve in our lives.[32]

---

[1] The idea that the four statements in the Mishnah are all stages in doing one act, as opposed to being four separate qualities, is expressed in *Da'as Torah* 1:181–182 and *Alei Shur* 2:255.

[2] See Rashi (Pesachim 112a ד"ה הוי עז), who explains this part of the Mishnah as meaning, "exert yourself for a mitzvah more than your capabilities."

[3] Rashi (Yirmiya 13:23) identifies namer as the leopard.

[4] D. I. Rubinstein and R. W. Wrangham, eds., Ecological Aspects of Social Evolution (Princeton, NJ: Princeton University Press, 1986), 433.

[5] See Milei D'Avos.

[6] Stuart Napier, Nova transcript #2519, "Leopards of the Night," December 1, 1998.

[7] Theodore N. Bailey, The African Leopard (New York: Columbia University Press, 1993), 331–334, 341.

[8] See Tiferes Yisrael; R' Yerucham Levovitz quoted in Alei Shur 2:255.

[9] Tiferes Yisrael.

[10] Of course, the trait of boldness must be applied appropriately or it can be a terrible and destructive force. As the end of the Mishnah states, "The brazen-faced person goes to Gehinnom." When we discuss boldness, we are referring to being bold for spiritual matters, to do mitzvos and teach Torah (Magen Avos, Hachassid Yaavetz). The Mishnah makes this point clear when it concludes that we should be bold as a leopard "in order to do the will of your Father in Heaven" (Rambam, Ksav Sofer).

[11] There is a widespread dispute as to the precise identity of the nesher. It is commonly translated as an eagle, and indeed Sefer Ha'itur (Sha'ar 2, Hilchos Shechita 45a) and Chizkuni (Vayikra 11:13) identify it as such. However, Tosafos (Chullin 63a ד"ה נץ) object to this translation because Chullin 61a says that the nesher has no kosher signs. Since one of the signs of a kosher bird is an extra toe, and an eagle possesses an extra toe, the nesher cannot be the eagle.

R' Saadia Gaon (Vayikra 11:13) translates nesher as nasr, which is Arabic for a griffon vulture. Ibn Ezra (Vayikra 11:13), Ramban (Chullin 62b), and Chiddushei HaRan (Chullin 61a) appear to concur (see Sichas Chullin, 422). However, even this translation has its difficulties (see ibid.).

Since it does not alter the understanding of the Mishnah, I translate nesher as an eagle, which is the familiar and widely accepted translation.

[12] Bartenura, Derech Avos.

[13] Merriam-Webster's Collegiate Dictionary, 11th ed., s.v. light.

[14] Devarim 28:49 describes the nesher as "swooping." Both understandings of nesher (see note 11) are compatible with this verse, as both the eagle and the

griffon vulture are capable of soaring for long periods of time (see *Encyclopedia Britannica*, 2004 DVD ed., s.v. vulture).

[15] Seton Gordon, *The Golden Eagle: King of Birds* (London: Collins, 1955), 60, 116–118.

[16] Gordon, *Golden Eagle*, 114, 176–177.

[17] *Yeshaya* 40:31.

[18] See *Bartenura*.

[19] The principle of using drives other than *yiras Shamayim* in order to make it through *nisyonos* is laid down by R' Yisrael Salanter, *Ohr Yisrael* §4. See also *Tnuas Hamussar* 4:287.

[20] The authorities dispute the identity of a *tzvi*. Rashi (*Chullin* 59b ד"ה והרי צבי) translates it as *steinbok*, an Old French word for an ibex, or wild goat (*Targum Hala'az*). *Tosafos* (*Chullin* 59b ד"ה והרי צבי) translate it as a deer, and R' Saadia Gaon (*Devarim* 14:5) identifies it as *ṣvi*, which is Arabic for a gazelle. Some suggest that Rashi also agrees that it is a gazelle (see *Sichas Chullin*, 415).

[21] Of course, a person has to know his limitations and not overextend himself.

[22] *Bamidbar* 23:24.

[23] See note 27.

[24] When describing the lion's food, the verse uses the word *teref*, a word which could refer to any food an animal wishes to eat, meat or vegetable (see *Bereishis* 8:11). *Targum Yerushalmi*, however, uses the word *basar*, which means meat, showing that the verse is to be understood as saying that the lion does not rest until it has specifically devoured meat.

[25] *Chagiga* 13b.

[26] See note 24. Additionally, when hunting animals, lions are more regal in their choice of prey, killing much larger specimens than do other carnivores, such as leopards, cheetahs, and wild dogs. See Dr. David Macdonald, ed., *The Encyclopedia of Mammals* (London: Allen & Unwin, 1984), 31.

[27] Chazal see the image of the lion "not lying down until it eats its prey and drinks the blood of its slain" as alluding to the Jew who does not retire for the night until he has recited *Shema*, and also to Moshe, who did not pass away until he defeated the Midianites (see Rashi, *Bamidbar* 23:24). According to both interpretations, the lion is used as the image of not resting until a task is complete, supporting the idea that "being mighty as a lion" means properly

finishing off whatever one is doing, without compromising his standards. See also *Targum Onkelos*, *Targum Yonasan ben Uziel*, and *Targum Yerushalmi*.

[28] *Tanna D'vei Eliyahu*, *Eliyahu Rabba*, chap. 21.

[29] *Yeshuos Yaakov* on *Tanna D'vei Eliyahu*, note 7.

[30] *Tanna D'vei Eliyahu*, loc. cit.

[31] *Me'orei Eish* on *Tanna D'vei Eliyahu*, note 11.

[32] See also *Me'orei Eish*, loc. cit., and *Yeshuos Yaakov*, note 8.

The Stages
of Life

פֶּרֶק ה׳ מִשְׁנָה כ״ה: הוּא הָיָה אוֹמֵר, בֶּן חָמֵשׁ שָׁנִים
לַמִּקְרָא, בֶּן עֶשֶׂר לַמִּשְׁנָה, בֶּן שְׁלֹשׁ עֶשְׂרֵה לַמִּצְוֹות,
בֶּן חֲמֵשׁ עֶשְׂרֵה לַתַּלְמוּד, בֶּן שְׁמוֹנֶה עֶשְׂרֵה לַחֻפָּה, בֶּן
עֶשְׂרִים לִרְדּוֹף, בֶּן שְׁלֹשִׁים לַכֹּחַ, בֶּן אַרְבָּעִים לַבִּינָה, בֶּן
חֲמִשִּׁים לָעֵצָה, בֶּן שִׁשִּׁים לַזִּקְנָה, בֶּן שִׁבְעִים לַשֵּׂיבָה,
בֶּן שְׁמוֹנִים לַגְּבוּרָה, בֶּן תִּשְׁעִים לָשׁוּחַ, בֶּן מֵאָה כְּאִלּוּ
מֵת וְעָבַר וּבָטֵל מִן הָעוֹלָם.

Chapter 5, Mishnah 25: *He used to say: A five-year-old for Chumash, a ten-year-old for Mishnah, a thirteen-year-old to observe mitzvos, a fifteen-year-old for Gemara, an eighteen-year-old for marriage, a twenty-year-old to pursue, a thirty-year-old for strength, a forty-year-old for understanding, a fifty-year-old for advice, a sixty-year-old for wisdom, a seventy-year-old for seiva, an eighty-year-old for might, a ninety-year-old for speech,[1] a hundred-year-old is as if he were dead, moved on, and gone from the world.*

P eople have always been interested in human development. In fact, over the past century developmental psychology has become a full-fledged scientific field. Initially these psychologists predominantly studied child development, the early years of life, which are filled with rapid changes. Only later did they begin observing adults, recognizing that development continues throughout a person's life.[2]

In this Mishnah, the stages of a person's development are delineated from childhood to old age. Chazal understood that although the changes in a person's understanding are most pronounced in the formative years, a person develops throughout his life, never ceasing to grow and reach new levels of maturity.

The stages mentioned in the Mishnah can be understood, on one level, as describing particular tasks a person should begin performing at given ages. In other words, he should start learning Chumash at five and Mishnayos at ten; he should be performing mitzvos at thirteen, getting married at eighteen, and so on.

On a deeper level, however, the Mishnah is describing new levels of understanding that a person reaches throughout the stages of his life. According to this approach, the statement "*ben chamesh laMikra*" is not just an instruction for a child of five to begin learning Chumash, but a description of the intellectual ability reached by a five-year-old, the result of which is his readiness to understand Chumash.

Similarly, the statement "*ben shelosh esrei lamitzvos*" is not just saying that the thirteen-year-old becomes obligated to perform mitzvos at that age, but rather, that he reaches a new level of maturity at thirteen, which makes him capable of maintaining a commitment to G-d. Until thirteen (twelve for a girl), a child is too consumed with his own needs and concerns to fully relate to the fact that there is a Higher Being to Whose will he must submit. At thirteen, however, he is mature enough to accept that he must follow G-d's command whether he feels like it or not.

Likewise, *ben shemoneh esrei* is not simply the time at which a young adult should begin finding his match, but a description of the person's emotional growth, the outcome of which is his readiness to commit to another human being. Having steadily kept mitzvos for five years and experiencing that he is not free to do whatever he wishes whenever he wishes, the young adult should be ready for marriage, where he will have to conform on a higher level to the will of another being.[3]

As we will see, each stage of development presents numerous challenges and opportunities for personal growth. In the following chapters we will discuss the ages from twenty onward and elaborate on what each age holds.

The Roaring Twenties: *Learning to be a Grown-Up*

בן עשרים לרדוף

A Twenty-Year-Old to Pursue

The commentators explain the word "pursuit" in various ways — pursuit of Torah and mitzvos,[4] pursuit by the Heavenly Court for punishment,[5] and pursuit of a livelihood.[6] All three explanations, however, point to the same underlying idea: independence, a time when childhood ends and adulthood begins.[7] Let us further examine these explanations.

An Age of Responsibility

Independence is evident in a person's attitude toward his Torah learning and mitzvah observance. Before he turns twenty, a boy's father is the one who is primarily responsible for ensuring that he learns and develops properly. Once he reaches twenty, however, a young man becomes responsible for himself and can no longer rely on his father to do things for him. He must "pursue" knowledge and good deeds on his own.[8] A child can fall back on the excuse that he never learned and didn't know better, but once he turns twenty, he can't say, "No one taught me." If he wasn't taught something by twenty, it is *his* responsibility to teach himself.

One young man "got away" with not learning Biblical Hebrew in school. While his friends were in the classroom learning, he was out playing and having fun. Later, in yeshiva, when he didn't know the correct translation of a certain word, he excused himself to a friend by saying that he had never studied Hebrew grammar. The friend commented that "I didn't take the course" may have been a good excuse in grade school but would not serve him in yeshiva. If there was something he didn't know, he should take it upon himself to learn it.

The friend's comment is true not only of *dikduk* but of every area in Torah. After a person reaches twenty, he becomes an adult and cannot justify his ignorance by citing his lack of childhood education. Having reached the age of twenty, he must "pursue" knowledge on his own.

The "pursuit" of a twenty-year-old also refers to his being pursued by the Heavenly Court.[9] Although obligated in mitzvos from age thirteen, a person is not punished by the Heavenly Court for his sins until he turns twenty.

This is a second example of how a person becomes a full-fledged adult at twenty. From thirteen to twenty, he is in a state of quasi-accountability. On the one hand, he is obligated to keep mitzvos, but on the other, he is not fully culpable for them. Once he turns twenty, however, he becomes fully responsible and must bear the consequences of his actions.

The "pursuit" of a twenty-year-old could also refer to the pursuit of a livelihood.[10] As a child, he is supported by his parents and doesn't have to worry about his finances. At twenty, though, the burden of earning a living falls on his shoulders, and money ultimately becomes his responsibility. This is another example of twenty being a time of full maturity.

Chazal say that Adam and Chava were created as twenty-year-olds.[11] Bearing in mind that twenty is the age of independence, we understand why of all the ages G-d could have chosen to create them, He picked twenty. Twenty is the time of adulthood in the full sense of the word and was thus the most fitting age to create Adam and Chava.[12]

The Torah writes that Moshe "grew up," and left Pharaoh's palace to share in his brothers' suffering.[13] According to one opinion in the Midrash, this happened when he turned twenty.[14] His leaving the place where he had grown up represented his becoming independent, and his voluntarily joining in his fellow Jews' suffering signified his taking on responsibility.[15]

Until twenty, most of a person's life decisions are made for him by his parents: his schooling, his vacation plans, his extracurricular activities, and so on. At twenty, a person begins to stand on his own feet, taking control of his life and mapping out his destiny. This is a major change in a person's life and marks a breaking away from the protection of his parents.

He should take charge of his life and not let others make important decisions for him. He should remember that he is now fully accountable for his actions and that it is he alone who will one day have to give a *din v'cheshbon* for how he lived his life. Of course, he should seek advice from his parents and teachers; they are older and more experienced than he is. But when all is said and done, it must be *his* decision and no one else's, for ultimately it will be he and no one else who will have to account for what he chooses.

This transition is often difficult for parents, who find it hard to let go of their children and watch them make decisions that they may not agree with.

Let them recall the time their twenty-year-old was just a toddler taking his first steps. Just as they stood back then, giving him the space he needed to learn to walk on his own, so must they stand back now. Their instinct then, too, was to reach out and protect their precious one from falling. But they restrained themselves, realizing that to help would in fact prevent their child from ever learning to walk. Similarly, now they must show the same restraint again in order that their child will learn to walk through life on his own.

Thirty-something: *Mastering Maturity*

בֶּן שְׁלֹשִׁים לַכֹּחַ
A Thirty-Year-Old for Strength

Upon reaching thirty, a person achieves his full strength. We learn this from the *Levi'im*, who began working in the *Mishkan* when they were thirty years old. They assembled and disassembled the *Mishkan*, carried its vessels, and loaded its beams onto wagons. From the fact that they began doing this only at age thirty, we derive that thirty is the age of strength.[16]

This may seem straightforward enough, but there are two difficulties with such a statement. Firstly, most people are stronger, more robust, and more energetic in their twenties than they are in their thirties.[17] And secondly, if *ko'ach* refers to physical strength, why would the Mishnah, which delineates spiritual milestones, exalt it as a major landmark?

In order to understand in what way thirty is in fact a time of strength, we first need to understand what true strength really is.[18]

True Strength: *A Unification of Energy*

True strength comes from focusing all one's energies into a concentrated area. Martial arts experts who are able to break slabs of wood and concrete with their bare hands explain that the way they achieve this startling feat is by focusing all their body's energy into one point — their hand. The force of the blow comes from their ability to channel and concentrate all their internal energy into one specific part of their body in a cohesive, harmonized fashion.

We find this concept of strength in Chazal, regarding Yaakov Avinu.

When Yaakov was on his way to Lavan's house, he met a group of shepherds standing around a well, which was covered with a large stone. The stone was so big that the shepherds were unable to move it until they had all gathered together. Yaakov, however, was able to single-handedly roll the stone off the well.[19]

From the use of a superfluous word in the verse, Chazal learn that Yaakov moved the rock as effortlessly as one removes a plug from the mouth of a flask. The Torah specifically included the extra word to teach us how incredibly strong Yaakov was.[20]

But if the strength of Yaakov was due to his powerful muscles, why would the Torah bother to teach us about it? Moreover, Yaakov's act is mentioned in our annual prayer for rain, *Tefillas Geshem*. If all he used was brute strength, why do we mention his feat as a merit for which G-d should bless us with rain?

The answer is that Yaakov possessed more than mere physical strength. As the text of *Tefillas Geshem* reads, he had *yichud lev*, the ability to unite all his energies. By concentrating on his great desire to help the shepherds, he focused all his energies together, attaining superhuman levels of strength. It is Yaakov's *yichud lev* — his ability to direct his inner strength and desires into a concentrated area — that we recall every year as a merit to receive rain.[21]

Similarly, the strength of a thirty-year-old refers to the ability to focus all his energies into one area.[22]

When a person is in his twenties, he explores different options. With regard to Torah learning, he may try one *kollel* and then another. Or he may experiment with different methods of learning, trying to determine which style and approach suit him best. The same holds true for his occupation. He may begin taking one course in one field, and then switch to a different one, until he discovers which particular specialty or line of work is most appropriate for him.

The twenties, then, are a time when he gets to know himself, learning what his capabilities are and in which areas he is particularly talented. One could say that a person spends his twenties "pursuing" different life experiences.

But by the time he reaches thirty, he should have learned enough about himself to know what his talents and unique qualities are. At this stage, he can concentrate on these strong points, developing them and devoting his life to achieving what he alone can achieve. Having discovered his strengths, he can dedicate himself to fulfilling his mission in life, be it in Torah learning or in any other field.

Thus, the strength of the thirty-year-old refers to his ability to focus and concentrate his energies into one area, thereby allowing him to attain his full strength and potential.

Back to the *Levi'im*

Upon further reflection, we find that the *Levi'im* are the source for this kind of strength as well. As a group, they had many jobs: singing, playing musical instruments, guarding the *Mishkan*, and opening and closing its gates. As individuals, however, each *Levi* had a specific task that he had to perform. In fact, if he switched tasks, he could be liable for the death penalty.[23]

Although a *Levi* began working at thirty, he first had to train for five years.[24] During this time, he learned all the laws pertaining to the *Levi'im's* work, including those laws that did not pertain to his particular specialty. In other words, even if he himself was going to become a gatekeeper, he was still required to study all the other laws the *Levi'im* had to know for their various tasks.[25]

Hence, thirty was the age when each *Levi* focused on one specific area.

According to some opinions, the *Levi'im* could begin working at twenty-five, but they weren't assigned to any particular job until thirty.[26] In other words, a *Levi* was free to work at different jobs and didn't have to commit himself to one specific duty until his thirtieth birthday. Thus, the *Levi'im* are, in a very real sense, the classic source of this idea of specializing at thirty. Not only did they study different lines of work, they actually tried their hands at various occupations until they settled on the one that suited them best.[27]

Sometimes, zeroing in on one's special interest requires strength of character. This is because, having discovered his talents, a person may find that his strengths and interests are different from those of his friends. Social pressure may push him to abandon his unique capabilities and just follow the crowd. In order to bring out his individuality, he would need to overcome his fear of being different.

In this sense, thirty is the natural progression after twenty. At twenty a person breaks away from his parents in order to become an independent personality. Instead of being considered merely an extension of his parents, he begins his own life and forms his own identity. At thirty he breaks away from the rest of the world, setting himself apart from his friends and peers in order to fulfill his unique mission in life. Instead of being concerned about what others may say, he should use his spark of individuality to illuminate the world with the specific task for which he was created.

The Forties: *Midlife Opportunity*

בן ארבעים לבינה

A Forty-Year-Old for Understanding

A person's power of reasoning and ability to think are strongest at forty.[28] At this age he is able to perceive matters with a greater depth than previously possible.[29] Indeed, Chazal say that only after a student reaches forty can he, in retrospect, truly comprehend his teacher's words. Although he certainly understands what he learned before, he does not fully appreciate the impact of the teachings until he turns forty.[30]

The reason that a person's mental abilities are strongest at forty is because his physical strength begins to wane. As his body weakens, his intellectual capabilities become sharper and more pronounced.[31] It is in recognition of this heightened intellectual capacity that the Sages ruled that a person should not decide halachic matters[32] or learn Kabbala[33] until he reaches the age of forty.

Contrast the Mishnah's positive view of forty to the negative one often taken by the secular world.

In secular circles, forty is "thought to be the quintessential age at which men and women experience a midlife crisis."[34] Forty-year-olds commonly experience intense feelings of restlessness and unhappiness, and undergo great emotional and professional instability. Carl Jung noted that "statistics show a rise in the frequency of mental depressions in men about forty."[35]

Perhaps Chazal's observation about people's physical drives weakening at forty could explain why many individuals go through such trauma at that age.

People map out their lives in their twenties and thirties based on their strong physical desires and energies. But as they enter their forties, their energies begin to wane and they no longer derive the same satisfaction from physical pleasures as they used to. As a result, they become dissatisfied with life and begin searching for something new. Unfortunately, without a clear sense of purpose and direction, this search often leads them to change jobs or enter new relationships that suffer from the same lack of meaning as their previous ones.

Rather than solve the problem at its root, which could be achieved by pursuing mentally stimulating activities, they merely discover new forms of physical stimulation. But trying to use new physical pursuits to appease dissatisfaction with old ones is as futile as trying to compensate for missing puzzle pieces by rearranging the puzzle's order.

If he were truly wise, the forty-year-old would utilize his newly powerful mental abilities to strengthen his relationship with G-d. This is a special opportunity for him to study new *sefarim* and relearn the old ones with added depth. For both men and women it can be an ideal time for a new look at daily mitzvos that might previously have been observed by rote and understood only superficially. With one's increased intellect, these mitzvos can now be restudied, so that one begins to perceive their inherent beauty, depth, wisdom, and subtle interconnectedness.

Reaching forty is a joyous occasion, not a depressing one. It is a time to undertake new learning projects and rejoice in the deeper insight and heightened powers of perception with which a person has now been blessed. Instead of making superficial adjustments, the wise forty-year-old will make fundamental changes, increasing his attachment to spiritual pursuits and embracing his *Yiddishkeit* with even more enthusiasm and understanding.[36]

The Fifties: *Somebody Finally Cares What You Think*

בן חמישים לעצה

A Fifty-Year-Old for Advice

The ability to offer advice does not, on the face of it, appear to be a milestone in a person's development. While being able to counsel people is certainly an important stage in life, in comparison to the previous stages of development — independence, specialization, heightened intelligence — it does not seem to be of such significance.

In order to appreciate the importance of this phase, we need to understand what is meant by advice.

When Chazal speak about giving advice, they are not referring to the relaying of technical information from one person to another, such as offering your opinion on what should be worn to a particular event or suggesting where to find good travel deals. Rather, what Chazal are referring to is the ability to help people resolve life-issues and overcome personal challenges.

In order to give this kind of advice effectively, one needs the ability to enter into another person's world. It is not enough to think about how *you* would handle the situation, or what *you* would do. You must be able to think through the issue based on the other person's needs and personality: What is best for *him*? What are *his* strengths and weaknesses? Where do *his* talents lie?[37]

Seeing Through Another's Eyes

Rabbi Eliyahu Meir Bloch describes how his father, Rabbi Yosef Leib Bloch, would give people advice by first attempting to understand their character. He didn't advise them based on his own perspective, but would attempt, in effect, to "become" the questioner, viewing the problem through the other's eyes. By doing so, he was able to suggest a course of action that would be best for that person.

On a number of occasions, Reb Eliyahu Meir entered his father's study to find him sitting, brow furrowed and deeply engaged in thought, with a layman from the community. Reb Eliyahu Meir assumed that the person had asked his father about a difficult Gemara, or had presented him with a contradiction in the Rambam. But he soon realized that the man had come to ask his father's advice about a personal problem, and that in order to arrive at the right counsel, his father was struggling mightily to comprehend the questioner's essential nature and character so that he could offer him an appropriate solution.[38]

To arrive at a proper understanding of another person's inner self and his needs is not a simple matter. It is often complicated by the fact that the advice-seeker himself may be out of touch with his own reality and may not be able to see the real issues underlying his dilemma. He may ascribe importance to areas that are in fact irrelevant and may be emphasizing the wrong points altogether. In such cases, the advice-giver would need to have the ability to perceive the unspoken messages that are hidden beneath a person's words, and see beyond what is being directly presented. He must be able to decipher what lies at the heart of the problem. In doing so, he will often need to arrive at a better understanding of the other person than that person has of himself.

Shlomo Hamelech compares the process of offering advice to the process of drawing water from the depths of a well. "*Mayim amukim eitzah b'lev ish, v'ish tevuna yidlena* — Counsel is like deep water in the heart of man, but the wise man will draw it out."[39] The reason he mentions deep water is because true advice is often resting deep beneath the surface, obscured beyond recognition by the waters that cover it. To offer good advice requires one to delve into the recesses of another person's character in order to find what is buried in the depths of his being and then to draw it out like water from the bottom of a well.

But giving advice is not just about putting yourself into another person's shoes. It requires connecting to other people on an emotional level as well as an intellectual one.

Imagine someone with a food disorder seeking advice on how to overcome his love of chocolate and being presented with all the latest medical findings on the dangers of overeating. Such "advice" may frighten the person into controlling his bingeing for a few days, but it will not provide any long-term solutions. Scientific evidence only addresses a person's intellect, not his emotions, and unless the problem is dealt with on an emotional level as well, no solution will be reached.

The human personality consists of two parts: the cold, intellectual aspect of a person (*sechel*) and the emotional and feeling aspect (*regesh*). One may think that in order to arrive at an accurate decision, one needs to use his *sechel* alone. After all, *sechel* is the root of logic and rational thought, while *regesh* tends to cloud one's thoughts, causing a person to think irrationally.

The truth is, however, that in order to help another person, one must be able to relate to his emotional needs and desires. One has to be able to sense what it is that excites him, so that he can arrive at a workable solution. Ignoring the *regesh* part of a person may at first seem to provide a simpler and easier solution, but eventually the *regesh* returns, destroying the well-laid-out plan.[40]

A man once came to Rabbi Shlomo Wolbe for advice on what to do about his son's over-involvement in soccer. The father wanted to know if it was reasonable to place a limit on his son's playing time. Rabbi Wolbe replied that it was, to which the father then asked if half an hour would be an appropriate time limit.

"Half an hour?!" exclaimed Rabbi Wolbe. "You can't play anything in half an hour!"[41]

Rabbi Wolbe was eighty-six years old at the time and had never played a game of soccer in his life, yet he managed to relate to the boy's attachment to the sport, sensing his love for the game. He thus understood that half an hour would do nothing to satisfy his need to play. The boy's father, on the other hand, who was forty years Rabbi Wolbe's junior and much closer to the boy's age, had tried to deal with the issue on a purely intellectual level, ignoring the boy's passion for the game.[42]

In order to give proper advice, one needs to connect to another person's feelings without permitting himself to be overcome by those emotions. Had Rabbi Wolbe felt the boy's excitement for soccer as strongly as the boy himself felt it, Rabbi Wolbe would not have been able to examine the issue objectively and offer his sagacious advice. Yet, had he not empathized with the boy's excitement at all, he would have ignored an intrinsic part of the young boy's personality, which would have prevented him from reaching an effective solution. One needs to reach a fine balance between feeling what the other person feels and retaining an appropriate sense of detachment.

Giving advice, then, demands the gift of being able to view things through another person's eyes without allowing that to become the only source of vision. It requires opening one's heart to be moved by what moves the other, without being completely overwhelmed by those feelings.

The Greatness in Being Able to Give Advice

Once we understand some of the issues involved in giving solid advice, we begin to realize how reaching "the age of advice" marks a major stage of development in a person's character.

On one level, it signifies the ability to lead others and bring out their potential. Until this point, the stages of development centered on the person himself and on his own growth: *his* reaching adulthood, *his* discovering *his* unique talents, and *his* becoming wiser. At fifty he finally branches out to others, helping other people reach their potential. Indeed, Chazal say that when choosing a leader, one should make certain to select a person who is over fifty years old.[43]

In this sense, fifty is a natural transition from the previous stages. Having actualized his own potential during the previous years, the fifty-year-old is now in a position to help others do the same.[44]

On another level, fifty marks a new plateau in his own maturity. If he can give advice to others, which, as we mentioned, requires feeling their excitement without being swept away by it, then he can do the same for himself. In other words, he can relate to his own emotions, giving them their appropriate weight and taking them seriously, without allowing them to carry him away and control him.

In his younger years, a person is controlled mainly by his emotions. Should a child set his heart on something, he will not easily be swayed by reasoning, for logic holds no place in his psyche. He is totally at the whim of his emotions. That is why children erupt into laughter and burst into tears with much more ease and frequency than adults. They do not engage in serious thought, and are more happy-go-lucky. Indeed, the Hebrew word for a youth, *na'ar*, comes from the root *er*, awake, because his emotions are in a heightened state of alertness and are the driving force behind his actions.[45]

As a young person develops into full maturity, however, his ability to think increases and he becomes more logical and rational. Whereas he used to be more excitable, he now becomes more reserved, and less capricious and erratic. At fifty, his *sechel* and *regesh* strike a unique balance, giving him the ability to listen with one ear to what his emotions desire, while taking a step back and weighing in his mind what logic dictates.

This weakening of emotions can sometimes cause people to feel dejected, wondering why they find it so much harder than before to laugh or cry. But instead of dejection they should experience delight, for this new stage has many advantages: they are now able to carry out projects and pursue endeavors with more lasting power, logic, and reason, and without the vagaries that are an inevitable part of a more emotional nature.

Giving good advice is no easy matter: it requires a deep understanding of other people as well as an ability to think clearly about what is best for them. The effective adviser is not only able to view situations from the perspective of others, but has developed the ability to connect with others both intellectually and emotionally. These attributes do not simply occur by chance. They are the result of a great amount of life experience and decades of concern for the welfare of others. Only someone who has reached the age of fifty and has been working on connecting with others on several levels can acquire such attributes.[46]

Little wonder that the commentators say that if you need guidance in life — make sure to go to someone over fifty.[47]

The Sixties: *More than a Senior-Citizen Discount*

בן ששים לזקנה

A Sixty-Year-Old for Wisdom

At sixty, a person attains a new level of wisdom, known as *zikna*. The word *zakein* (from which *zikna* is derived) is an acronym for *zeh shekana chochma* — the one who has acquired wisdom.[48] The wisdom a sixty-year-old attains is the wisdom of life that is gained from many years of living in and experiencing the world.[49]

Zikna is often mistranslated as "old age." "Old" refers to something that has passed its "sell-by date," something whose usefulness has expired. Indeed, the word for "old" in Hebrew — *yashan* — has the same root as *sheina* (sleep), and *ishon* (darkness), both of which portray negative images of inactivity and withdrawal.[50] Translating *zikna* as "old" implies that the sixty-year-old is past his prime and is of secondary importance, like an old product that is better replaced by a new one.[51]

This misnomer is taken from the Western world. Western culture tends to measure people according to their level of productivity, and therefore regards elderly people, who are no longer as productive as the younger generation, as being of lesser importance. Consider the justification often heard for why elderly people deserve respect, namely, that they worked for many years and contributed a lot to society. The emphasis is on what they achieved in the past — what they *did* and who they *were* — rather than on who they are now.[52]

The negative light in which secular society regards aging is clear from the way people react to the mention of growing old. If a person comments that he is getting old, his acquaintances will usually try to deny it, saying, "It's not true," as if "growing old" were a negative and derogatory term, a phenomenon to be avoided at all costs, to the point that anyone who even suggests the thought must be comforted or corrected.[53]

Chazal, on the other hand, view the aging process positively, noting the new level of understanding that the sixty-year-old attains. In fact, the word *zakein* is often used as a form of praise to connote wisdom. The Torah, for example, refers to the leaders of the generation as the *zekeinim*,[54] and when the Gemara wants to rule authoritatively on a matter, it states, "*Kevar hora zakein* — the *zakein* has already ruled,"[55] implying that there is nothing more to argue about.[56]

The Age of Wisdom

An elderly person's importance does not stem from what he achieved in the past, but from who he is at this point in his life. His many years in this world afford him a level of wisdom and a breadth of vision unmatched by his younger counterparts. Having watched regimes and governments rise and fall, and having lived through times of war and peace, he is not easily flustered by difficulties that arise, but is able to look at the wider picture, viewing the situation thoughtfully and calmly. He has lived through enough, and has gained enough experience, to be able to rise above petty issues and not be swept away by the fads of the day.[57]

Secular culture often portrays old age as a "second childhood," a time when the elderly regress to engaging in the same fun and games as children. One newspaper article, entitled "The Fun Life for Young and Old," offered "a guide to August activities for senior citizens and children" — a puppet show, a magic act, and so forth.[58] Obviously this is an extreme example, and most elderly people would be offended if they considered the full implications. But when we think about other activities in which elderly people commonly participate, ones which Western culture deems appropriate for them, we realize that these, too, are childish in that they don't utilize the older person's talents and wisdom.

Golf, bridge, and bingo, to name a few, can all be played by youngsters just the same as they can by the elderly. In engaging in these pastimes to the exclusion of more serious things, the older person ignores the wealth of wisdom he has accumulated during his long life in this world, whiling away his time with the mindless expectations of the society around him.

The wise and perceptive sixty-year-old will take his hard-won knowledge and use it constructively to benefit those around him. He will, for example, volunteer to help the poor or deprived, the sick or the lonely, comforting them in a way that only someone with his experience can. He may not have been the president of the United States, a high-powered CEO, or a renowned *talmid chacham*, but by virtue of his experience he will always have something to teach others. By so doing, he will enlighten and uplift those around him with his discerning visions of the future and his insightful memories of the past.[59]

The Seventies: A Wrinkle in Time

בן שבעים לשיבה

A Seventy-Year-Old for Seiva

The word *seiva* refers to the fact that by the time a person reaches the age of seventy, most of his hair has turned white.[60] When Rabbi Elazar ben Azaria's hair miraculously went white overnight at the age of eighteen, he commented that he was now like a seventy-year-old.[61] He specifically mentioned seventy, and not sixty or eighty, because seventy is the time associated with white hair.[62]

Seiva also refers to the general signs of physical weakness that accompany old age.[63] Indeed, the word *seiva* is related to the word *yavesh* (dry),[64] for it is the body's drying up that causes a person's hair to turn white and his body to grow weak.[65]

This stage of development does not seem consistent with the rest of the Mishnah. The previous stages described spiritual progressions that take a person to new levels of understanding and maturity. Turning white and growing weak, on the other hand, are physical signs of aging, ones that do not appear to reflect any spiritual growth.

In order to appreciate how the stage of *seiva* does indeed mark a spiritual development, we need to understand that according to Chazal, the physical changes a person's body undergoes are there to remind him of his mortality and his need to do *teshuva*.[66]

Physical Signs, Spiritual Reminders

The Western world would have us believe that the symptoms of old age — loss of hair, wrinkling skin, weakening body, lack of energy — are just an unfortunate biological eventuality, one that is best covered over. Indeed, millions of dollars are spent each year trying to do just that.

The Torah, however, teaches us that G-d specifically incorporated the symptoms of old age into the natural processes of our bodies in order to remind us of something very significant: that we are nearing the end of our lives and should prepare accordingly.[67]

The fact that as a person ages his eyesight fades and he grows weaker isn't an accident of nature, but an intentional part of G-d's plan of creation. The Designer par excellence formed us with a built-in wake-up mechanism, drawing our attention to the fact that we are traveling day and night toward our final resting place.

When you are on an airplane that is about to land, you notice the signs: the air pressure changes, your ears begin to pop, your stomach momentarily flies upward, the fasten-seat-belt sign appears. If you want to have a smooth and safe landing, you stop wandering around the plane and return to your seat. Ignoring the warning signals and continuing to roam around the plane as if you were in mid-flight would be foolish.

The symptoms of old age play the same sort of role, reminding us that we are nearing the end of our trip in this world and that if we want to have a safe and smooth landing at our final destination we should heed the warning signs.

Thus, although *seiva* describes a physical development, it is meant to lead to a spiritual awakening,[68] which is consistent with the rest of the Mishnah.

Retirement: *A Time for Spiritual Work*

As a wise and thoughtful person ages, he begins to withdraw from the physical pursuits of this world and concentrate on refining his character and increasing his share of Torah and mitzvos. Indeed, as his time left in this world decreases, his commitment to spiritual pursuits increases.[69]

This lesson is particularly important today when the average age of retirement is steadily rising.

Throughout most of the previous century and up until the mid-eighties, the average age of retirement gradually decreased and people retired earlier and earlier. That trend has reversed itself, however, and increasing numbers of people are opting to delay their retirement. For those at the lower end of the socioeconomic spectrum, the decision to continue working isn't one of personal choice but one of financial necessity. Those who have financial security, however, could afford to retire but choose to continue working in order to derive satisfaction[70] and personal fulfillment[71] from their professions. Considering the loss of identity that often accompanies retirement,[72] perhaps people also choose to continue working as a way of avoiding this difficult adjustment.

The secular world views retirement as a time to take life easy and indulge in more physical pursuits, such as buying a second home and traveling to far-off places. Faced with such emptiness and lack of purpose, it is no wonder that many people experience a loss of identity and prefer to continue working than face the feelings of uselessness that retirement often brings with it. Work provides a sense of meaning and fulfillment — leisure doesn't.

If we look at the Torah's outlook on retirement we will see why this issue does not exist.

The Torah provides one instance of a group that worked only until a certain age. This group was the *Levi'im*. At fifty, they stopped carrying the vessels of the *Mishkan* and began advising the younger *Levi'im*.[73] But they didn't stop working completely at that point; they simply switched from performing more physical duties to performing less physical ones that were better suited to their age.

We see that according to the Torah, a person never stops working in the sense of being productive and active. All he does is switch from one type of work to another. Less physical? Yes. Less creative or mentally demanding? Not at all. On the contrary, the job of advising the younger *Levi'im* required more knowledge and expertise than that of hauling the vessels.

Retirement is not a time to leave work in order to fill one's time with trivialities, but rather, a time to shift from one form of productivity to another, a time to begin achieving more spiritually. The Torah informs us that Moshe was eighty and Aharon eighty-three when they first went to Pharaoh to request permission to leave Egypt.[74] According to one of the commentators, the Torah deliberately records their ages to emphasize that in the Torah's eyes the latter years of one's life are meant for increased achievement and productivity.[75]

We don't have to look far back in history to see examples of people achieving tremendous things in their old age. Rabbi Shlomo Wolbe opened a yeshiva when he was eighty. Furthermore, he wasn't just a figurehead, but was actively involved with each of the students.[76]

The Bostoner Rebbe, Rabbi Levi Yitzchak Horowitz, established his shul and chassidic court in Jerusalem when he was sixty-five. At an age when most people are going into retirement and taking life easy, he was building a new community.[77]

These *Gedolim* didn't feel a loss of identity in their older years. On the contrary, they felt an *added* sense of identity, as they were doing what they did best, bringing together all the skills and wisdom they had gathered throughout their lives and using them for the benefit of the community. Their golden years are a culmination of their life's work, the most thrilling and stimulating years of their existence.[78]

As we will see in the next section, when a person uses his remaining years to benefit others and to occupy himself with spiritual pursuits, he merits long life.

The Eighties and Going Beyond

בן שמונים לגבורה בן תשעים לשוח בן מאה כאילו מת ועבר
ובטל מן העולם

An Eighty-Year-Old for Might, a Ninety-Year-Old for Speech, a Hundred-Year-Old Is As If He Were Dead, Moved On, and Gone From the World

The final stages of the Mishnah continue to delineate the spiritual powers that a person attains as he ages. At eighty, a person's desire for physical pleasure weakens, thus granting him "might" over his evil inclination and the ability to concentrate more easily on spiritual matters like Torah and mitzvos.[79] At ninety, he enters the stage of speech, devoting his time to speaking words of Torah,[80] prayer, and praise of G-d.[81] And at a hundred, he reaches such a state of purity and elevation that it is as if he has already left this physical world and moved on.[82]

Although the length of a person's life is determined by the strength of his body and other physical factors, when he uses his time to cling to G-d and follow His ways, he merits living longer than was originally ordained.[83] As the verse says, "*yiras Hashem tosif yamim* — Fear of G-d increases one's days."[84]

When the *Tanna'im* were asked why they merited long life, they listed mitzvos and good *middos* in which they were particularly scrupulous,[85] thus teaching us that it is not just physical causes but also spiritual ones that lead to long life.[86]

The Midrash tells of a very old woman who would arise early every morning for shul, even when there were other matters she needed to attend to. The woman grew so old that she became tired of living in this world and wanted her life to come to an end. She sought advice on what to do and was told to stop going to shul. She died three days later.[87]

The point of this Midrash is not that elderly women should get up for shul every morning, but to show us that it is in the merit of striving for higher goals that a person is granted long life. People naturally want to tend exclusively to their own needs, without having to concern themselves with matters outside their own world. The Midrash teaches, however, that it is precisely those acts like going to shul, which push a person beyond his own domain and require special effort, that earn him extended time in this world.

The Chasam Sofer writes that a person may have fulfilled his mission in life and yet be kept alive for the sake of the benefit he brings others.[88]

When Rabbi Eliyahu Lopian was almost eighty, he was offered a position as a *mashgiach* of a major yeshiva, but declined, expressing his desire to spend his final days learning. When he went to see the Chazon Ish about the matter, the Chazon Ish told him that the promise of freshness, youthfulness, and vigor in old age ("*Od yenuvun b'seiva, desheinim v'ra'ananim yiheyu*") is dependent on spreading G-d's Name in the world ("*Lehaggid ki yashar Hashem...*").[89] Rabbi Lopian accepted the post, which he held for another twenty years, until he passed away when he was almost one hundred![90]

The above are spiritual considerations which suggest why strengthening one's service of G-d leads to long life. But there is also a more down-to-earth, psychological factor for this phenomenon.

People have a deeply rooted need to grow. G-d embedded this need into our psyche so that we may fulfill the purpose for which we were created, which is to strive to grow ever closer to G-d and earn our place in the World to Come. An easy life may not present any challenges, but it also provides no opportunities for growth. As far as the human spirit is concerned, that spells death. Chazal summed this up when they said, "*Ein adam meis ella mitoch habatala* — Man only dies as a result of inactivity,"[91] a fact that gerontologists are only beginning to discover 2,000 years after Chazal made this statement.[92] Vitality comes from accomplishing and striving to reach beyond one's present level. Concentrating solely on one's own needs strips a person of this vitality, causing him to sink into depression and decay.

When the time came for Moshe Rabbeinu to die, Moshe refused to leave this world. He pleaded to be allowed to remain alive in the form of an animal, and, when that request was denied, in the form of a bird. After that failed as well, he fought the *malach hamaves* with all the strength he had, refusing to yield his soul under any circumstances.[93]

Moshe was one hundred twenty years old at the time and had already accomplished more than any other human being. Yet he tried with all his might to gain just one more moment of life in this world, for perhaps in that brief moment he might attain an even higher level of spirituality.

Upon reaching Moshe's age and achievements, most people would become complacent, satisfied with their lives, and resigned to leaving this world. But for the one who truly lives Torah — no matter how young or old — there are just not enough hours in the day. Every moment is another precious opportunity to acquire more knowledge and do more good deeds.

The ages of man: how quickly they pass. The twenty-year-old, filled with vigor and ambition, soon finds himself, as if in the blink of an eye, sixty years old, then seventy and eighty. If he is wise, he will welcome each new milestone, for each one has its own precious qualities and unique characteristics. The Sages of this remarkable Mishnah teach us that, whatever our age, it presents us with special gifts with which to grow personally and to relate more effectively to others and to our Creator. For those who take this Mishnah seriously, there are no midlife crises, and no traumas upon reaching certain points in life.

People often say to one another, "Act your age." But our Sages teach that it is not enough to behave a certain age. It is even more important to *be* that age, for each new decade of life provides a new challenge to become that which we were truly meant to be.

The endnotes to this chapter are found in the Appendix.

The Source and
the Secret

פרק ה' משנה כ"ו: בֶּן בַּג בַּג אוֹמֵר, הַפֹּךְ בָּה וַהֲפֹךְ בָּה,
דְּכֹלָּא בָהּ. וּבַהּ תֶּחֱזֵי, וְסִיב וּבְלֵה בָהּ, וּמִנַּהּ לָא תְזוּעַ,
שֶׁאֵין לְךָ מִדָּה טוֹבָה הֵימֶנָּה.

Chapter 5, Mishnah 26: *Ben Bag Bag says: Turn it [Torah] over and over for everything is in it. See with it, grow old and gray with it, and do not budge from it, as there is no better measuring rod than it.*

"Rabbanim, don't interfere with politics," David Ben-Gurion admonished the *Gedolim* in 1951 when they stated their opinion on the topic of women's national service.[1] His remark, which has often been echoed by others,[2] is founded on the mistaken belief that the Torah only deals with so-called ritualistic matters, like the kashrus of a pot or the height of a sukka, but has nothing to do with worldly affairs, such as the running of a country.[3]

Delve into Torah, says the Mishnah, *d'chola ba* — for *everything is in it:* every facet of creation and every wisdom of the world.[4] The Torah offers direction on the most diverse topics, from how to become a leader and speak in public, to how to view world events and care for the environment. As Reb Yitzchak of Volozhin put it, "There is no question in the world whose answer cannot be found in Torah…. One only needs to open his eyes to find where it is written."[5]

Everything Is in the Torah

The greatest men in our history sought and derived all of their knowledge from the Torah. Shlomo Hamelech, the wisest man who ever lived, gleaned all of his knowledge in astrology, botany, medicine, the language of animals, birds, reptiles, demons, and spirits from the Torah.[6]

Dovid Hamelech referred to the Torah's testimonies as his "men of counsel."[7] Whereas most rulers have a cabinet of ministers to whom they turn for advice, Dovid Hamelech sought guidance from the Torah. Moreover, the Torah provided better advice than the finest of ministers. Ministers can only offer advice in their particular fields of expertise, whereas the Torah was equivalent to *all* Dovid's "men of counsel," providing him with direction in all areas and circumstances.[8]

Even in our generation there are those whose study and understanding of the Torah is so in-depth that they are able to gain clarity on scientific subjects and other areas of worldly knowledge. The Chazon Ish had a profound understanding of human anatomy and was able to guide doctors on how best to perform surgeries, even drawing detailed diagrams for them.[9] Yet he never attended medical school or any lectures on the subject.[10] He learned everything from the Torah.

A distraught Jew came to him one night for advice. His son was deathly ill and the doctors were faced with a dilemma. On the one hand they felt that without an operation he would not have long to live. On the other hand the operation itself was fraught with danger and had a low success rate, with many patients not surviving the surgery.

The Chazon Ish listened to the man's predicament while he was lying down with his eyes closed. He lay still for almost fifteen minutes, buried in thought. When he finally opened his eyes, he asked the boy's father which doctor would be performing the surgery. Upon hearing the name, the Chazon Ish said that they should proceed with the operation, and he instructed the father to tell the doctor in his name that the operation should be carried out.

When the doctor heard what the Chazon Ish had said, he commented, "It is true that the Chazon Ish is always accurate with his prognoses, but in this case he is mistaken. There is no hope." Nevertheless, he acceded to the father's plea and performed the surgery. When he emerged from the operating room six hours later, he told the father that if his son regained consciousness in the next twenty-four hours it was a good sign, but if not, the end was surely near.

Twenty-four hours passed and the son was still unconscious. The doctor threw up his hands in despair. The broken father hurried to the Chazon Ish, who told him, "Our allotted time is seventy-two hours." To the father's great joy, the boy opened his eyes after seventy-two hours and within a few weeks made a complete recovery.

Afterward, those close to the Chazon Ish asked him what he had been thinking about for so long when the father had first come. They also wanted to know from which source he had derived the seventy-two-hour wait.

The Chazon Ish replied that when he heard the doctor's report about the child not having long to live without the operation, he mentally reviewed the Gemara's discussion about whether we are allowed to put momentary life at risk for a chance of effecting a long-term extension of life, until he arrived at the conclusion that this is indeed permitted.[11] As for the number seventy-two, that was an explicit Mishnah, he said.[12]

We see that the Torah is not just a dry set of laws, but a living entity, encompassing all areas of life.

Dig and Discover

What is unique about the Torah is the way its knowledge needs to be retrieved. All the information is there, but in order to access it you have to "turn it over and over," digging for answers — just as one turns over layers of earth when searching for a lost object.[13]

Why is the Torah organized in this manner? Why couldn't G-d have presented the Torah's attitude on all kinds of topics in an organized and easy-to-find manner, like an encyclopedia? Why the need to excavate answers with toil, sweat, and a lifetime of effort?

To answer this question we first need to understand why the Torah is described as being deep.[14]

For any medium to have depth, it must simultaneously exist on higher and lower levels. For example, were the sea only to have an upper layer without any water below, it would be shallow like a pond. Yet if it only had a lower layer without any water on top, it would simply be low, but it would not be deep. Depth requires that an upper and lower layer coexist together.[15]

The Torah is described as deep because it contains infinite layers of meaning, all of which are true and exist in complete harmony. When a child learns Bereishis he understands the verses on one level. As he grows older and learns the same verses again, he reads more into the text and attains new levels of understanding. In fact, a person can read the same verse in the Torah again and again throughout his life, uncovering new layers of meaning each time. Indeed, the Vilna Gaon perceived that the details of every creation that ever existed and that will ever exist — human, animal, plant, and inanimate object — are all contained in Bereishis.[16]

The new levels of perception a person discovers in the text do not negate his original interpretation of the text; they add to it. The Torah is able to accommodate multiple layers of understanding simultaneously. The cheder boy's understanding of the verse is as true as the Vilna Gaon's interpretation. Most other books are not like that. They are either easy to understand, such as a child's spelling book, or difficult to understand, such as quantum physics, but they cannot be both at the same time. The Torah, however, contains an infinite number of layers, all existing side by side.[17]

Hard-Earned Wisdom

The reason that the Torah could not be laid out "flat," like an encyclopedia, is because the Torah is G-d's way of revealing Himself to the world, and, as such, its words must infuse us in a very deep, intrinsic way.[18]

When you read an encyclopedia, you connect to the information it contains on a purely intellectual level. But Torah is not meant to enter just our minds, like a cold textbook of information. It is meant to permeate our entire being, forming the very core of our existence and becoming the center of our lives. The only way to form a strong, inner bond of this sort is by chiseling away at its words, using all one's heart and soul to uncover hidden layers of meaning.

This explains the meaning of the coming phrase in the Mishnah, which says that one should "grow old and gray" with Torah.[19]

With an encyclopedia, once you have read a particular entry there is no reason to read it again, unless you want to refresh your memory or you did not fully understand the material the first time. But either way, you will not discover any new insights or uncover depth that was not there before. With Torah, however, you can reread it until you're gray, for the more you dig away at the surface, the more you uncover.[20] You never outgrow or tire of learning Torah, for as you delve deeper into its words, you uncover new layers of meaning. It's like digging in a mine where the soil is abundant with precious stones. You till the earth and discover a rare gem, a new insight. After unearthing your treasure and rejoicing over it, you continue to dig more, finding yet more jewels and new levels of comprehension.[21]

The Mishnah concludes by saying that there is no better measuring rod than Torah. In other words, the levels of knowledge and understanding that man attains through his own intellect will never reach the level of truth contained in the Torah.[22] It is clear that besides offering a unique, G-d-oriented perspective on every conceivable topic and moral issue, the Torah's dictates and insights always contain more discernment and profundity than any other system of thought.[23]

Secular wisdom is referred to as *chochma chitzonis*, external wisdom.[24] The reason is that it derives its knowledge from analyzing the world itself, whereas the Torah derives its knowledge from examining the very source of the world.[25]

The previous Mishnah about the developmental stages a person goes through in each phase of life provides an excellent example.

The way psychologists learn about human development is by observing many people and recording their observations. They watch how children play and note when they begin developing various skills. They interview adults and conduct polls to assess how people grow throughout their lives.

The Torah approaches the topic from a different perspective entirely. Its insights into human development are not based on surveys or on what we observe to be true, but on G-d's plan for life and what He teaches us about human development.

G-d formed man as a twenty-year-old because that is the beginning of adulthood. He commanded the Levi'im to begin working in their particular field in the Mishkan at thirty because that is when man should specialize. That forty is a time of deeper understanding was not arrived at by testing the IQs of thousands of forty-year-olds, but by analyzing what the Torah has to say about turning forty. The same idea holds true for all the other ages mentioned in the Mishnah.

Psychologists can only describe what they see. The Torah reveals man's essence: who we really are, what our strengths are, and what we are capable of achieving at each stage of life.

The same idea applies to the natural sciences. Scientists can only reveal the nature of the world by looking at it from the outside, experimenting, observing, and postulating various theories. But the reasons why various phenomena exist and their intended roles in creation are beyond the realm of science — as scientists themselves admit. These truths can only be revealed by the Torah.

And so it is with history. Historians can record which events took place when, and offer theories for what caused various wars and revolutions to happen. But the underlying reasons and causes behind the surface events, and what we are meant to learn from them, are only revealed to Chazal. That is why the Chazon Ish once commented that "to write history you have to be a prophet."[26]

One author, who noted that "rabbis frequently hear the complaint that Orthodox Judaism is not 'with it,'" decided to write a book showing how "traditional Judaism does have something to say on contemporary matters." Without meaning to, he actually belittles the value of Torah. Torah does not just have "something to say" about the world and modern issues — it has everything to say, for it contains priceless wisdom and insights that far outweigh what any contemporary philosophy posits about the world.

The Torah's wisdom stems from G-d and will always surpass human wisdom. In fact, if after learning what the Torah has to say on a certain topic, it seems to be something we could have derived on our own from outside sources, we can be certain that we have not fully understood what the Torah is saying, and that we still need to uncover more layers.[27]

It has been this idea, together with the subject of the whole Mishnah, which has comprised the theme of this book.

While learning just a selection of the Mishnayos from *Pirkei Avos* we have been given a taste of the *"d'chola ba,"* that everything is dealt with in Torah: from how to acquire a friend, to how to control anger; from how to view the process of aging, to what we can learn from eagles and lions; from the right attitude to earning a livelihood, to the right way to use MP3 recorders.

It is noteworthy that, despite the profundities of the teachings, in each case they were compacted into no more than a few words, and only by paying close attention to every nuance of Chazal's language were their insights revealed to us. The use of the word "buy" in the phrase "buy for yourself a friend" taught us three things, and the choice of the singular word *friend* as opposed to the plural taught us another. The same is true of many of the Mishnayos we examined. The insights we uncovered, however, do not even scratch the surface of the depths contained in Torah, whose treasures still lie far beyond us.

We do not learn Torah just because we are commanded to. We learn it because it teaches us how to live and how to behave, how to think and relate to everything that happens in our lives with unmatched wisdom and clarity.[28] It is *Toras chaim* — a living Torah.

When we enter a new phase of life, or are faced with a dilemma of any sort, the first place we should turn to for direction is the Torah. After finding the area where the Torah deals with the general subject of our issue, we need to immerse ourselves in its words, prodding and poking and churning until — with the help of our teachers — the Torah's guidelines emerge from beneath the surface. We will then discover that not only does the Torah contain a viewpoint on every facet of life, but that its teachings surpass all others and are the most relevant aspect of our lives.

---

[1] *Pe'er Hador* 5:27.

[2] See R' Avi Shafran, "What *Da'at Torah* Really Means," *Jewish Week*, March 21, 2003; and R' Moshe Grylak, "Point of View," *Mishpacha*, June 23, 2004.

[3] In a letter, the Chazon Ish writes that one who subscribes to the Torah's authority in regard to halachic rulings but not in other areas of life distorts the Torah and has no place in the World to Come (*Pe'er Hador* 5:52–53). Part of the letter has been reprinted in *Igros Chazon Ish* 3:§92.

[4] Rabbeinu Yona (Vilna Shas ed.), Rabbeinu Ephraim (quoted in the last line of *Midrash Shmuel*), *Peirushei Rabbeinu Yitzchak ben Harav Shlomo MiToledo*, *Pirkei Moshe*, *Sefer Mussar*, *Mirkeves Hamishneh*, *Roshei Avos*, *Milei D'Avos*. See also Ramban (introduction to *Bereishis*), Rabbeinu Bachya (introduction to *Bereishis*), *Ma'oz Hadas* (chap. 6), and Vilna Gaon (commentary to *Sifra Ditzniusa*, chap. 5). Cf. Meiri and *Midrash Dovid*, which offer a different explanation of the Mishnah.

[5] Chofetz Chaim in the name of R' Itzele, quoted in *Kovetz Ma'amarim V'igros* 1:229.

[6] Ramban (introduction to *Bereishis*).

[7] *Tehillim* 119:24 with *Seforno*.

[8] R' Avrohom Chaim Feuer, *Tehillim*, 1427.

[9] *Pe'er Hador* 4:106–146. When Professor Yerachmiel Ashkenazi, head of the neurology department at Beilinson Hospital in Petach Tikva, was provided with a diagram of the brain showing how to carry out a surgical procedure, he asked the family which expert had given them the drawing, solving the patient's complicated problem (ibid., 138).

[10] Ibid., 127–128.

[11] The reference is to the passage in *Avoda Zara* 27b: אי חיישינן לחיי שעה.

[12] *Pe'er Hador* 4:144–146.

[13] See *Lechem Shamayim*.

[14] *Sanhedrin* 44b with Rashi ד"ה עתה באתי.

[15] R' Reuven Leuchter.

[16] Vilna Gaon, commentary to *Sifra Ditzniusa*, chap. 5.

[17] See *Midrash Shmuel*.
Chazal compare Torah scholars to fish in water (*Berachos* 61b) to bring out this point. Land creatures move in two dimensions: left-right and forward-backward, thus remaining on one plane. Fish are unique in that they move in three dimensions, gliding smoothly between upper and lower layers of water. The reason Torah scholars are compared to fish is because they are able to move between different layers of understanding in Torah, much as fish move in water.

[18] R' Reuven Leuchter.

[19] *Menoras Hama'or* (Al-Nakawa), chap. 5, "Talmud Torah," 317. See also Meiri.

[20] *Roshei Avos* mentions the idea of reading other books once, and the Torah many times.

[21] As Dovid Hamelech writes: "I rejoice over Your word like one who finds abundant spoil" (*Tehillim* 119:162).

[22] *Nachalas Avos*. See *Hachassid Yaavetz*.

[23] The Midrashic saying (*Eicha Rabba* 2:13) "*chochma bagoyim ta'amin…Torah bagoyim al ta'amin*" portrays this point: While non-Jews do possess wisdom (*chochma*), they cannot reach the highest form of wisdom referred to as *Torah*. See *Da'as Chochma U'mussar* 2:163.

[24] The phrase *chochma chitzonis* is mentioned in the *Rishonim*: Ibn Ezra (introduction to *Bereishis*), Rashba (Responsa 1:§418), Meiri (introduction to *Avos*), and Rosh (Responsa 55:§9).

[25] This difference between Torah and other wisdoms is discussed in *Drashos HaRan* §1. Cf. *Pachad Yitzchak, Chanuka*, 39, which explains the phrase *chochma chitzonis* differently.

[26] *Yemos Olam*, 7. A pointed example of the Torah's perception of history is Chazal's analysis of the Purim story. See *Michtav Me'Eliyahu* 1:76–77.

[27] On the verse "For it [the Torah] is not an empty thing *from you*" (*Devarim* 32:47), Chazal expound that if the Torah does seem empty it is only *from you*, that is, due to a lack of exertion in understanding its words. *Midrash Tanna'im, Devarim*, loc. cit. See also *Sifri, parashas Eikev, piska* 12.

[28] See *Michtavim U'ma'amarim* 4:125.

Appendix: Endnotes to "The Stages of Life"

[1] This reading of the word לשוח follows the commentators who read it as *lasuach* with the letter *sin* (*Sha'arei Teshuva* 2:§9 and others cited below in note 81). Cf. *Bartenura*.

[2] Robert Kastenbaum, ed., *Encyclopedia of Adult Development* (Phoenix: Oryx, 1993), 7.

[3] Although the commitment to a husband or wife is not to be compared to one's commitment to G-d, on one level the commitment to a spouse — with new challenges and tests that arise almost daily — is more challenging than a commitment to G-d, Whose demands do not change. The commitment to a spouse is different in kind than commitment to G-d. One requires the ability to meet changing circumstances and needs, while the other requires deepening commitment to a Being Whose demands remain constant.

[4] *Mirkeves Hamishneh.*

[5] Rashi; Rabbeinu Bachya; *Bartenura.*

[6] *Machzor Vitri; Bartenura; Mirkeves Hamishneh; Hachassid Yaavetz.*

[7] See *Yalkut Shimoni* (*Mishlei, remez* 929) that quotes R' Yishmael as saying that *na'arus* (childhood) ends at twenty. Other opinions in the Midrash there define *na'arus* as ending at twenty-five or thirty (ibid.).

[8] *Mirkeves Hamishneh.*

[9] Rashi; Rabbeinu Bachya; *Bartenura*. Cf. *Noda BiYehuda, Mahadura Tinyana, Yoreh De'ah* §164; *Chasam Sofer, Yoreh De'ah* §155.

[10] *Machzor Vitri; Bartenura; Mirkeves Hamishneh; Hachassid Yaavetz.*

[11] *Bereishis Rabba* 14:7.

[12] R' Reuven Leuchter.

[13] *Shemos* 2:11 with Rashi.

[14] *Shemos Rabba* 1:27. According to the other opinion in the Midrash he was forty.

[15] Rashi, *Shemos* 2:11, cites an opinion that Pharaoh appointed Moshe chief

officer over his palace. This would be another example of Moshe's assuming responsibility.

[16] See Rashi; *Bartenura*; *Machzor Vitri*; Vilna Gaon.

[17] See *Oznayim LaTorah* (*Bamidbar* 4:3), which wonders how the age of army conscription — which requires much more physical strength than working in the *Mishkan* — was twenty, while the draft age for *Levi'im* was not until thirty.

[18] R' Dovid Orlofsky.

[19] *Bereishis* 29:2-10.

[20] The verse states: "ויגש יעקב ויגל את האבן" — Yaakov came forward and rolled the stone." The superfluous word is *vayigash* ("came forward"), which teaches us that he rolled the stone as soon as he came forward — in other words, effortlessly (*Bereishis* 29:10 with Rashi and *Nachalas Yaakov*, cited in *Sifsei Chachamim*).

[21] *Sichos Mussar* 5731:§5, 5732:§9, 5733:§8.

[22] *Lev Avos* writes that the various stages delineated in the Mishnah are stages of character development, and that at thirty a person attains the characteristics of *gevura* and *ometz lev*. His words support the idea that the "strength" mentioned in the Mishnah does not refer to physical strength, but to strength of character, and, in particular, to the ability to fuse one's energies into what he does. *Derech Chaim* also understands the thirty-year-old's strength as *kochos hanefesh*, strength of character, and not physical strength.

[23] *Arachin* 11b.

[24] Rashi, *Bamidbar* 8:24.

[25] *Sifrei D'vei Rav, Beha'alosecha* §63.

[26] Ramban, *Bamidbar* 8:24; *Kesef Mishneh, Hilchos Klei Hamikdash* 3:7 (second answer).

[27] From the verses in I *Divrei Hayamim* 9:14-34 it is clear that each family of *Levi'im* had particular jobs assigned to it. If so, upon reaching his thirtieth birthday, a *Levi* would not have been free to pick whichever task he felt best suited for, but would have had to continue his family's tradition. It seems, however, that there must have been some flexibility in this regard. After all, a *Levi* who was not musically inclined, or who did not have a pleasant voice, would not have been able to play an instrument or sing, even though that was his family's tradition, and he would have had to find a more fitting assignment (R' Zev Leff). Moreover, even within each family's position, there was room for specialization, such as which instrument to play or which vessel to carry (see Ramban, *Bamidbar* 4:32).

[28] Rabbeinu Bachya, Meiri. Rambam (*Hilchos Avoda Zara* 1:3), Radak (*Bereishis* 26:5), and Meiri (on this Mishnah and in his introduction to *Avos*) write that Avraham was forty years old when he recognized G-d's existence. *Bereishis Rabba* (30:8), however, states that he was either three or forty-eight. *Kesef Mishneh* (*Hilchos Avoda Zara* 1:3) points out that Rambam must have had a different version of the Midrash, and indeed, in some manuscripts of the Midrash "forty" appears in place of "forty-eight" (see *Yalkut Shinuyei Nuschaos* at the back of the Shabse Frankel edition of Rambam).

[29] In particular, *bina* refers to the ability to logically derive one thing from another (Rashi). It comes from the word *ben* (son) because by analyzing the information he already knows, he creates new information, like one who gives birth to a son (Maharal, *Nesivos Olam, Nesiv Hayissurin*, chap. 3, and *Chiddushei Aggados* 3:234).

[30] *Avoda Zara* 5b with Rashi. Although *Tosafos* (*Sota* 22b ד"ה ועד כמה) learn that the Gemara means forty years after he began to learn, Rashi and Rabbeinu Bachya (both on our Mishnah) learn that the Gemara means age forty. See also *Tosefos Yom Tov*.

[31] Rabbeinu Bachya. See a similar idea in *Derech Chaim* in regard to age sixty. That forty is a time of physiological slowdown is noted in *Shabbos* 151b–152a. The enhancement of mental capabilities that accompanies the waning of physical strength might be due to the increased amount of resources now available to the mind. Thus, this enhanced *bina* only lasts as long as the body as a whole functions well, supplying sufficient energy to the brain. However, in later years, as the overall energy level of the body decreases, or when the brain itself begins to degenerate, mental capacity will also weaken.

[32] *Avoda Zara* 19b. The Gemara does not make clear if the reference to forty means forty years old, or forty years after one has learned the material. Rashi (*Avoda Zara* 19b ד"ה עד ארבעין שנין) interprets it to be the former; *Tosafos* (*Sota* 22b ד"ה ועד כמה) explain it to be the latter. Rema rules like Rashi (*Yoreh De'ah* 242:31 with *Shach*).

Note that the forty-year stipulation does not apply where there is no one more qualified in the city (Rema loc. cit). It also does not apply to the citation of well-known, codified halachos, but rather to rulings concerning novel cases (*Shulchan Aruch, Yoreh De'ah* 242:8).

[33] *Yalkut Me'am Lo'ez* and *Shach* (*Yoreh De'ah* 246:6). Cf. Rabbeinu Chananel, *Chagiga* 13a, who says that R' Elazar did not want to learn *ma'aseh merkava* until age fifty. Additionally, see *Sefer Habris* 1:4, subsection 16.

[34] Stanley Brandes, *Forty: The Age and the Symbol* (Knoxville: University of Tennessee Press, 1986), 18.

[35] Ibid., 20.

[36] *Derech Avos* and *Pele Yo'etz* (s.v. זקן) mention the need to rethink one's life-direction at forty.

[37] This idea actually runs deeper. Ask people whether advice comes from the person posing the question, or from the person offering the counsel, and most people will respond that it comes from the person giving the counsel. After all, he is the one who suggests the solution. While they are correct on one level, on a more subtle level, the advice is ultimately contained within the heart of the person with the difficulty. To be sure, it takes another person to extract it and bring it to the surface, but he only brings to the surface that which is contained within the heart of the questioner.

This idea may be alluded to in *Mishlei* 20:5, which compares decision-making (see Malbim) to water that must be drawn from a well by someone standing outside the well (see Ibn Ezra). This metaphor is very revealing because it teaches us that the solution to a person's problem emanates from within the person himself, like the water in a well, which, although drawn by an outsider, comes from inside the well itself. (The commentators themselves, however, interpret this verse differently.)

Further in the text, this verse is used to illustrate a different point about giving advice.

[38] R' Eliyahu Meir Bloch, *Shiurei Da'as*, 100–101.

[39] *Mishlei* 20:5.

[40] Shlomo Hamelech asked G-d for a *lev shome'a* — "a listening heart" (I *Melachim* 3:9). One usually associates listening with the ears or the head. Shlomo Hamelech, however, asked for a *heart* with which to listen, because, as Chazal say, the heart is the source of both desire *and* thought (*Shulchan Aruch, Orach Chaim* 25:5). Shlomo Hamelech, who was the supreme leader, wanted to be able to guide those who sought his counsel in the best manner possible, employing both his intellect and his feelings, both of which emanate from the heart (R' Reuven Leuchter).

[41] Heard from the father.

[42] Ibid.

[43] *Yalkut Shimoni* (*Yeshaya, remez* 394). Cf. *Chagiga* 14a.

[44] *Lev Avos.*

[45] That the word *na'ar* stems from the root *er* is found in *Haksav V'hakabbala*, *Shemos* 2:6; Malbim, I *Shmuel* 1:24; *Sfas Emes, Likkutim, parashas Vayeshev* ד"ה ובות. Cf. R' Hirsch, *Bereishis* 8:21.

[46] The need for life experience is mentioned in *Nachalas Avos*, Meiri, and *Milei D'Avos*.

[47] *Mirkeves Hamishneh, Midrash Shmuel*.

[48] *Kiddushin* 32b with Rashi. See *Birkas Peretz* (*parashas Kedoshim*), which discusses how we can know that the acronym refers to *chochma* even though the word is not included in the abbreviation.

[49] Meiri on *Tehillim* 120 [119]:100; *Midrash Shmuel*; Malbim (*Vayikra* 19:32); *Torah Temima* (*Vayikra*, loc. cit.). Perhaps that is why the Mishnah doesn't say *ben shishim la'chochma*. After all, if *zikna* is just a way of referring to *chochma*, the Mishnah should have written *chochma* explicitly, just as it did regarding forty, where it mentioned *bina* directly. The answer may be that the wisdom of the sixty-year-old is a particular type of wisdom, the kind acquired through age and experience, and this kind of wisdom is better captured through the word *zikna*. (Note that some texts [mentioned in *Midrash Shmuel*] do read: *ben shishim la'chochma*.)

[50] R' Hirsch, *Bereishis* 24:1.

[51] *Zikna U'vacharus*, 56–58.

[52] Abraham J. Twerski, *Let Us Make Man* (New York: Traditional Press, 1987), 57.

[53] *Zikna U'vacharus*, loc. cit.

[54] *Bamidbar* 11:16 according to *Kiddushin* 32b.

[55] *Shabbos* 51a.

[56] *Targum Onkelos* to *Bereishis* 37:3 translates the phrase "*ben zekunim*" as "*bar chakim*" (wise one).

[57] *Kinnim* 3:6 says that as *talmidei chachamim* grow older, *da'atan misyasheves*, their minds become "seated," meaning they become more firmly based and solid (R' Reuven Leuchter).

[58] Betty Friedan, *The Fountain of Age* (New York: Simon & Schuster, 1993), 56–57. A poster entitled "Have a Senior Birthday Party at McDonald's" offered to provide cake, party favors, and paper hats for the "birthday kid" who is "young at heart" (ibid.).

[59] While space constraints do not permit full elaboration, it is obvious that the elderly person also has personal intellectual challenges that he can now address,

such as Torah study and aspects of Jewish thought that may have been ignored in his younger years.

[60] Rashi. See *Iyov* 41:24 with Ibn Ezra, Ralbag, and *Metzudas Dovid*; *Yerushalmi, Berachos* 4:1 (where it says that R' Elazar ben Azaria's hair was filled with *seivus*, meaning it turned white). See also R' Hirsch to *Vayikra* 19:32. The word *seiva* is phonetically related to the word *ziv*, which means "bright" or "shining." Matityahu Clark, *Etymological Dictionary of Biblical Hebrew* (Jerusalem: Feldheim, 1999), 277.

[61] *Berachos* 28a.

[62] Rashi (on this Mishnah).

[63] *Hoshea* 7:9 with *Targum Yonasan*, Rashi, *Metzudas Dovid*, Radak, and *Mahari Kara*. According to this understanding of *seiva*, R' Elazar ben Azaria would have been stressing his becoming weak like a seventy-year-old due to all his Torah learning (see *Rosh Yosef, Berachos* 12b). *Magen Avos* mentions both aspects of *seiva*: white hair and weakness.

[64] Abarbanel (*Hoshea* 7:9). Cf. *Yalkut Shimoni* (*Tehillim, remez* 804), which connects *seiva* with *yeshiva* (sitting), and *Derech Chaim*, which connects it with *sevi'a* (satisfaction).

[65] Chofetz Chaim, *Zachor L'Miriam*, chap. 13.

[66] *Sha'arei Teshuva* 2:§9; Meiri (*Mishlei* 16:31).

[67] Ibid.

[68] Meiri (on this Mishnah); Radak to *Hoshea* 7:9.

[69] *Sha'arei Teshuva* 2:§9.

[70] *Reinventing Aging: Baby Boomers and Civic Engagement* (Boston: Harvard School of Public Health, 2004), 13–16.

[71] In its October 2005 newsletter, Benefits Management, Inc., reported that 55 percent of older employees surveyed said they were not planning to retire on schedule because they found their jobs interesting.

[72] Kathleen C. Buckwalter, *Elderly Loss: Treat It With Respect* (University of Iowa Health-Science Relations, 2000).

[73] That they stopped carrying the *klei hamikdash* at fifty is stated in *Bamidbar* 8:25 (see Rashi there). That they began guiding others at that age is mentioned in Rashi, *Machzor Vitri*, Rabbeinu Yona (MS ed.), and Rabbeinu Bachya.

[74] *Shemos* 7:7.

[75] *Oznayim LaTorah, Shemos* 7:7.

[76] Heard from R' Reuven Leuchter.

[77] Heard from R' Dovid Gottlieb.

[78] The Torah describes the latter years of several righteous people using the term *ba bayamim* (coming in days): Avraham and Sarah (*Bereishis* 18:11), Yehoshua (*Yehoshua* 13:1), and Dovid (I *Melachim* 1:1). *Kli Yakar* (*Bereishis* 24:1) remarks that, on the face of it, *yatza min hayamim* (going out of days) would seem to be a more appropriate description for the final years of life. He therefore explains that the phrase alludes to the fact that among the righteous the later years of life are more glorious than their younger years, because later life is more conducive to attaining wisdom. Hence the phrase "coming in days" is more suitable.

[79] *Lev Avos, Tiferes Yisrael. Midrash Shmuel* makes the opposite point: The eighty-year-old *needs* might to overcome his evil inclination and should not assume that he is now beyond temptation. After all, Yochanan Kohen Gadol became an apostate after eighty years of serving as the high priest, showing that a person is never beyond the clutches of the evil inclination.

[80] Rabbeinu Yona (MS ed.); *Midrash Shmuel* quoting the Rama.

[81] *Sha'arei Teshuva* 2:§9. The word *suach* is used in reference to prayer in *Bereishis* 24:63 (ibid.). Meiri, *Roshei Avos*, and *Hachassid Yaavetz* also interpret *suach* as referring to prayer.

[82] *Tiferes Yisrael*. Although the phrase "it is as if he were dead" implies a negative stage, that the person's body and mind are no longer of use (see Rashi), one of the commentators points out that this cannot be the Mishnah's intent, because: (1) *Kinnim* 3:6 states that *talmidei chachamim* grow wiser as they grow older, and if this did not apply after the age of a hundred, the two Mishnayos would contradict each other. (2) Moshe Rabbeinu, R' Yochanan ben Zakkai, Hillel, and R' Akiva all taught Torah until one hundred twenty, showing that one hundred does not mark the end of one's life in any way.

[83] Ibn Ezra, *Shemos* 23:26.

[84] *Mishlei* 10:27, cited by Ibn Ezra, *Shemos* 23:26.

[85] *Megilla* 27b–28a.

[86] See *Tnuas Hamussar* 2:113.

[87] *Yalkut Shimoni* (*Eikev, remez* 871).

[88] *Chasam Sofer*, introduction to responsa on *Yoreh De'ah*.

[89] *Tehillim* 92:15–16. Heard from R' Mattisyahu Salomon. Note that Malbim (*Tehillim*, loc. cit.) makes the same connection between the verses.

[90] See R' Avrohom Chaim Feuer's commentary to *Tehillim*, 1156.

[91] *Avos D'Rebbi Nasan* 11:1.

[92] Thomas A. Glass et al., "Population-Based Study of Social and Productive Activities as Predictors of Survival Among Elderly Americans," *British Medical Journal* 319 (1999):478–483. See also "Rowe and Kahn's Model of Successful Aging Revisited: Positive Spirituality — The Forgotten Factor," *Gerontologist* 42 (October 1, 2002):613–620.

[93] *Devarim Rabba* 11:10.

Glossary

Ahava Rabba: second blessing said before *Shema* in the morning prayers

Am Yisrael: the Jewish nation

Amora'im: Sages of the Gemara

aseh: make

av beis din: head of a Jewish rabbinical court

avodas Hashem: service of G-d

avos: fathers

ayin hara: evil eye

Ba'alei mussar: those who strive to live by ethical teachings and undertake introspection toward spiritual growth

bachur(im): unmarried yeshiva student(s)

baruch Hashem: "blessed be G-d"; expression of gratitude to G-d

beis midrash (battei midrash): study hall(s)

Beis Hamikdash: the Holy Temple in Jerusalem

ben Torah: someone who molds his behavior and way of thinking according to Torah ideals

Borei Olam: Creator of the world

bracha: blessing

Chasan: groom

chavrusa(s): study partner(s)

chelek: portion

chesed (chasadim): act(s) of loving-kindness

chillul Hashem: act that desecrates G-d's Name

chinuch: education

chol hamo'ed: intermediate days of the festivals of Sukkos and Pesach

Daf Hayomi: study of one page of Gemara every day according to an internationally fixed schedule

d'chola ba: Aramaic for "everything is in it"

derech eretz: literally, "the way of the land," referring to everything required for life in this world, specifically earning a livelihood and courteous social interaction

dikduk: Hebrew grammar

din v'cheshbon: spiritual judgment and accounting

dvar Torah (divrei Torah): word(s) of Torah

Erev Shabbos: the day before Shabbos

erev Yom Kippur: the day before Yom Kippur

esek: work

Gadol baTorah: Torah sage

gadol hador: leading Torah sage of the generation

Gedolim: Torah leaders

gemilus chasadim: performing acts of loving-kindness

Hachnasas orchim: hosting guests; engaging in hospitality

hakhel: the commandment to gather in Jerusalem every seven years to hear the king read from the Torah

Kaddish: prayer publicly recited by mourners after the death of a close relative

kapparos: a ritual of atonement before Yom Kippur

kedusha: holiness

kiddush Hashem: act that sanctifies G-d's Name

klal: the public

kollel(im): place(s) of post-yeshiva studies

korbanos: offerings

Levi('im): Levite(s)

Makom Torah: place of Torah

malach hamaves: angel of death

masechta: volume of Talmud

mashgiach: spiritual adviser in a yeshiva

mehalech b'derech yichidi: traveling alone

melachos: types of work

mema'et b'esek: reduce work

me'od me'od: very, very

midda (middos): character trait(s)

midda kenegged midda: G-d's method of rewarding or punishing people's deeds "measure for measure"

min haShamayim: ordained by Heaven

Mishkan: Tabernacle

mispallelim: people who gather together for davening; congregants

Na'aseh v'nishma: "we will do and we will listen"

nasi: a high-ranking position of Jewish leadership

neshama: soul

nisyonos: challenges

Parsa(s): Talmudic unit for measuring distance

Regesh: emotion

Roshei Yeshiva: deans of yeshivos

Sechel: intellect

sefer (sefarim): Torah-related book(s)

seiva: general signs of physical weakness that accompany old age

seuda: meal

seudas hoda'a: festive meal held to give thanks to G-d for an important event occurring in a person's life

sheitel: Yiddish for "wig"

sheva brachos: festive meals during the week after a wedding, at which seven blessings, *sheva brachos,* are recited

shidduch(im): date(s) or the process of dating for marriage

shiur(im): class(es) on a Torah-related topic

shtender: Yiddish for "lectern"

sifrei Torah: Torah scrolls

simcha: joyous event; happiness
Siyum HaShas: the completion of study of the entire Talmud

T a'amei hamitzvos: reasons for the mitzvos
talmid(im): student(s)
talmid chacham (talmidei chachamim): Torah scholar(s)
Tanna('im): Sage(s) of the Mishnah
tefilla (tefillos): prayer(s)
teshuva: repentance or return
tzedaka: charity

Y etzer hara: evil inclination
Yiddishkeit: Yiddish for "Judaism"
yiras Shamayim: fear of Heaven

Z akein(im): elder(s)
zikna: old age; a level of wisdom

Selected Bibliography

The bibliography has been divided into two sections, the first containing works on *Avos*, and the second containing other works. In the first section, the places and times in which the authors lived are given along with the bibliographic information. An author who lived at the turn of a century is identified by the century in which he produced most of his work.

Authorities such as Rashi, Malbim, and Hirsch, who are cited in the text by their names or acronyms rather than by the names of their works, are also listed this way in the bibliography.

I have not included entries for the books of Tanach, or Talmudic and Midrashic texts, such as *Sifri, Targum Onkelos,* and *Tanna D'vei Eliyahu.*

Works on *Avos*

Bartenura. R' Ovadia ben Avraham Yarei of Bertinoro (15th century, Italy and Eretz Yisrael). In Vilna Mishnayos.

Baruch She'amar. R' Baruch ben Yechiel Michel HaLevi Epstein, author of *Torah Temima* (20th century, Russia). Tel Aviv: Am Olam, n.d.

Be'er Ha'Avos. R' Menachem Mordechai Frankel-Teumim (20th century, Eretz Yisrael). New York, 5704.

Beis Avos. R' Shlomo Zalman ben Eliyahu (19th century, Lithuania). Berlin: Itzkovski, 5649.

Chelek Yaakov. R' Yaakov ben Naftali Greenwald (20th century, Romania). Sieni: S. Warohl, 5683.

Derech Avos. R' Meir ben Eliyahu (19th century, Lithuania). Vilna, 5596.

Derech Chaim. R' Yehuda Loew ben Betzalel, the Maharal (16th century, Bohemia). Israel, 1980.

Dvar Moshe. R' Moshe Rosemarin (contemporary, Eretz Yisrael). Jerusalem, 5749.

Dvar Yerushalayim. R' Yoel Shwartz (contemporary, Eretz Yisrael). Jerusalem: Dvar Yerushalayim, 5763.

Ethics from Sinai. Irving M. Bunim (20th century, America). 3 vols. Jerusalem: Feldheim, 2002.

Hachassid Yaavetz. R' Yosef ben Chaim Yaavetz (15th century, Spain and Italy). Jerusalem: Mechon Ma'oz HaTorah, 5750.

Lechem Shamayim. R' Yaakov Yisrael ben Tzvi Emden (18th century, Germany). In *Eitz Avos*. Sighet, 5672.

Lev Avos. R' Shlomo ben Yitzchak HaLevi (16th century, Salonika). Salonika, 5325.

Machzor Vitri. Attributed to R' Simcha ben Shmuel (11th century, France). In back of Vilna Mishnayos.

Magen Avos. R' Shimon ben Tzemach Duran (15th century, Spain and Algeria). Leipzig, 5615.

Meiri (Beis Habechira). R' Menachem ben Shlomo HaMeiri (13th century, Provence). Jerusalem: Yad Harav Herzog, 5724.

Midrash Dovid. R' Dovid ben Avraham, grandson of Rambam (13th century, Egypt). Jerusalem, 5704.

Midrash Shmuel. R' Shmuel ben Yitzchak D'Uzeda (16th century, Eretz Yisrael). Bnei Brak: S.L.A., 5752.

Milei D'Avos. R' Yosef ben Avraham Chayon (15th century, Portugal and Turkey). In *Peirushei Rishonim L'maseches Avos,* eds. R' Moshe Shlomo Kasher, R' Yaakov Yehoshua Blecherowitz. Jerusalem: Mechon Torah Sheleima, 5733.

Mirkeves Hamishneh. R' Yosef ben Moshe Al-Ashkar (16th century, Algeria). Lod: Speigel, 5753.[1]

Mishel Ha'Avos. R' Moshe Levi (contemporary, Eretz Yisrael). 4 vols. Bnei Brak, 5752–55.

Nachalas Avos. R' (Don) Yitzchak ben Yehuda Abarbanel (15th century, Spain and Italy). Jerusalem: Feldheim, 5764.

Peirush Maseches Avos L'Rebbi Mattisyah HaYitzhari. R' Mattisyah ben Moshe HaYitzhari (14th century, Spain). Jerusalem: Yad Ben Tzvi, 5766.

Peirushei Rabbeinu Yedaya Hapenini. R' Yedaya ben Avraham Hapenini (14th century, Provence). In *Peirushei Rishonim L'maseches Avos,* eds. R' Moshe Shlomo Kasher, R' Yaakov Yehoshua Blecherowitz. Jerusalem: Mechon Torah Sheleima, 5733.

Peirushei Rabbeinu Yitzchak ben Harav Shlomo MiToledo. R' Yitzchak ben Shlomo (14th century, Spain). Eds. R' Moshe Shlomo Kasher, R' Yaakov Yehoshua Blecherowitz. Jerusalem: Mechon Torah Sheleima, 5732.

Peirushei Rabbeinu Yosef ben Shoshan. R' Yosef ibn Shoshan (14th century, Spain). Eds. R' Moshe Shlomo Kasher, R' Yaakov Yehoshua Blecherowitz. Jerusalem: Mechon Torah Sheleima, 5728.

Pirkei Moshe. R' Moshe ben Baruch Almosnino (16th century, Turkey). Salonika, 5323.[1]

Rabbeinu Bachya. R' Bachya ben Asher (14th century, Spain). In *Kisvei Rabbeinu Bachya,* ed. R' Chaim Dov Chavel. Jerusalem: Mossad Harav Kook, 5730.

Rabbeinu Yona. R' Yona ben Avraham of Gerona (13th century, Spain). In Vilna Shas and manuscript editions, eds. R' Moshe Shlomo Kasher, R' Yaakov Yehoshua Blecherowitz. Jerusalem: Mechon Torah Sheleima, 5729.

Rambam. R' Moshe ben Maimon (12th century, Spain and Egypt). Various editions.

Rashi. R' Shlomo ben Yitzchak (11th century, France).[2] Various editions.

Rav Yosef ben Nachmias. R' Yosef ben Yosef ibn Nachmias (14th century, Spain). Paks: Rosenbaum, 5667.

Roshei Avos. R' Yitzchak ben Shlomo Al-Achdab (14th century, Spain). Jerusalem: Mechon Beis Aharon, 5762.

Ruach Chaim. R' Chaim ben Yitzchak MiVolozhin (18th century, Lithuania). Jerusalem, 5754.

Sefer Mussar. R' Yosef ben Yehuda ibn Aknin (13th century, Syria). Berlin: Mekitzei Nirdamim, 1910.

Seforno. R' Ovadia ben Yaakov (16th century, Italy). In *Kisvei R' Ovadia Seforno,* ed. R' Dr. Zev Gottlieb. Jerusalem: Mossad Harav Kook, 1987.

Sfas Emes. R' Yehuda Aryeh Leib ben Avraham Mordechai Alter (19th century, Poland). Petrokov: Koppelman, 5693.

---

[1] These texts appear on *The Responsa Project* CD-ROM, ver. 13.0 and on.

[2] Although there is some debate as to whether the "Rashi" commentary on *Avos* is authentic, the consensus is that it is. Mossad Harav Kook published an annotated edition of Rashi and various other commentaries to *Avos* in *Mishnas Reuven* (Jerusalem, 2005). The introduction to that volume contains a synopsis of the above debate.

Tiferes Tzion. R' Yitzchak Zev Yadler (19th century, Eretz Yisrael). Jerusalem, n.d.

Tiferes Yisrael. R' Yisrael ben Gedalya Lifschitz (19th century, Germany). In Vilna Mishnayos.

Toldos Yehoshua. R' Yehoshua ben Aharon Heller (19th century, Lithuania). Jerusalem: Mechon Sha'arei Yosher, 5754.

Tosafos Chadashim. Various authors. In margin of Vilna Mishnayos.

Tosefos Yom Tov. R' Yom Tov Lipman ben Nasan HaLevi Heller (17th century, Bohemia and Poland). In Vilna Mishnayos.

Vilna Gaon. R' Eliyahu ben Shlomo Zalman (18th century, Lithuania). *Maseches Avos im Peirush HaGra*, ed. R' Meir Zev Etrog. Bnei Brak, 5751.

Yalkut Me'am Lo'ez. R' Yitzchak ben Moshe Magriso (18th century, Turkey). Trans. and expanded by R' Shmuel Yerushalmi. Jerusalem: Wagschal, 5732.

Other Works

Abarbanel. Commentary on Tanach by R' (Don) Yitzchak ben Yehuda Abarbanel. 3 vols. Jerusalem, 5715–39.

Akeidas Yitzchak. R' Yitzchak ben Moshe Arama. 6 vols. Warsaw: Edelstein, 5643–44.

Alei Shur. R' Shlomo Wolbe. 2 vols. Jerusalem: Beis Hamussar, 5746–48.

Aruch Hashulchan. Commentary on *Shulchan Aruch* by R' Yechiel Michel Epstein. Various editions.

Aruch Laner. R' Yaakov Ettlinger. 4 vols. Bnei Brak: Sifrei Ohr Hachaim, 5757.

Ateres Paz. Responsa by R' Pinchas Zevichi. 3 vols. Jerusalem: Tiferes Rafael, 5750–58.

Bayis U'menucha. R' Moshe Aharon Stern. Jerusalem, 5759.

Beis HaLevi al Drush U'milei D'aggadeta. R' Yosef Dov Soloveitchik. Warsaw: Goldman, 5644.

Beis Yechezkel (Hilchos De'os). R' Moshe Yechiel HaLevi Tzuriel. Bnei Brak, 5741.

Binyan Olam. Anon. Jerusalem, 5739.

Binyan Tzion. Responsa by R' Yaakov Ettlinger. Altona: Bonn, 5628.

Binyan Yehoshua. Commentary on *Avos D'Rebbi Nasan* by R' Yehoshua Falk ben Yitzchak Izak. In Vilna Shas.

Birkas Peretz. R' Yaakov Yisrael Kanievsky, the Steipler. Bnei Brak, 5750.

Be'ur Halacha. See *Mishnah Berurah*.

Chasam Sofer. Responsa by R' Moshe Sofer. 5 vols. Pressburg, 5601–22.

Chayei Olam. R' Yaakov Yisrael Kanievsky, the Steipler. Bnei Brak, 5750.

Chiddushei Aggados. R' Yehuda Loew ben Betzalel, the Maharal. 4 vols. Israel, 1980.

Chiddushei HaRan al Maseches Chullin. R' Nissim ben Reuven. Bnei Brak: Frankel, 5741.

Chiddushei HaRitva al HaShas. R' Yom Tov ben Avraham Al-Ashbili. Various editions.

Chiddushei Ge'onim on *Ein Yaakov*. Various authors. In *Ein Yaakov*. 4 vols. Vilna: Romm, 5643.

Children in Halachah. R' Simcha Bunim Cohen. New York: Mesorah, 1993.

Chinuch Habanim L'mitzvos V'dinei Katan. R' Yehoshua Y. Neuwirth. Jerusalem, 5756.

Chizkuni. R' Chizkiyahu ben Mano'ach. Ed. R' Chaim Dov Chavel. Jerusalem: Mossad Harav Kook, 5754.

Chofetz Chaim al HaTorah. R' Yisrael Meir Kagan. Ed. R' Shmuel Greineman. Bnei Brak: Sifriati, 5717.

Chofetz Chaim al Hilchos Lashon Hara U'rechilus. R' Yisrael Meir Kagan. Various editions.

Chovos Halevavos. R' Bachya ben Yosef ibn Pakuda. Trans. R' Yehuda ibn Tibbon. 2 vols. Tel Aviv: Hamenora, 5744.

Da'as Chochma U'mussar. R' Yerucham HaLevi Levovitz. 3 vols. New York: Daas Chochmo Umussar, 1966–72.

Da'as Tevunos. R' Moshe Chaim Luzzatto. Ed. R' Chaim Friedlander. Bnei Brak: Sifriati, 5758.

Da'as Torah. R' Yerucham HaLevi Levovitz. 6 vols. Jerusalem: Daas Torah, 1976–95.

Divrei Chanina al Gidrei Talmud Torah. R' Chanina Yisrael Rottenberg. Jerusalem, 5752.

Drashos Chasam Sofer. R' Moshe Sofer. 3 vols. Jerusalem: Mechon Chasam Sofer, 5749.

Drashos HaRan. R' Nissim ben Reuven. Ed. R' Aryeh L. Feldman. Jerusalem: Mossad Harav Kook, 2003.

Dvar Shmuel. Responsa by R' Shmuel ben Avraham Abuhav. Venice, 5462.

Eimek HaNetziv. Commentary on *Sifri* by R' Naftali Tzvi Yehuda Berlin. 3 vols. Jerusalem: Va'ad L'hotzaas Kisvei HaNetziv, 5720–37.

Eitz Yosef. Commentary on *Midrash Tanchuma* by R' Chanoch Zundel ben Yosef. In *Midrash Tanchuma*. 2 vols. Jerusalem: Eshkol, 5732.

Emunos V'de'os. See *Saadia Gaon*.

Encyclopedia Talmudit. Eds. R' Meir Berlin, R' Shlomo Yosef Zevin et al. 26 vols. Jerusalem: Yad Harav Herzog, 5733–64.

Ha'amek Davar. R' Naftali Tzvi Yehuda Berlin, the Netziv. 5 vols. Jerusalem: Bamberger, 5697.

Hagahos Yaavetz. R' Yaakov Yisrael ben Tzvi Emden. In back of Vilna Shas.

Haksav V'hakabbala al HaTorah. R' Yaakov Tzvi Meklenberg. 2 vols. Frankfurt am Main: Kaufman, 5640.

Halichos Bas Yisrael. R' Yitzchak Yaakov Fuchs. Jerusalem, 5744.

Halichos Shlomo. R' Shlomo Zalman Auerbach. Eds. R' Yitzchak Trager, R' Aharon Auerbach. 2 vols. Jerusalem: Feldheim, 5760–63.

Hamashgiach Reb Meir. Shulamit Ezrachi. Jerusalem: Feldheim, 2001.

Hirsch. Commentary on Torah by R' Shimshon Raphael Hirsch. 5 vols. Jerusalem: Mossad Yitzchak Breuer, 5762.

Horeb. R' Shimshon Raphael Hirsch. Trans. Dayan Dr. I. Grunfeld, 2 vols. London: Soncino, 1975.

Ibn Ezra. Commentary on Torah by R' Avraham ben Meir ibn Ezra. In *Mikra'os Gedolos*.

Iggeres HaTeshuva. R' Yona ben Avraham. Jerusalem: Mussar HaRishonim, 5751.

Igros Chazon Ish. R' Avraham Yeshaya Karelitz. Ed. R' Shmuel Greineman. 3 vols. Bnei Brak, 5750.

Igros HaRambam. See *Rambam*.

Igros Moshe. Responsa by R' Moshe Feinstein. 7 vols. New York, 1959–85.

Judaism Eternal. R' Shimshon Raphael Hirsch. Trans. Dayan Dr. I. Grunfeld. 2 vols. London: Soncino, 1956.

Kad Hakemach. R' Bachya ben Asher. In *Kisvei Rabbeinu Bachya*, ed. R' Chaim Dov Chavel. Jerusalem: Mossad Harav Kook, 5730.

Kaf Hachaim. R' Yaakov Chaim Sofer. 8 vols. Jerusalem: M. Sofer, 5723–26.

Karyana D'igarta. R' Yisrael Yaakov Kanievsky, the Steipler. 2 vols. Bnei Brak: 5746–50.

Kesef Mishneh. R' Yosef Karo. In various editions of *Mishneh Torah*.

Kiryat Sefer. R' Moshe ben Yosef MiTrani, the Mabit. Jerusalem: Mossad L'idud Limud Torah, 5754.

Kisvei R' Ovadia Seforno. R' Ovadia ben Yaakov. Ed. R' Dr. Zev Gottlieb. Jerusalem: Mossad Harav Kook, 1987.

Kli Yakar. R' Shlomo Ephraim ben Aharon. In *Mikra'os Gedolos*.

Kovetz He'aros L'maseches Yevamos. R' Elchanan Bunim Wasserman. Jerusalem: Yeshivas Ohr Elchanan, 5756.

Kovetz Ma'amarim V'igros: part 1, R' Elchanan Bunim Wasserman; part 3, R' Elazar Simcha Wasserman. Jerusalem: Mechon Ohr Elchanan — Ohel Torah, 5760.

Ksav Sofer al HaTorah. R' Avraham Shmuel Binyomin Sofer. Tel Aviv: Sinai, 1980.

Kuzari. R' Yehuda ben Shmuel HaLevi. Trans. Even Shmuel. Tel Aviv: Dvir, 5737.

Leket Reshimos B'inyenei Elul V'yamim Nora'im. R' Nosson Meir Wachtfogel. Lakewood: Mechon Meir Einei Chachamim, 5759.

Lerei'acha Kamocha. R' Dovid Ariav. 3 vols. Jerusalem: Mechon Lerei'acha Kamocha, 5760–63.

Lev Eliyahu. R' Eliyahu Lopian. Ed. R' Shalom Mordechai HaKohen Shwadron. 3 vols. Jerusalem: Hava'ad L'hotzaas Kisvei Maran, 5739–43.

Mahari Kara. Commentary on *Nevi'im* by R' Yosef ben Shimon Kara. In *Mikra'os Gedolos*.

Maharsha. Commentary on Talmud Bavli by R' Shmuel Eliezer HaLevi Eidels. In back of Vilna Shas.

Malbim. R' Meir Leibush ben Yechiel Michel:

       • Commentary on Tanach. Various editions.

       • *Ya'ir Ohr*. Jerusalem: Mossad L'idud Limud Torah, 5754.

Masores Hachinuch. R' Elazar Menachem Man Shach. Bnei Brak: Talmud Torah Darchei Ish, 5765.

Matnas Chaim, Elul–Yamim Nora'im. R' Mattisyahu Salomon. Eds. R' Yisrael Yaakov Neuman, R' Zev Gottlieb. Jerusalem: Mechon Soferim, 5765.

Matnas Chaim, Kinyanim 1. R' Mattisyahu Salomon. Ed. R' Yaakov Chaim Dinkel. Jerusalem: Y. C. Dinkel, 5764.

Mayim Chaim. R' Chizkiyahu ben Dovid D'Silva, author of *Pri Chadash* on *Shulchan Aruch.* Amsterdam: M. Frankfurt, 5490.

Ma'oz Hadas. R' Yehoshua ben Aharon Heller. Brooklyn: Ahavas Hakadmonim, 5734.

Meiri. R' Menachem ben Shlomo HaMeiri:
> • Commentary on *Tehillim.* Jerusalem: Mekitzei Nirdamim, 5696.
> • Commentary on *Mishlei.* Jerusalem: Otzar Haposkim, 5729.
> • Commentary on Talmud Bavli: *Beis Habechira.* Various editions.

Mekor Baruch. R' Baruch ben Yechiel Michel HaLevi Epstein. 4 vols. Vilna: Romm, 5688.

Menoras Hama'or. R' Yitzchak Abuhav. Jerusalem: Mossad Harav Kook, 5721.

Menoras Hama'or. R' Yisrael ben Yosef Al-Nakawa. New York: 1929–32.

Me'orei Eish. Commentary on *Tanna D'vei Eliyahu* by R' Avraham ben Aryeh Leib Yehuda. Jerusalem: Lebovitz-Kest, 5754.

Mesillas Yesharim. R' Moshe Chaim Luzzatto. Various editions.

Metzudas Dovid. R' Dovid ben Aryeh Leib and his son R' Yechiel Hillel. In *Mikra'os Gedolos.*

Michtav Me'Eliyahu. R' Eliyahu Eliezer Dessler. Eds. R' Aryeh Carmell, R' Alter Halperin. 5 vols. Jerusalem: Sifriati, 5752–62.

Michtavim U'ma'amarim. R' Elazar Menachem Man Shach. 6 vols. Bnei Brak, 5748–56.

Mikra'os Gedolos. Generic name for volumes of Torah, *Nevi'im,* and *Kesuvim* containing many commentaries.

Mishnah Berurah (including *Be'ur Halacha* and *Sha'ar Hatziyun*). Commentary on *Shulchan Aruch, Orach Chaim,* by R' Yisrael Meir Kagan. Various editions.

Mishneh Torah. See *Rambam.*

Moreh Nevuchim. See *Rambam.*

My Disciple, My Child. R' Noach Orlowek. Jerusalem: Feldheim, 1993.

Nachalas Yaakov. Commentary on *Maseches Soferim* by R' Yaakov ben Baruch Nomburg. In back of Vilna Shas.

Nefesh Hachaim. R' Chaim MiVolozhin. Bnei Brak, 5749.

Nefesh Shimshon, Igros U'ma'amarim. R' Shimshon Dovid Pincus. 5765.

Nesivos Olam. R' Yehuda Loew ben Betzalel, the Maharal. 2 vols. Israel, 1980.

Nitzotzei Eish. Anon. Bnei Brak: Korlanski, 5756.

Noda BiYehuda. Responsa by R' Yechezkel Landau. 2 vols. Jerusalem, 5729.

Ohr Hachaim. R' Chaim ben Moshe ibn Atar. In *Mikra'os Gedolos.*

Ohr Yechezkel. Commentary on *Orchos Chaim LehaRosh* by R' Yechezkel Levinstein. In *Orchos Chaim LehaRosh Hamevo'ar.* Bnei Brak, 5754.

Ohr Yisrael. R' Yisrael Lipkin Salanter. Vilna: Metz, 5660.

Orach Yesharim. Commentary on *Orchos Chaim LehaRosh.* Various authors. In *Orchos Chaim LehaRosh Hamevo'ar.* Bnei Brak, 5754.

Orchos Rabbeinu. R' Avraham HaLevi Horowitz. 5 vols. Bnei Brak: Horowitz, 5751–65.

Orchos Tzaddikim. Anon. (14th century). Jerusalem: Ohros Chaim, 5746.

Orchos Yosher. R' Chaim Kanievsky. Bnei Brak, 5757.

Oznayim LaTorah. R' Zalman ben Ben-Tzion Sorotzkin. 5 vols. Jerusalem: Mechon Hade'ah V'hadibbur, 5756.

Pachad Yitzchak, Chanuka. R' Yitzchak Hutner. New York: Gur Aryeh, 1998.

Pe'er Hador. Ed. R' Shlomo Cohen. 5 vols. Bnei Brak: Netzach, 1966–73.

Pele Yo'etz. R' Eliezer Papo. Jerusalem: Toshia, 5747.

Peninim Mishulchan HaGra. See *Vilna Gaon.*

Pirkei Emuna. R' Mordechai Gifter. Jerusalem: Tochen, 5760.

Rabbeinu Chananel. Commentary on Talmud Bavli. In margin of Vilna Shas.

Rabbeinu Bachya al HaTorah. R' Bachya ben Asher. Ed. R' Chaim Dov Chavel. 3 vols. Jerusalem: Mossad Harav Kook, 5754.

Radak. R' Dovid ben Yosef Kimchi:
- Commentary on Torah. In *Toras Chaim.* 7 vols. Jerusalem Mossad Harav Kook, 1986–93.
- Commentary on *Nevi'im* and *Kesuvim.* In *Mikra'os Gedolos.*
- *Sefer Hashorashim.* Jerusalem: Wagshal, 5727.

Rambam. R' Moshe ben Maimon:
- Commentary on Mishnah. In Vilna Shas.
- *Igros HaRambam.* Ma'aleh Adumim, Israel: Shilat, 5755.
- *Mishneh Torah*, Shabse Frankel ed. 13 vols. Jerusalem: 5735–63.
- *Moreh Nevuchim.* Jerusalem: Aharon Barazani, 5720.

Ramban. R' Moshe ben Nachman:
- Commentary on Torah. In *Mikra'os Gedolos*.
- Commentary on Talmud Bavli: *Chiddushei HaRamban*. Various editions.

Rashash. Glosses to Talmud Bavli by R' Shmuel Strasson. In back of Vilna Shas.

Rashba. Responsa by R' Shlomo ben Aderes. Various editions.

Rashi. R' Shlomo ben Yitzchak:
- Commentary on Tanach. Various editions.
- Commentary on Talmud Bavli. In Vilna Shas.

Rema. Glosses to *Shulchan Aruch* by R' Moshe Isserles. Various editions.

Rishon L'Tzion. R' Chaim ben Moshe ibn Atar, author of *Ohr Hachaim*. Jerusalem: Levi, 5675.

Rosh. Responsa by R' Asher ben Yechiel. Jerusalem: Mechon Yerushalayim, 5754.

Rosh Yosef. R' Yosef ben Meir Te'umim, author of *Pri Megadim*. Lemberg: Flekir, 5623.

Saadia Gaon. R' Saadia ben Yosef:
- Commentary on Torah. In *Toras Chaim*. 7 vols. Jerusalem Mossad Harav Kook, 1986–93.
- *Emunos V'de'os*. Berlin: B. Cohen, 5688.

Sedei Chemed. R' Chaim Chizkiyahu Medini. 9 vols. New York: Friedman, 5727.

Sefer Habayis. R' Yosef Yitzchak Lerner. Jerusalem: Mechon Sha'arei Ziv, 5755.

Sefer Habris. R' Pinchas Eliyahu ben Meir. Jerusalem: Yerid Hasefarim, 5750.

Sefer Hachinuch. Attributed to R' Aharon HaLevi. 3 vols. Jerusalem: Mechon Yerushalayim, 5748.

Sefer Ha'itur. R' Yitzchak ben R' Abba Mari. 2 vols. Jerusalem, 5747.

Sefer Hamitzvos. See *Rambam*.

Sefer Hashorashim. See *Radak*.

Sefer Hayira. R' Yona ben Avraham. Jerusalem: Mussar HaRishonim, 5751.

Sefer Hazikaron L'maran Ba'al HaPachad Yitzchak. Anon. New York: Gur Aryeh, 5757.

Seforno. Commentary on *Tehillim*. See *Kisvei R' Ovadia Seforno*.

Selected Writings. R' Shimon Schwab. Lakewood: C.I.S., 1988.

Sfas Emes, Likkutim. R' Yehuda Aryeh Leib ben Avraham Mordechai Alter. 2 vols. Petrokov: Koppelman, 5694–97.

Sha'ar Hatziyun. See *Mishnah Berurah*.

Sha'arei Teshuva. R' Yona ben Avraham. Jerusalem: Ohros Chaim, 5761.

Shach (Sifsei Kohen). Glosses *to Shulchan Aruch by* R' Shabsai HaKohen. Various editions.

She'ifos. R' Yitzchak Hershkovitz. Jerusalem: Hershkovitz, 5763.

Shem Olam. R' Yisrael Meir Kagan, the Chofetz Chaim. Various editions..

Shemiras Halashon. R' Yisrael Meir Kagan, the Chofetz Chaim. Various editions.

Shevet Mussar. R' Eliyahu Shlomo HaKohen. Ed. R' Chaim Yosef Waldman. 2 vols. Jerusalem: Mechon L'hafatzat Sifrei Mussar, 5749.

Shiurei Da'as. R' Eliyahu Meir Bloch. Jerusalem: Feldheim, 5732.

Shiurei Da'as. R' Yosef Yehuda Leib Bloch. 2 vols. Jerusalem: Feldheim, 5749.

Shiurei U'fninei Da'as. R' Eliyahu Meir Bloch. Ed. R' Nasan Tzvi Baruch. Wickliffe, OH: Peninei Daas, 2004.

Shelah (Shnei Luchos Habris). R' Yeshaya ben Avraham Horowitz. 5 vols. Jerusalem: Mechon Sha'arei Ziv, 5753.

Shulchan Aruch. R' Yosef Karo. Various editions.

Sichas Chullin. R' Amitai Ben-David. Jerusalem: Midrash Bikkurei Yosef, 5756.

Sichos Mussar. R' Chaim Leib Shmulevitz. Jerusalem, 5740.

Sifrei D'vei Rav. R' Dovid ben Yaakov Ferdo. Salonika, 5559.

Sifsei Chachamim. R' Shabsai Meshorer. In *Mikra'os Gedolos*.

Strive for Truth. R' Eliyahu Eliezer Dessler. Trans. Aryeh Carmell. 3 vols. Jerusalem: Feldheim, 1978–89.

Targum Hala'az al HaShas. R' Yisrael Gukovitzki. London, 1985.

Tashbatz. Responsa by R' Shimon ben Tzemach Duran. 4 vols. Jerusalem, 5720.

Tehillim (ArtScroll Tanach Series). Commentary of R' Avrohom Chaim Feuer. 2 vols. New York: Mesorah, 1991.

Teivas Gomeh. R' Yosef ben Meir Te'umim, author of *Pri Megadim* on *Shulchan Aruch*. Lublin, 5660.

The Torah Profile. Ed. Nisson Wolpin. New York: Mesorah, 1988.

Tnuas Hamussar. R' Dov Katz. 5 vols. Jerusalem: Feldheim, 1996.

Torah Temima. R' Baruch ben Yechiel Michel HaLevi Epstein. 5 vols. Tel Aviv: HaTalmud, 5751.

Toras Avraham. R' Avraham Grodzenski. Bnei Brak: Yeshivas Toras Avraham, 5738.

Toras Moshe. R' Moshe Sofer, the Chasam Sofer. 5 vols. Jerusalem: Mechon Chasam Sofer, 5755.

Tosafos. In Vilna Shas.

Tziporen Shamir. R' Chaim Yosef Dovid Azulai, the Chida. Amsterdam: Propps, 5584.

Vilna Gaon. R' Eliyahu ben Shlomo Zalman:
   • Commentary on *Sifra Ditzniusa*. Vilna, 5642.
   • Commentary on *Mishlei*. Ed. Moshe Philip. Petach Tikva, 5745.
   • *Peninim Mishulchan HaGra al HaTorah*. Ed. R' Dov Eliach
     Jerusalem: Mechon-Moreshes HaYeshivos, 5757.

Ya'aros Devash. R' Yehonasan Eibeshitz. 2 vols. Jerusalem: Mechon Ohr Hasefer, 5748.

Ya'ir Ohr. See *Malbim*.

Yabia Omer. Responsa by R' Ovadia Yosef. 8 vols. Jerusalem: 5746–55.

Yalkut Lekach Tov, Chaim Shel Torah. R' Yaakov Yisrael HaKohen Beifus. 3 vols. Rechasim, Israel: Tashbar Harav, 5760–63.

Yalkut Me'am Lo'ez. R' Yaakov ben Machir Culi et al. 31 vols. Jerusalem: Wagshal, 5727–50.

Yam Shel Shlomo. R' Shlomo ben Yechiel Luria. 4 vols. Jerusalem: Mechon Mishnas Dovid, 5756.

Yemos Olam. R' Yoel Shwartz. Jerusalem: Dvar Yerushalayim, 5740.

Yeshuos Yaakov. Commentary on *Tanna D'vei Eliyahu* by R' Yaakov ben Naftali Hertz. In *Tanna D'vei Eliyahu*. Jerusalem: Lebovitz-Kest, 5754.

Zachor L'Miriam. R' Yisrael Meir Kagan, the Chofetz Chaim. Jerusalem, 5725.

Zikna U'vacharus. R' Yoel Shwartz. Jerusalem: Lebovitz-Kest, n.d.

Index

Credits

In memory of

Chaim Schreiber, ל״צז

חיים שמואל בן אברהם ויענטי, נפטר י׳ אייר תשמ״ד

of whom it may be said,
"The crown of a good name rises above
them all" (*Avos* 4:17).

Sara Schreiber
Judy Schreiber
Jonny and Ayala Finn
Gershon Roth

In memory of

Dovid and Rachel Roth, ל״צז

דוד בן יצחק ואסתר מלכה, נפטר י״ג ניסן תשס״ג
רחל בת צבי וליבע, נפטרה כ״א תשרי תשנ״ז

who embodied a deep love of
Torah, *derech eretz,* and Eretz Yisrael.

Yitzchak and Ada Roth
Jonny and Ayala Finn
Gershon Roth

In memory of

Rabbi Reuven Poupko, זצ״ל
ראובן בן אליעזר ופעשא חיה, נפטר כ״ב תמוז תש״ט

a *talmid* of Baranovitch and Radin,
who developed in his short life the nobility, modesty, wisdom,
and intuition of *Gedolei Torah.* His insight and respect made him
revered and beloved by people of all ages.

Felice Poupko
Gary and Joy Poupko

In memory of

Dr. William W. Brickman, זצ״ל
זאב בן שלום דוד וחיה שרה, נפטר ט״ו סיון תשמ״ו

an educator's educator, who instructed with compassion,
scholarship, and humor, and most of all taught by example as a
Torah Jew. *Roshei Yeshiva*, governments, and schools all over the
world sought his expertise and counsel.

Sylvia Brickman
Gary and Joy Poupko
Chaim and Hassidah Brickman
Shlomo and Sara Sudry

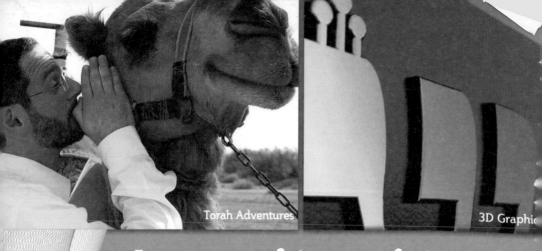

Torah Adventures

3D Graphic

Interested in applying the WISDOM OF THE SAGES to TODAY'S WORLD?

Torah Live presents practical and engaging videos on a variety of Jewish topics.

201
SCHOOLS!

218
ORGS!